THE MAN
WITH
THE PLAN

Contents

Acknowledgements 7

Prologue: The Real Class of 92 9

Mr S and Mr F 13

The Apprentice 29

The Graduate 49

Winds of Change 68

The Man with a Plan 80

The Crusade 93

Separating the Wheat from the Chaff 105

Bournemouth 129

Freshmen 154

That Difficult Second Season 173

TV Personalities 187

A Touch of Chic 204

Toughing It Out 223

Blowing It 241

Kidulthood 264

Remake/Remodel 284

Master Blaster 305

Brolin 321

Lower Than a Snake's Belly 331

The Sell-Out 348

'Twere well it were done quickly 360

A Post-Leeds World 371

Bibliography 398

Acknowledgements

FOR HOWARD Wilkinson, for his kindness, his insights and his time, and for what he did for Leeds United Football Club and those who supported them during the darkest of days.

For those who left us too soon, Leslie Silver, Bill Fotherby, Peter Gunby and Gary Speed.

Prologue
The Real Class of 92

Next time I'm coming back as a personality.

CEDAR COURT Hotel, Harrogate, 29 April 2022.

There is a reverent atmosphere as you leave the modern reception area and enter the wood-panelled rooms where the evening's events are about to begin. It is 30 years since an unsung set of players showed what team spirit and grit could accomplish, and we're here to pay homage.

There's Mel Sterland, the life and soul of the party, gregarious and constantly laughing, as big a character now as he always was on the field.

There are the towering giants, Jon Newsome and Chris Whyte, refusing to show their age and comparatively quiet in the company of legends.

There are the shorter Tony Dorigo and Steve Hodge, the Aussie sharp and snappy in his suit, the Englishman in comfy, zip-up woollen top. To quote Sterland, 'Smart casual, they said. Look at him, four million on his head, what a tramp!'

There is the even shorter Gordon Strachan, now old and craggy, his red hair turned snowy grey, always ready with the quick wit, the sharp put-down and a million anecdotes.

And finally, there is the captain of the crew – The Sergeant, Wilko, Howard Wilkinson – holding court and commanding the room, the audience falling silent whenever he chooses to speak.

It's incredible to be here, talking to these men and taken back 30 years to when they were young, to a time when football hadn't sold its soul for the sake of filthy lucre.

* * *

For Wilkinson, it was the team that mattered; it was all about the team, first, last and always. Not the media, not the individual players, not the directors and, often, not even the fans.

'Team spirit is never easy to develop,' Wilkinson says. 'A team willing to accept the work ethic as a fundamental principle and then nurture collective aspirations is ideal.'

For John Sheridan, Eric Cantona and Tomas Brolin, the gems, those who were bigger than the unit, even if only in their own minds, there was never a chance. They were not Wilkinson players and not one of them lasted more than a year with the Sarge.

It was not that Wilkinson couldn't handle big players – Mel Sterland, Lee Chapman, Gordon Strachan, Chris Kamara, Vinnie Jones, Gary McAllister, Tony Yeboah and Carlton Palmer were hardly shrinking violets – but they subjugated themselves to the needs of the collective, to Wilkinson's design, and their standing ebbed and flowed with the success of the team.

Those who shared Wilkinson's ethos, got behind the plan, earned the manager's fierce, fierce loyalty. Indeed, he was probably too loyal for his own good in his later years at Elland Road. But that was his way, his virtue and his folly, a constant that characterised his entire career, which became an anachronism when money was all that mattered in football.

He was obsessed with authenticity and refused to participate in the media game.

'People want their leader to be himself, they don't want a leader who's trying to be someone else. They want him to be knowledgeable, they want him to be good at what he does. But above all, above all, they want you to be honest and they want you to be authentic, because what you're giving out are messages. I want people to recognise that I know what I'm doing, but more importantly, the thing that I want them to do. The messages from me have got to be authentic and my responses have got to be authentic, and they need to know that they can trust me.'

He has a distinctive outlook and a distinctive look, does Wilkinson. Even in younger, more carefree days, he always seemed to sport a worried frown, his eyes screwed up into a pained grimace, tight-lipped and wary of the world. The look fits the stereotype of a dour Yorkshireman, his voice slow and reflective and his words peppered with 'as it were' stock phrases and hard vowels.

He acknowledges how he is perceived, though he feels the view is misinformed. 'I don't know anybody in my circle of friends who would have that view. They would say no, that's nothing like him. Maybe I was, maybe I was suspicious of the media.'

Gary Speed said once, 'Howard Wilkinson is a scholar of the game and knows as much about football as anyone I know. Howard may come across on the telly as a dour man but, when you get to know him, he's a great guy and funny with it.'

Close mate Dave Bassett comments, 'Among friends, Howard is completely different from his public image.'

An unfinished novel ('a bit like *Kes*') might have confirmed that, or maybe a quote about his heroes: 'Lester Piggott, Frank Sinatra, Fidel Castro has done a magnificent job in some respects, the fellow who invented red wine and the outside-right I used to have at Boston United.'

Wilkinson's wit is Sahara-dry, but constantly there, ready to cut you down with a sharp, well-considered phrase.

He certainly took the rise out of me when I interviewed him for this book.

Distracted by having to take an urgent phone call, Wilkinson wandered off to another room, leaving me to consider my next inane question. Then he seemed to remember me and returned, still on the phone, talking to whoever it was on the line.

'I'm currently talking to a gentleman who I think is writing a book. But I'm worried about the content and the questions I'm being asked, the content he seems to require. I'm scared that he's recording everything I say and he's going to use it against me later in court.'

'Howard, I'm really sorry if I've offended you. That's sincerely not the intention, and I'm quite happy once I've taken the transcription of our discussion, I'm quite happy to destroy everything.'

Wilkinson leaned close into the phone, as if to confide in me. 'I don't know where you've got that impression from. I don't know what you're worried about or scared of.'

'I just don't want to offend you.'

'If you were offending me … I always told my staff and I'm telling YOU, if you're not afraid to think it, you should not be afraid to say it. So, if I have anything to say that I think is really important, believe you me, I will say it.'

I could sense him silently chuckling; it's the closest Howard Wilkinson ever gets to a full-scale belly laugh.

I didn't mind, I wasn't upset, just immensely pleased to be in his company. I'm not afraid to think it and I'm certainly not afraid to say it. This is Howard Wilkinson, a remarkable man, a deity of football management.

Mr S and Mr F

*I came home knowing that I'd
met a gentleman.*

IN THE early hours of Sunday, 30 September 1888, Elizabeth Stride became the third victim of Jack the Ripper. The murder occurred in Dutfield's Yard, just off Berners Street in the east London borough of Tower Hamlets. The yard, adjacent to a Jewish socialist club, housed the printing and publication of a radical Yiddish newspaper.

Interrupted before he could mutilate the body, the killer struck again within the hour. He slaughtered Catherine Eddowes less than a mile away in Mitre Square.

A few blocks away, a chalk message was found scrawled on a wall: 'The Juwes are the men that will not be blamed for nothing.' A police officer hurriedly washed away the writing, fearing that it would incite anti-Semitism in an already tense neighbourhood.

Between 1880 and 1914, the tens of thousands of Jewish refugees fleeing economic hardship and religious persecution transformed London's small Jewish community. More than half of the immigrants settled in the East End in the area between Spitalfields and Whitechapel, drawn to the area by the idea of cheap housing and an abundance of work.

The unfamiliar language, diet and religion of the 'strange exotics' sparked suspicion; crimes that appeared to be 'foreign to the English style', such as the Ripper murders, were commonly blamed on Jews.

A fog of resentment swirled around the newcomers. Newspapers crackled with scornful rhetoric, branding the immigrants as 'pauper foreigners', 'a pest and a menace to the native-born East Ender'. Trade unions and rabble-rousing politicians alike called for tough limits on immigration and protested that England was becoming 'the human ashpit for the refuse population in the world'.

A stone's throw from this maelstrom of anti-immigrant sentiment, tucked away in the underbelly of Dutfield's Yard, lay a narrow, cobblestoned thoroughfare named Severne Street. It was typical of the area, lined either side with grimy back-to-backs. Yet, it was the beacon of hope for many, including Isaac and Sarah Silverstein. The couple had fled their home in Poland in search of a better life with their son Ashy. They settled on Severne Street, and on 22 March 1899, their humble abode echoed with the first cries of their second son, Harry.

Severne Street soon beckoned another Polish family — Shmuel and Hannah Hoffman, and their daughter Bessie. They took up residence next door to the Silversteins, their lives intertwined by shared stories of displacement and dreams of belonging.

Life was hard. Anti-Jewish sentiment escalated following the passing of the Aliens Act in 1905. The *Manchester Evening Chronicle* promised that 'the dirty, destitute, diseased, verminous and criminal foreigner who dumps himself on our soil … shall be forbidden to land.' The Act established a mechanism for deporting such undesirables, including Jews fleeing racial persecution in their homeland. Despite such oppression, the Silversteins and the Hoffmans were content. An attraction grew between Harry and Bessie and it came as no surprise when the couple married in February 1923.

On 22 January 1925, Bessie gave birth to their first child, a boy they named Leslie Howard.

This febrile atmosphere allowed a British fascist movement to gain traction, spearheaded by Sir Oswald Mosley, 'the most polished literary speaker in the Commons'. Mosley quit the Conservative party in 1922 to become an independent, and two years later he shifted his allegiance to Labour. Mosley was given responsibility for resolving the unemployment crisis after the party's victory at the 1929 general election. He advocated a programme that would nationalise vital industries and introduce tariffs to protect British firms from imports. When the cabinet rejected his recommendations, Mosley resigned to become the leader of the British Union of Fascists, embracing the ideologies of Hitler and Mussolini. His supporters became known as the Blackshirts for their all-black, long-sleeved and high-necked uniform. They were little more than organised thugs who roamed the streets of London attacking elderly Jews and picking on young boys on their way home from school.

Observing such developments with dread, the Silversteins became overtly political, espousing left-wing thinking. On 4 October 1936, Leslie, then 11, took part in the Battle of Cable Street, a series of clashes that occurred in the locality after members of the Metropolitan Police were sent to protect a march by Blackshirts through the East End. The police clashed with anti-fascist protestors, who rallied 100,000 to their cause and erected roadblocks and barricades to disrupt the march.

A 6,000-strong police force attempted to clear the route so the march could pass. The demonstrators would have none of it, and Mosley was forced to abandon his plans.

In August 1938, Harry and Bessie paid ten shillings to change the family name to Silver, reasoning that the new surname would reduce antagonism and make life easier.

Leslie left school at 14 and found work in tailoring through his father. Harry worked as a junior manager for the tailors Stanley Morrie, and he wangled an opening for his son.

Leslie despised the tedium and monotony but there was soon more to be concerned about than boredom. In the autumn of 1940, air raids killed over 43,000 civilians.

One of the first bombs landed on the Stanley Morrie factory – no one was hurt but the owners of the firm considered it wise to relocate to Yorkshire. Harry decided that the family should follow suit and rented a property in Leeds in December 1940.

This new life appealed to Leslie. He became an active member of the Chapeltown branch of the Young Communist League, working in the League's bookshop on Woodhouse Lane, a job that was far more to Leslie's liking than tailoring. He became a fervent advocate for communism, arguing that the party was the only one prepared to stand up to fascism.

It was a decision he regretted in later life, telling an after-dinner audience in 1998, 'It was a mistake and beyond comprehension how my generation could have been so misguided.'

Silver volunteered for the RAF in 1943 and was assigned to Bomber Command as a flight engineer. He flew with four different squadrons in Europe and the Far East, completing his maximum allocation of 250 hours of missions.

During his travels, Silver received a letter from Anita Feddy, a girl he had left behind in England. After being introduced at Young Communist League meetings, the couple had begun dating casually and Anita was now keen to understand Silver's intentions.

He had no reservations and the couple married on 31 August 1946 in Chapeltown.

Uncle Joe, who attended the wedding, inquired about Silver's plans after he was demobbed.

Silver paused for a second. He hadn't really thought about it, other than knowing with all his being that tailoring was off the agenda. He had toyed with the idea of a job as a salesman, but his thinking was vague.

Uncle Joe, a production and development chemist in the nitro-cellulose industry, suggested that he should go into the paint trade. Silver was bewildered – paint? He knew nothing about it.

Joe pooh-poohed Silver's apprehension, offering to supply cellulose thinners for Silver to sell if he could find a warehouse to use in Leeds. Joe assured him there was a national shortage for the car refinishing market, and he'd make enough money to retire in three years.

Taken by the suggestion, Silver scraped together a £1,000 investment. Uncle Joe put up £250 to supplement a £250 demobilisation gratuity and a few hundred made from selling alcohol while serving in the Far East. And so, the Silver Paint and Lacquer Company Ltd was born.

Silver started making cellulose thinners before moving on to domestic paint, all from a small warehouse off Woodhouse Lane. In 1963, he moved to larger premises in Batley, and then to Birstall. By then, the company had been renamed Kalon, taken over Leyland Paints and become a public limited company.

Silver rose to prominence in the paint industry, serving as president of the Oil & Colour Chemists' Association, the Paint Industries Club, the Paintmakers Association of Great Britain and the Paint Research Association.

Hailing from a generation that understood the needs of both the Leeds and wider Jewish community, Silver was generous to the extreme. He became involved with many organisations in Leeds, making significant contributions to life in the city without regard for personal gain. 'Leeds has given a lot to me,' responded a humble Silver when told that he had given a lot to Leeds. He was about to give so much more.

'I say, I say, I say, young man, how would you feel about joining our board of directors?'

Leslie Silver smirked at the suggestion that he was a youngster. At 56, he had long since stopped thinking of himself as young. By comparison to his colleague, though, Silver was young, juvenile even.

Manny Cussins, the chairman of Leeds United Football Club, was 20 years Silver's senior but looked even older, worn down by his association with the club. Silver was in his prime, a touch overweight perhaps, but otherwise ruddy with health, sporting a thick mane of greying, wavy hair and an easy smile.

The pair were attending a charity event at the home of local philanthropist Arnold Ziff, the president of the Leeds Jewish Welfare Board.

'Smiling at the thought, are you, Leslie?'

'It would be a great honour. How much will it cost me?'

Cussins' turn to chuckle now, relishing the parallels to a conversation from two decades earlier, when it was he who had been tapped up for an investment by a United chairman.

He was now the father figure at Elland Road, the elder statesman, having been invited on to the board by former chairman Sam Bolton back in 1961.

Cussins took over as United figurehead in 1974 and was now trying to persuade Silver to join a once-great club that was back in the doldrums.

'Nothing, Leslie,' came Cussins' reply to the query about the cost. 'This isn't about money. We'd welcome an investment, surely, but this is about energy, commitment and enthusiasm, getting someone in who can lead this club back to where it belongs, where we were when Don Revie was around. What d'you say? Interested?'

'I am, Manny, of course I am.'

Cussins was lying, of course – the interest payments on the money borrowed to pay for signings like Peter Barnes, Kenny Burns and Frank Worthington had pushed United to the brink of insolvency. Silver had to advance £200,000 to keep the club afloat, though he later claimed it was more like £2m over the years.

And thus, the die was cast. Cussins had recruited the man who would succeed him in steering a dying football club back to the top of the game in England.

Silver's lifelong passion for football was sparked in his youth. It was 1935 when Silver first witnessed the legendary Alex James command the field for the indomitable Arsenal side. James wasn't the archetypal superstar with his baggy shorts and mature demeanour. Yet, the artistry with which he caressed the ball and retained possession intelligently before releasing one of his team-mates marked him as a titan of the pre-war game.

It was Silver's uncle who took him to Highbury that fateful day. Surrounded by the roar of the crowd and the colour of the afternoon, Silver stood, mouth agape in awe. In that moment, 'I just fell in love with football.'

Silver began attending Leeds United games after the war and quickly became a devoted fan. He was present when the legendary John Charles made his debut in April 1949.

Silver befriended Leeds manager Don Revie, whom he adored. On occasion, the two holidayed together with their wives.

Silver jumped at Cussins' invitation to get involved in Leeds United in 1981. He was enthralled by the opportunity to make a meaningful contribution to one of the area's great institutions.

He had the money, the time and the energy, and he made a mark on the history of Leeds United in much the same way that Revie's mentor, Harry Reynolds, did in the 50s and 60s. Silver, like Reynolds, made a significant contribution to the club.

Silver's Jewish background helped his relationship with Cussins and United, a club with long-standing ties to the local Jewish community.

Les Goldberg, born in Leeds, played right-back for United in 1937, but he reflected the fears of many in his community by changing his surname by deed poll to Gaunt.

Cussins joined the United board in 1961, along with two other Jews, Sidney Simon and Albert Morris, who briefly chaired the club until his death in 1968.

Their appointments reflected the growing influence of Jews in the local community – between 1880 and 1920, approximately 2.5 million Jewish migrants, many of them impoverished, fled Russia. Many were drawn by the prospect of working in Leeds' thriving tailoring industry – the city had the third-largest Jewish population in the country.

Leeds' Jews formed a community centred on Chapeltown. Revie moved to nearby Alwoodley in 1969 and settled at 'Three Chimneys', the five-bedroom house formerly owned by Cussins.

The Jewish community became avid supporters and benefactors of the club after being drawn to Elland Road by Revie's success.

Leeds United appeared to be designed for a man like Silver. He had lofty ambitions and was determined to do for Leeds United what he had done for Kalon. His energy revitalised a sagging board and one of his early moves paved the way for a force of nature to blow through Elland Road's stagnant corridors.

Silver had become a patron of the 100 Club, a charitable body formed by United-supporting local businessmen to help replace the West Stand after it was destroyed by fire in 1956. The 100 Club grew into a powerful pressure group whose members included many eminent locals – it was only natural that Silver should join up.

Among the other patrons was Bill Fotherby, another local entrepreneur and a close friend of Silver's.

Fotherby was charismatic, an ebullient salesman with the gift of the gab and a penchant for fedora hats, large cigars and self-promotion. He adopted the stereotypical persona of a used car salesman, someone who 'could sell sand to the Arabs'. His extraordinary public persona was crowned with a crest of black curls and huge, horn-rimmed spectacles atop a spiv moustache – truly, Fotherby was, to misquote from *Billy Bunter*, the Owl of Elland Road (alternatively, a footballing version of *Hi-De-Hi*'s Ted Bovis).

Fotherby was not a Jew, despite once joking, 'I would never deny it if someone said I was.' He became a close friend of the Jewish community, taken under the wing of a tailor as a young boy and running Cussins' clothing factory.

He played for the club's junior side, the Leeds United Stormcocks, but lacked the talent to make it as a footballer and instead focused his energies on business.

During the 70s, Fotherby began stockpiling United shares but was always blocked from joining the board by a dubious Cussins, who habitually mocked his ambitions.

Despite Cussins' reluctance, Fotherby wangled a way into the boardroom by virtue of a conditioned business transaction.

As Silver recounted, Fotherby's involvement was not entirely selfless. 'The first director we had who drew a salary was Bill

Fotherby. He came to me one day and we gave him a job as commercial director. A nominal salary, but he got a commission on business and did a very good job. He was crazy, Bill!'

Fotherby adored Silver; he never had a bad word for him. 'A wonderful chap, a real gent.' But he was equally clear that it was he, not Silver, who ran the club. 'From the day I joined, I made a difference at Leeds United. I changed Leeds United. God gave me a gift of convincing people that Leeds United was the best club in the world. I would have stayed there until I died. It was my club.'

Fotherby was not everybody's cup of tea as evidenced by fans' graffiti on a bridge on Whitehall Road East, a couple of miles north of Elland Road. 'Fotherby = Liar Thief Crook Cheat'. The accusation was daubed there after one of Fotherby's rumoured big transfers came to nothing. Such a teller of tall tales could not but attract critics.

There were other newcomers in the boardroom: Maxwell Holmes and builder Peter Gilman joined a board which also included Rayner Barker, Jack Marjason and Brian Woodward.

The club Silver and Fotherby inherited was in dire straits – football fans across the land oozed hatred for anything different, but those who followed Leeds were in a different league.

Racist chants filled the Elland Road stadium, which was rarely more than half-full at the time. Matchdays were a magnet for the far-right National Front, doing a roaring trade in sales of its magazine, *The Flag*, outside the ground.

The club was on its financial uppers. Revie's legacy when he left to manage England in 1974 was £200,000 in the bank and one of the strongest squads in the country. By the time they were relegated in 1982, there was an overdraft of £1.8m secured against the stadium. The club only made it through the next year by selling off the few players who could command a fee, slashing the payroll by 23 per cent, and banking donations of £200,000 from the 100 Club. There were few positives – a mediocre team meandered without direction in a mediocre Second Division.

The club's accounts carried the doomy warning from the auditors that 'the company has incurred substantial losses during the year and is dependent upon the financial support of its bankers and its directors through their guarantees'.

The magnitude of the club's problems didn't deter Silver and Fotherby; their resolve only grew stronger. As Fotherby remembered, 'We needed money, and I was commercial; my job was to bring money into Leeds United and get us publicity, because what were Leeds? Who were Leeds? Don Revie had gone ... how do you follow that?'

Following that was exactly what Silver and Fotherby had to do, and it wouldn't be easy.

Their first season on the board wasn't a pleasant one – Leeds United were relegated after 18 years in the First Division. It was a miserable campaign and manager Allan Clarke paid the price with his job.

Eddie Gray, another United legend, was named player-manager. Gray, like Revie 20 years earlier, pinned his hopes on youth. That went down well with supporters, made for some pleasant afternoons and brought an exciting breeze to Elland Road, but ultimately Gray's time ran into the sand.

* * *

Cussins believed that in hiring Silver, he had found the man who could succeed him as chairman.

Silver had substance that the other directors lacked, a gravitas that made him the obvious choice when Cussins' thoughts turned to retirement.

Silver was appointed vice-chairman when he arrived and assumed the chair when Cussins stepped down in 1983.

Cussins was named vice-chairman, but it was always clear that Fotherby was Silver's right-hand man. They spent hours playing snooker together, with Fotherby always contriving to lose, keen on remaining 'in' with the chairman.

The pair were at the snooker table when Silver revealed that he had been invited on to the United board. 'How the hell did you pull that one off, Leslie? You're not a fan of Leeds like I am. I'll have Manny's ears for this.'

They were in the same location when Silver's financial adviser told him that he had disposed of his shares in Kalon in 1991. 'Get a bloody bottle open!' exclaimed Fotherby at the news.

He knew what side his bread was buttered, did Fotherby.

There was no honeymoon period for Silver – within a couple of years, the new chairman had become one of the city's most disliked men as he took the steps he believed to be necessary to improve the club's fortunes.

Leeds hinted for three seasons in a row that they could reclaim their top-flight status under Eddie Gray, but the closest they got was seventh in 1985. It was hugely disappointing – a decent start suggested that Leeds might be able to secure the promotion they craved, and they sustained their push through the winter months but they couldn't finish the job.

Silver was forced to accept a harsh reality as he thumbed through the club's financial results, pondering how to keep United's heads above water. If Leeds could not return to the First Division – and there was no indication that this was going to happen any time soon – then something had to be done.

The interest on a bank overdraft, which remained stubbornly above £1.5m despite the club's penny-pinching over the previous three years, was the biggest expense after players' wages.

It was obvious to Silver that this was madness – the only option was to sell off the club's one concrete asset, the Elland Road stadium.

Silver opened discussions with Leeds City Council to see if a deal could be done. Elland Road was a vital municipal amenity, attracting thousands of visitors to the city each year, and the council saw the value in keeping such a local business going. Leeds United's demise would be disastrous for the city.

The club's valuation was an issue. The stadium and the land on which it stood were valued at £8.5m on the balance sheet. The council would not accept such a fee, and beggars cannot be choosers. Recognising that the accounts showed the ground's replacement value as a sports stadium, Silver accepted a £2.5m offer as a more realistic estimate of its commercial value and closed the deal.

That sum enabled the club to clear its overdraft and reduce operating costs. The agreement included a 125-year lease of the pitch and stands, ensuring that football would continue at Elland Road.

The shareholders approved the sale of the freehold at an extraordinary general meeting in September 1985, with Silver reporting that the transaction 'removed the intolerable burden of debt'.

The motion was approved, but its passage was far from smooth.

Dr Aubrey Share, a serial agitator, demanded to know how the proceeds had been used. Silver informed the meeting that all the club's debts had been paid in full, including directors' loans of £368,000, with the remainder placed on deposit. He emphasised the reduction in operating expenses and bank charges, which would lower the break-even figure from 16,000 to 12,000 spectators.

Mutterings that 'the directors are taking their money and running' were clearly audible in the room.

When it was suggested from the floor that the cash would be gone within three years, Silver said Leeds United were in a better financial position than 75 per cent of Football League clubs.

Responding to questioning, Silver confirmed that there was no buy-back clause in the agreement and that the council would be the beneficiary of the revenue generated by hosting rugby games at the stadium.

United's increasingly cynical supporters saw the sale as a hugely symbolic admission that the club was in terminal decline. If their reaction to the sale was hostile, their outrage at Eddie Gray's dismissal was even more intense – for a time, Leslie Silver was the most unpopular man in West Yorkshire, his Rolls-Royce vandalised by enraged fans.

A disastrous opening to the 1985/86 season saw Leeds dip as low as 20th after winning just three of their first 11 games. A 6-2 defeat at Stoke City was especially humiliating, forcing the board to admit that enough was enough.

Silver drove youth-team coach Keith Mincher to a League Cup game at Walsall in early October with the intention of announcing that he would be taking over from Gray after the game if Leeds failed to win.

The players had not read the script and a comfortable 3-0 victory stayed Silver's hand. It was a temporary reprieve – Gray was fired on Friday morning.

The decision wasn't unanimous. Barker, Cussins, Fotherby, Marjason and Gilman backed Silver, but Holmes and Woodward voted against.

Woodward was so adamantly opposed that he resigned from the board.

A resolute Silver followed through and showed Gray the door, putting coach Peter Gunby in temporary charge.

The sacking sparked outrage among fans and players alike, with veteran skipper Peter Lorimer reading out an angry statement of protest before the following day's game against Middlesbrough.

Leeds won 1-0, though Lorimer was said to have considered messing up his penalty winner to express his displeasure with the board's decision. Supporters called for Silver's resignation, but he resisted their demands, helped by Gray's dignified words as he urged the players to act professionally.

Gray's departure cost the club its greatest advocate of youth development. Following his exit, there would be a sharp volte-face in approach.

Prompted by a recommendation from Revie, Silver persuaded Doncaster Rovers to release legendary former United captain Billy Bremner. The Scot set about reshaping the squad, ditching the youngsters in favour of more experienced journeymen who he believed were better equipped to win promotion.

There was no new-manager bounce – Leeds struggled to keep their heads above the quicksand of relegation. They finished 14th, the same position they were in when Gray was dismissed.

Even the cash injection from the stadium sale could not fully address Leeds United's financial problems. Silver reported a loss of more than half a million and net liabilities of nearly £200,000.

'I trust ... you will join me and my fellow directors,' Silver begged the shareholders, 'in the confidence that the alterations are already showing the desired improvement in the financial and playing position of the club.'

His words rang hollow as he was forced to acknowledge the increase in costs from 'rent to our new landlords'.

Silver looked around a cold boardroom but there were no solutions there, just the bonhomie and madcap schemes of Fotherby.

Leeds United was a club in crisis, seemingly doomed to struggle forever in the mind-numbing limbo of the Second Division.

That is, for as long as they could avoid the dreadful prospect of bankruptcy.

A shaken Silver held his head in his hands, knowing that the task ahead of him was far more challenging than Manny Cussins had suggested.

Silver sighed as he considered an uncertain future. 'What on earth can I do?'

The Apprentice

I'm not coming here to carry the balls.

'I'VE FOUND our boy, Jack.'

Jack Dunnett, chairman of Notts County, leant forward. 'Oh yes?'

'Aye, he'll do for us,' came the thick Glaswegian burr from across the table. 'Ah've never been surer of anything in ma life.'

His eyes bulged with excitement; his hair, still black despite his advancing years, was swept back from his brow but curly and out of control; a bulbous nose was misshapen from clashes during his playing days; his uneven teeth were even more asymmetrical, giving him a trademark smile, 'resembling the broken keyboard of an old piano', according to one wag.

Jimmy Sirrel's was a distinctive look. He appeared much older than his 57 years. However, Sirrel was bouncing along like a man half his age at that moment. He was elated at persuading Howard Wilkinson to join him at County, where Sirrel was manager.

Sirrel was synonymous with Notts County, the world's oldest professional association football club. He had led them from the bottom of the Football League to the upper echelons of the Second Division. Now, though, he was struggling to take them any further and needed someone who could.

That was where Wilkinson, one of the brightest young coaches in British football, came in.

Sirrel tracked him down to Loughborough University where he was delivering a coaching course. Wilkinson had been relaxing in the staff room at lunchtime when Sirrel called.

'What do you want?'

'Could you come over to our ground, please?'

'Okay, but what's it about?'

'Working with me.'

Wilkinson was taken aback by the request but a colleague at the FA persuaded him to take a chance. 'You've got nothing to lose. Why don't you get yourself over there?'

So it was that one sweltering summer day in 1979, Wilkinson drove to Meadow Lane in Nottingham to meet Sirrel. Wilkinson suited and booted, Sirrel in his habitual tracksuit, the two met in Sirrel's rabbit warren of an office under the stand.

'Why do you want me?' began Wilkinson.

'Because I saw what you did at Boston. I saw what you did when you took the England non-league team. I watched those three games. And I've seen you at Lilleshall various times.'

'I don't want to come here just to carry the balls for you and put the cones out.'

'No, no, no … we dinna want you to do that.'

'What do you want me to do?'

'I canna get the buggers to run, they dinna listen to me anymore. You shall coach them and you shall decide how we play and you shall pick the team and I shall do the rest.'

After a brief discussion about exactly what Sirrel meant by 'the rest', the pair went to see Jack Dunnett.

Dunnett was a large, imposing figure, balding with huge horn-rimmed glasses. His manner was straightforward.

'Is there anything you want to ask me, Howard?'

'For this to work I need to know you are happy with it. You're the chairman responsible for the money, Jimmy is the manager responsible for the acquisition and signing of players. I get on with coaching and picking the team. If I want a player I tell Jimmy, he tells you, you decide if we can afford him, we give you a valuation, if we can get him for that or less, we're in.'

'That's correct, Howard. That's what we've agreed.'

That was enough for Wilkinson. He agreed to be the man in charge at Meadow Lane.

* * *

Howard Wilkinson was born on 13 November 1943 in Sheffield's Netherthorpe district. The place was almost exactly at the centre of the three miles that separated the football stadia of the Wednesday and United clubs.

The Steel City clubs were nearly as old as Notts County – Wednesday were formed in 1867 and United followed 22 years later – but were both pre-dated by Sheffield FC, established in 1857 and the world's first football club.

In the Steel City, there was a fierce rivalry. 'You are either blue and white or red and white, Wednesdayite or Unitedite. And ne'er the twain shall meet,' according to Richard Crooks in his book, *Wednesday v United: The Sheffield Derby.*

Wilkinson, a winger, was Wednesday from the off, so it was with mixed feelings that he accepted an invitation to a trial at United in 1959. He had been good enough to play for Yorkshire and England Grammar Schools and was hopeful of making his way in the game, but he never came close to the Blades' first team.

Gordon Jago, the Charlton defender who had been appointed coach for the UEFA Under-18 Championship, called Wilkinson up to the England youth team in 1962.

He made his debut on 17 March against Wales, alongside future Leeds United players Paul Madeley and Rod Johnson.

Wilkinson scored the final goal in a 4-0 victory and looked set for a good summer.

The UEFA tournament was plagued by problems, with Europe divided by Cold War tensions at the time – the borders dividing Berlin's two halves were closed weeks before the tournament. The decision to hold the competition in Romania rather than Spain was made at the last minute as a symbolic gesture of support for football in the East.

On the understanding that professional players would be eligible, Jago selected a strong England party, many of whom had league experience, including Martin Peters, Jim Montgomery and George Armstrong. When UEFA announced that the competition was strictly for amateurs, Jago's plans were thrown into chaos, paving the way for Wilkinson.

He appeared in all three of England's games at the tournament, against Yugoslavia, the Netherlands and Bulgaria, but England were eliminated after taking a single point.

Wilkinson won a fifth cap against Northern Ireland in May and was given a boost when Sheffield Wednesday signed him as a professional on 25 June.

In September 1964, he made his league debut at Stamford Bridge against First Division pacesetters Chelsea. 'We forced a 1-1 draw and I quite enjoyed the match.'

Wilkinson made 12 appearances as Wednesday finished eighth. Two of those came over Easter in back-to-back games against a Leeds United team on the way to an unprecedented runners-up spot.

In the 3-0 victory at Hillsborough on 19 April, Wilkinson and team-mate Colin Dobson 'revelled in the freedom they were given. Sprake made a fine dive forward to kill a square centre by Wilkinson, who had got away clear to the line. Off went Wednesday for Wilkinson to sail round Bell on the outside and centre from the line. Charlton saved what looked a certain goal with a desperate sliding kick.'

After such a promising start, the following campaign was a disappointment with Wilkinson limited to eight appearances. Featuring England keeper Ron Springett and Scottish cap Jim McCalliog, Wednesday were strong enough to reach the FA Cup Final. Frustrated by a season of marking time, Wilkinson asked for a move.

He signed for Brighton a few days after England won the World Cup.

Wilkinson was straight into the first team, scoring on the season's opening day against Swindon. He was on the mark again two games later in a draw at Reading and he also scored in the season's high-point match when third-tier Albion defeated First Division Coventry in the League Cup. In December 1966, he suffered concussion and a fractured cheekbone during a match at Middlesbrough, halting his progress.

'I seemed to be out for an eternity after that injury,' Wilkinson recalled. 'They didn't have the technology back then that they do today to mend injuries like that. I had an operation, they reset it, and I was on fluids for ages. It wasn't nice.'

Wilkinson developed an interest in coaching, convinced that this was where his true talents lay. 'I realised one of my assets was passing on knowledge to others. I started coaching in 1966, when I did the B licence. From that moment on, I was coaching as well as playing. I coached Tuesday and Thursday nights at local grassroots clubs, and on Friday afternoons at a school.

'We'd never really had a serious coaching culture in England to compare with the coaching cultures in the Netherlands, France, Germany and much of the rest of Europe. We've come a long way since those pioneers in the coaching field were trying to prove that it was the right way to go. In England, we had the ridiculous idea that practising was "not what gentlemen did. Practising to get better? We don't do that! You play, and then you go and have a game of golf or go to the races.'"

In those days, there was an old school, stiff-upper-lip feel to coaching. *The Football Association Coaching Manual* carried this paragraph:

> The player who 'gives' up easily is another problem. There are some players who play well so long as they are winning, but as soon as their side is a goal behind, they give up trying. This is due to some weakness of moral fibre – lack of 'backbone'. The coach must try to spur on these players by encouraging every attempt which they make to show that they are trying. Occasionally, by judiciously ignoring such a player, the coach may stimulate him to make efforts to win approbation.

'It was during my last year at Brighton that I decided to try and do a teaching qualification combined with a degree, ready for when I finished playing,' Wilkinson continued.

'I was becoming increasingly bored with all the spare time we had. One morning, the reserve-team coach, Steve Burtenshaw, pinned a note on the board advertising an FA preliminary coaching course every Thursday night and Sunday morning. I went to the first session purely for something to do. But by the end of that session, I was convinced that coaching was for me. A new door had suddenly been opened in terms of structure, tactics, technique and how I looked at the game.'

Wilkinson's new-found interest brought fresh insights into football – 'Before, it had been a game with no real logic to it: you just played, and you did well, or you didn't do well.' Now, he realised it wasn't just about playing, there was depth and complexity to the game he hadn't appreciated. The realisation sparked an unquenchable curiosity, and he probed even deeper, seeking out books from renowned coaches.

His reading took in the golfer, Gary Player, who championed the value of visualisation. He also discovered 'this mad Australian coach', Percy Cerutty, who used the teachings of philosophy to help him develop a host of the world's greatest long-distance runners. And then there was Vince Lombardi, the legendary Green Bay Packers coach who led his team to five NFL Championships and two Super Bowls in seven years; his innovative work in cutting and splicing together video clips of games to pick over the good, bad and ugly with his players set the template for future generations of coach.

These trailblazers were visionaries, fantastic innovators who helped transform the sports industry at a crucial time. Wilkinson took bits and pieces from each of them in developing his own approach to coaching.

He took his first step on the path to becoming a coach when he enrolled for his A licence. Leading this course was Allen Wade, a man whose passion for the game was as infectious as his insight was profound.

'I can still feel the tingle as he conducted a session at a refresher course, illustrating a way of playing that mirrored the style of modern-day Barcelona.'

The air was thick with scepticism from the other attendees. 'No, no, this is never going to work … pie in the sky.' Thirty-five years down the line, his vision is now the accepted norm.

Away from the group, Wilkinson shared his ambitions with Wade. The latter suggested teacher training, a path that seemed daunting to a man with a young family to provide for. It sounded a bit of a risk, going back to school when he needed to earn a living. But Wade was absolutely right. The training taught Wilkinson a lot about how people learn, gave him a real insight. 'A lot of today's coaches would benefit from that grounding.'

It's interesting that Wilkinson was so taken with Wade, a proponent of possession-based football. Most people would have assumed he was more influenced by Charles Reep, who was 'credited' with inventing the long-ball game, especially given the latter's influence behind the scenes at Sheffield Wednesday in the late 50s.

Reep, described by Wilkinson as 'a zealot', was a pompous character who did not take criticism well. His status as the pioneer of match analysis resonated with Wilkinson.

Reep was inspired by Arsenal's style of play under Herbert Chapman in the 30s. Long balls were to be hit out to the wingers, who were to stay just onside without tracking back. They would try to win the ball as far up the pitch as possible, dispossessing defenders.

Reep was appointed head of football at RAF Yatesbury in Wiltshire after the war. He continued collecting and analysing football data and came up with a few key findings. Seven out of nine goals came from moves of three passes or fewer; moves beginning with a long pass from your own half were twice as likely to result in a goal as short passing moves; and most goals came from winning the ball back in the attacking quarter of the pitch.

Reep found that, regardless of the level of football, it took an average of nine shots to produce a goal. He referred to getting the ball into the final quarter as a 'reacher' and discovered that an average of three 'reachers' were required to produce a shot; with nine shots required to produce a goal, a team would need to reach the attacking quarter 27 times in order to score.

The game had never been examined in this manner before, and Reep quickly earned himself a reputation.

In January 1951, his all-conquering RAF side caught the eye of Brentford manager Jackie Gibbons, whose club was struggling in the Second Division at the time. A scout told him about a local team that had just won 12-1.

'There's some crazy fellow who stands on the touchline with bits of paper making notes,' he reported. '[He] produces a tactical plan which seems to work.'

Gibbons paid a visit to Bushy Park, and two days later, Reep was on the team's coach to Doncaster. Brentford, who had not won away since September, ran out 3-0 victors, much to Gibbons' delight.

He agreed to fully implement Reep's tactical plans, which resulted in 'an unbelievable and instant success', according to Reep.

Brentford had won nine of their 29 games prior to Reep's involvement; of their final 13, they won nine.

Reep went on to work closely with Wolves manager Stan Cullis, whom he met shortly after Hungary defeated England 6-3 at Wembley in November 1953. Cullis asked him to help devise a style of play that would combine the best of Hungary's approach while remaining true to the 'wholly English' principles of 'direct passing'.

Wolves won the championship for the first time in 1954, the success based on the Cullis/Reep methodology.

In 1955, Reep left Wolves for Sheffield Wednesday. He'd never been formally employed at Molineux, and the job at Hillsborough provided greater security and higher wages. He earned £750 for a one-year renewable contract as an analyst for manager Eric Taylor. He played a key role in the Owls' promotion to the First Division in 1956 before departing two years later when Taylor was fired.

'I must emphasise that my methods are not a declaration of how football should be played,' Reep was at pains to explain, 'but it is the most efficient way.'

His ideas were not universally accepted, but they left an indelible mark on English football. Charles Hughes, the FA's director of coaching in the 1980s and 1990s, was a staunch supporter. In his book, *The Winning Formula*, he stated that '85 per cent of goals were scored from moves of five or fewer passes.' Thus began the English obsession with the 'Position of Maximum Opportunity'. Thanks largely to Hughes' influence at the FA, POMO football became the norm in England.

This philosophy advocated that teams should get the ball as close to the opposition's far post as possible, as this was from where most goals were scored. This meant launching crosses and long diagonals as frequently as possible.

Such thinking would be exploited by Wilkinson in later years but it was Allen Wade who inspired his passion for coaching.

Wilkinson left Brighton in 1971 at the age of 27, having made only 18 starts under new manager Pat Saward. He applied for the manager's job at Wimbledon but was rejected. Jim Smith, the player-manager at Northern Premier League Boston United, offered Wilkinson the position of player-coach, which he eagerly accepted.

Smith was an old friend, a young pro making his way at Sheffield United when Wilkinson had a trial there.

'As a nervous 16-year-old I was shown into the dressing room,' recalled Wilkinson. 'Jim walked over with a huge grin on his face, shook my hand and wished me luck.

'Jim was intelligent, passionate, determined and honest. Never one to mince his words, he was a leader in the truest sense. He was liked and admired by everyone around him.

'Jim recommended me to look after the team with Keith Jobling and so we decided I would look after the team and again he would deal with matters not directly concerned with the players or with the games.

'In a sense, without knowing it, I'd had four years of practice at Boston where we were very successful, very successful, winning the league two or three times, winning the competition between the Northern Premier League and the Southern League.

'We'd had some good runs in the Cup, one of them ending at Derby County, who the year before had been champions. We got a 0-0 draw at Derby County and we were unfortunate because in the last five or ten minutes, Alan Tuly had a header that hit the post. The ball was stuck on the line in the mud, otherwise we would have been heroes. We got battered the following week.'

Wilkinson combined his management role with studying for a Physical Education degree at Sheffield University and working part-time as a teacher at Abbeydale Grange School.

Wilkinson took over full-time after Smith left Boston in 1975 and led the club to two more Northern Premier League titles. The club's chances of being elected to the Football League were thwarted because their stadium and facilities did not meet the League's standards.

He moved on to Mossley, combining the role with managing the England non-league team, and was part of Ron Greenwood's senior set-up.

Wilkinson was offered the job when Graham Taylor left Third Division Lincoln to take over at Watford in June 1977, but he declined, 'given my age at the time and Lincoln's limited potential'.

The decision didn't hold him back – the FA appointed Wilkinson as their regional coach for the Sheffield area and by 1978 he was assisting Dave Sexton and Terry Venables with the England Under-21s.

Such experiences set Wilkinson up nicely for Notts County. Considering his resignation discussion with Wade a formality, Wilkinson was astonished to receive a stony response.

'Your contract here ends at the end of this year and I'd like you to see it out.'

A downcast Wilkinson broke the news to Sirrel, thinking that was the end of it. He received another unexpected response.

'We didn't say WHEN we wanted you. We said we wanted you and if that's going to be 1 January next year, so be it.'

A relieved Wilkinson spoke again to Wade, thinking he might yet get released. Wade, however, was adamant that Wilkinson should see out his contract.

Wilkinson sat out the next six months, watching County whenever he could. Neither the players nor the media realised what was going on until his appointment as first-team coach was made public. Even then, most observers assumed Wilkinson would be a glorified gopher for Sirrel. To keep pressure off the new man, County didn't correct the misunderstanding.

Wilkinson was cool and detached, with a bookish demeanour, but his direct, adult approach helped him form a strong bond with the squad.

His first game in charge was against Cambridge United on New Year's Day 1980 at Meadow Lane. County were only four points clear of the drop zone.

With several Scots and one Irishman in the squad, Wilkinson was worried what they might get up to on New Year's Eve. He arranged for them to stay at the Post House Hotel in Sandiacre, ten miles from Nottingham, so he could keep an eye on them.

A phone call from the night porter woke Wilkinson up shortly after he went to bed. Some guests were complaining about a commotion in one player's room.

Wilkinson arrived to find the entire squad, bar two, partying. At 36, Wilkinson was little older than some of the players and unsure how to react.

'Have you got a glass for me, lads, before we have a little chat?' he said, quite calmly, before expressing 'my extreme displeasure at their behaviour, their failure to accept a code of conduct expected of top sportsmen and suggested they head straight to their beds. There may have been a temptation to try to win the players over by being their mate and turning a blind eye. I knew that was wrong and that a dividing line had to be drawn.'

There was no yelling, just a calm, assertive tone – and no grassing up to Sirrel.

It was a huge test, having to assert his authority at a critical time. The players appreciated his calm reaction, his decision not to make a fuss. The first test had been passed.

'Players fundamentally want honesty,' says Wilkinson. 'Certainly, you have to gain their trust. Players will trust you for two reasons. One is your competence. Is he good or not? When he makes a decision, has he proved that is the correct way to go? You have to build that up. Trust you in the second sense that he won't use us or abuse us. He will make decisions that we will all benefit from, not just him.'

Sirrel taught Wilkinson a lot. The Scotsman knew the ropes and gave Wilkinson the best grounding in management he could wish for. The two made an excellent team, a partnership way ahead of its time.

Sirrel did everything he could to shield his colleague from the worst ravages of the media. Wilkinson recalled an early example when Sirrel invited him to a press conference after a game at Leyton Orient.

The first question came. 'Mr Wilkinson, you've got a different style, can you tell us something about that?'

As Wilkinson was considering his response, Sirrel leapt in. 'Young man, young man, I suggest if you want to know answers to things like that, you get a f***ing coach education at Lilleshall.'

He led Wilkinson away, abruptly ending the press conference.

Wilkinson was more than a sponge – he developed his own distinct insights and approaches, years ahead of his time in terms of diet and nutrition, statistical analysis and sports science.

'I went to Nottingham University, spoke to the appropriate people and said, "Look, free tickets for a game if at the same time when you come to the game, you'll record stats based on what you see occurring during the game."'

Charles Reep would have been proud.

Diet became crucial. Wilkinson began taking the team to Holme Pierrepont, the National Water Sports Centre located just outside Nottingham. The meals there were designed to maximise performance, 'so the steak went and carbohydrates and so on'.

There were other innovations. Wilkinson habitually watched matches from a perch high up in the roof of the stand.

'I decided I'd go up there first half which meant me climbing up this ladder, then getting along the rafters and then sitting in this area underneath the stand roof above the dugout which gave me a perfect view for 44 or 43 of the 45 minutes because then I was off and down to be in the dressing room when they came in.

'If there's anything really crucial cropped up whilst I was up there, I'd write that down on a piece of paper and wrap it around one of the pebbles that I'd taken up with me and sling that down on to the track.'

Wilkinson steadied County's form after Christmas and they finished the season a comfortable eight points clear of relegation.

Wilkinson had devised a strategy for getting the most out of the players. There were some decent footballers at County, even if they had not realised their potential.

Chief among them was Don Masson, a cultured Scottish midfielder who returned to Meadow Lane in 1978 after four years away with Queens Park Rangers and Derby. He had been a member of Ally MacLeod's underperforming Scotland team at the World Cup and even at 33 was still one of the best schemers in the country.

'At Notts County, our strategy was clear: capitalise on our strengths and devise a game plan that would unsettle our opponents. Our team was full of players with excellent ball control and passing abilities. That was the cornerstone of our approach.

'Don Masson was like an orchestra conductor. He had very nearly a full set of clubs in his bag, and he was instrumental. He dictated the tempo with his ball control and vision. We had other skilled passers like Ray O'Brien, Tristan Benjamin, and Pedro Richards. Pedro – "Pedro Beckenbauer" we called him – played sweeper, playing the ball out from the back. He was the first sweeper in the country who did that.

'I decided that the best way for them to play, particularly with Don Masson in the middle of the park, was pass, pass, pass, with the goalkeeper not allowed to kick the ball. We had rotating full-backs, we invented underlapping. The full-back, instead of going around the wide player, went inside him. We played with a sweeper.

'This was how I tried to get Boston to play, passing football, but we didn't have the players. At Notts County, we had players who could pass.'

Wilkinson extended pre-season training to seven weeks, far longer than was customary. 'It gave me time to play, pick a team and work with the team ... decide how best to get each of those individuals doing what they do best in a team that performs at its best.

'We played to get out of that division, we played, as they call it today, beautiful football. Avramovic in goal was not allowed to kick the ball unless he had to, he had to throw it to people. We had rotation particularly at full-back and wide midfield. Don Masson would drop into the back four and it became a back five but then Richards would come out and we literally passed our way to success.

'I'd agreed friendlies … starting at like almost pub-team level which would allow us to do what we had been practising when we'd got the ball. We had rehearsal and then practice during the game and then rehearsal again and then practice until we got it grooved, then it came natural.

'I remember playing a friendly away at Bristol City. We passed the ball for fun but the game was a draw. They were running all over the place, chasing shadows.'

As Wilkinson came off at the end, he ran into one of Bristol's midfielders in the tunnel, Gerry Gow, a grizzled Scot, a bit of a hard man.

'Are you the new coach?'

'Yeah.'

'You'll get f***ing relegated trying to play like that.'

'Well, we'll see.'

It was a common response until the season began but the strategy worked for County. 'It was Christmas before anybody worked out what we were doing.'

Wilkinson's approach to the season would serve him well throughout his career. It contradicted the stereotypical assertion that 'we take each game as it comes'.

He divided the season into groups of games and estimated a points trajectory for each group. His players would be promoted if they could average seven or eight points per group (in the days when a win was worth two points).

'By all means, look at performance game to game because that's where you'll make the minor adjustments, but just as important is to look at results in a longer term. It can be groups of six, it can be groups of ten, and let's look at how many points we've got out of that group and how many would we have expected to get. It just takes a bit of the up and down nature away which is sometimes generated by results.'

Notts County went into their home game against Watford on 25 April knowing that they needed two points from their final three fixtures to seal automatic promotion in second place behind West Ham. County were three points ahead of Blackburn, who had two games remaining, and four better than Swansea, who had three to go.

When the news broke that Blackburn had beaten Newcastle and Swansea had seen off Chelsea, Wilkinson was left biting his nails after County's 2-1 defeat to Watford.

The result was not terminal, but County went into their penultimate game at Chelsea in anxious mood.

'The most important thing is that we continue to do what we're good at and trust each other, trust ourselves, trust what we do and then just give it our best shot. So that's always been my approach. We'd had enough dress rehearsals, so it's a matter of, "Listen fellas, forget it's Chelsea, forget it's away, forget promotion. The most important thing is come out of this game with a good performance and a good result and then we'll look at it."'

Trevor Christie put County ahead in the 15th minute, and Rachid Harkouk made it 2-0 in the second half with a solo effort.

As the clock ticked down, Chelsea fans staged a pitch invasion, forcing the players to go off. There was a Tannoy announcement saying the game might be abandoned if the pitch couldn't be cleared. The referee assured the County players, 'Don't worry, we'll finish this game even if it's at midnight.'

Eventually, the players returned to complete the 90 minutes and County confirmed their promotion.

Masson fully appreciated how much credit was owed to Wilkinson.

'There is not a hope in hell the club would have got promotion without Howard. He was key to it all. As far as the players were concerned, Howard was the boss. To supporters, Jimmy was the boss. Yes, Jimmy was there but he was in the background, he never interfered. It was fantastic judgement from Jimmy to be able to know when to let go and delegate. He now had someone who he could trust.

'Howard was comfortable dealing with top-quality players. He knew he could mould them and get them to do what he wanted them to.'

The fixture list was not kind to County – their first game in the top flight since 1926 was away to Aston Villa. Wilkinson's men were forced to watch Villa parade the championship trophy in front of their fans but it did his pre-match motivational talk for him.

Villa Park was silenced when Iain McCulloch headed home from a corner in the first half as County showed that they could compete in the First Division.

The victory gave Wilkinson confidence, but the league eventually worked out how to deal with County. By the first week of December, they were in the relegation zone and fearing the worst.

Fate suddenly intervened. In one of the worst winters in recent memory, snow fell heavily for weeks, and football was cancelled until 5 January. Wilkinson used the break to work out how to change things.

'The division we were now in, they had better coaches, they had better players and they were making life more difficult for us. We weren't allowed to play our game. The passing game was no longer effective.

'It started snowing beginning of December and that was football finished for five weeks. At the very beginning of that long lay-off, I sat them down. "Listen, fellas, what we're doing is not working, we're going to get relegated if we keep doing it, because we're not suddenly going to get better, coaches are getting to know what we're trying to do better, they're getting to know what works against us better. We need to change and here's what I propose. Obviously, I need your buy-in."

'To cut a long story short, in the Second Division, we played possession for position. We now had to work on position for possession. We had to stop giving the ball away or losing it in our own half. We needed to start playing up there, so we went to almost the opposite extreme.

'We worked very hard on the new way which was to play longer from our half. If we got it in their half, great, we play on from there. If they get it in their half, we work very hard at getting the ball back, but in their half.'

Wilkinson's solution could have been lifted directly from the teachings of Reep.

Success was not immediate; County lost 6-0 to Villa in the FA Cup in their first game back. The teams met again in the league a week later, with County winning 1-0. They then defeated local rivals Nottingham Forest 2-0, with Avramovic saving a John Robertson penalty.

Brian Clough's team won the European Cup in 1979 and 1980 and was regarded as one of the best in the country. This was a watershed moment for County fans, who had lived in their neighbours' shadow for decades.

It wasn't all plain sailing – Liverpool won 4-0 at Meadow Lane – but County bounced back instantly with victory at high-flying Ipswich, which Wilkinson remembers fondly.

'The longer ball was a solution to our predicament at the time but that's not to say that on those occasions when the opportunity presented itself you didn't use the strengths that hitherto you had been able to capitalise on. Away at Ipswich, the opportunity arises and we revert back to winning the ball in our half and finishing up with a goal up at the other end after making 18 passes. They weren't just passes, they were one-touch passes, all first-touch from one end of the pitch to the other, put the ball in the net, Gordon Mair. They never touched the ball.

'It was such a good goal that at half-time as we get up to go inside, Bobby Robson's waiting for me, walking up to where he stood at the dugout, puts his arm around my shoulder, shakes my hand and eulogises about the goal.'

County gathered enough points to finish 15th, five clear of relegation, but were widely expected to be one-season wonders.

There were some heavy defeats – 5-3 at Luton, 6-0 at home to Ipswich, 4-0 at Manchester United, 5-1 at Liverpool, 5-3 at Watford – but even a run of five losses in seven games in December and January saw them drop only as low as 15th.

Three consecutive victories in February and March were crucial, but a disastrous run of one win in nine games saw County slip dangerously close to relegation before beating Brighton at the end of April. On the final day, a famous 3-2 victory over Manchester United confirmed a third successive year in the First Division.

Wilkinson sat back, content, with a growing reputation as one of the brightest young coaches around.

The Graduate

The foundation stone to Wednesday's
success was invariably perspiration
rather than inspiration.

IN HIS time at Notts County, Howard Wilkinson created some wonderful memories for the fans – getting them into the First Division at all was one thing but keeping them there for two years was an achievement beyond most supporters' dreams. He built a team that, with wise investment, could have gone on to great things.

'There's a point where sometimes only money will make a difference,' admitted Wilkinson. 'That player would do us and improve us by five per cent or whatever, but he'll cost this. There has to be that ability to do that because the higher up you go the more the qualities of the players matter.'

Wilkinson was content at Meadow Lane and had no desire to leave, but his contract had expired by the summer of 1983. Jimmy Sirrel and Jack Dunnett wanted Wilkinson to stay, and initial talks about a new contract were promising. There was one issue: the salary. Wilkinson and Dunnett both had red lines and neither was willing to compromise. With Wilkinson's summer holiday approaching, there was still a difference of £1,000 between them.

If Dunnett had compromised, Wilkinson would have stayed, and history would have turned out very differently.

The County chairman, president of the Football League and a former Labour MP, however, was obstinate and refused to budge.

Wilkinson recalled, 'It wasn't £1,000 in 350 or 400 thousand, it was £1,000 in double figures, lower double figures. I left to go on holiday and left the contract business like that because of Jack's refusal to reconsider.'

Wilkinson was at East Midlands Airport waiting for a flight when there was a phone call for him. It was Bert McGee, the chairman of Sheffield Wednesday.

'Good morning, Howard. I wondered if you would be interested in joining us at Hillsborough?'

Jack Charlton had just resigned as Wednesday manager, claiming that he was no longer enjoying the job.

Charlton led Wednesday to promotion from the Third Division in 1980, missed a second promotion by a single point in 1982, and led Wednesday to the FA Cup semi-finals the following year. Nonetheless, Big Jack was gone, disgruntled at the fickleness of some fans.

McGee identified Wilkinson as someone who could take Wednesday to the next level. When he indicated his willingness to talk, a meeting with McGee and two fellow directors was scheduled.

'What I said made sense to them,' said Wilkinson. 'They were happy to recognise the fact that the money mattered and can accelerate progress. In those days Sheffield Wednesday could count on the support of over 30,000 fans if things were going well and at that time gates mattered in terms of revenue. It came with disadvantages but it was a blank piece of paper. It was to start from scratch in many respects.'

Wilkinson could not say no to the chance to manage his boyhood favourites. Even though Wednesday were in a lower division than County, he was drawn to the club's potential. 'Given God's grace and time and all the other things that one needs,' he told the media a year after he arrived, 'I came here to win the European Cup.'

More reflectively, he commented, 'When I came here, I looked at the whole situation. I decided what I'd like to do and I sat down and decided what I could do relative to the league we were in, relative to our pitch, relative to the players I'd got, relative to fixtures, relative to the expectations of the public. When I came here, I tried as much as I could to analyse the job as I've done in the past and then, having analysed the job, lay down what I thought was necessary to achieve some sort of success in it.

'I just feel that I better understand the people around here than perhaps I understand the people anywhere else, and I think that is an advantage. I also think that the same consideration applies the other way round. I think that maybe the supporters feel that as well, to a certain extent.'

At Hillsborough, there was the making of a decent squad and a backbone on which Wilkinson would rely that first season, with central defender Mick Lyons being the main man. He rose to prominence with Everton, but after nearly 500 appearances, he chose to start over with Wednesday in 1982. He liked Charlton, but he was even more taken with his successor. 'Out of all the managers I have played under, probably Howard Wilkinson has had the most effect on me. I believe that no matter what a player is, Wilkie would always be able to extract the most out of that player, even in some cases without the player knowing it himself.'

The contrast between Charlton and the highly organised Wilkinson was a culture shock for many. Mel Sterland, despite his aversion to Wilkinson's rigorous training regimen, coped particularly well with the transition.

Sterland was a staunch supporter of Wilkinson – 'A fantastic manager, brilliant' – and contrasted his approach with that of the chaotic Charlton.

'The two managers could not have been more different, but they were both great for me.

'Howard went through everything in detail and was very, very strict. He knew what he wanted and if we didn't get it right first time, we would stay there until we did.

'Jack, though, couldn't have been more different. I remember the first FA Cup semi-final we played against Brighton at Highbury. It was a huge day for the club and yet we managed to leave two players behind at the hotel. No one noticed until we were nearly there. Big Jack just forgot them both.

'Jack constantly forgot players' names. I always remember a practice match when we had 12 players on the pitch! I said, "Gaffer, you've got an extra man!" He just turned to John Pearson and said, "You're not playing. Get off!" It was so funny.'

Wilkinson bolstered his squad with the additions of goalkeeper Martin Hodge, strikers Imre Varadi and Tony Cunningham, and centre-back Lawrie Madden, who played under Wilkinson at Boston. He returned to Meadow Lane the following February to sign Northern Ireland international Nigel Worthington as he strengthened further.

Wilkinson, determined that Wednesday would hit the ground running, was a tyrant in pre-season, demanding that they become 'the fittest team in the league. The legend grew that I put Sheffield Wednesday through the most gruelling training sessions in the game. Whenever a player was involved in transfer talks, he would raise the hoary old chestnut about the cross-country runs and the physical fitness levels. The legend was, in fact, a myth.'

Wilkinson insisted that the reputation was nothing to do with him but dated back to the 60s when Alan Brown managed Wednesday.

He said that Brown had introduced the idea of runs through the countryside surrounding the city to keep the players fresh. Wilkinson credited assistant manager Peter Eustace with suggesting the change. He insisted the players never ran any further than they would have done inside the training ground.

Mick Lyons put a different slant on things. 'Every Monday in training we would be running. He'd have us running up and down hills for an hour or more non-stop. He ran our bollocks off!' One wag said, 'I heard a story that when he took over, he called all the players in, nine o'clock in a morning. He locked the gates and when they did come out eventually on their hands and knees, it was dusk.'

When asked about it, Wilkinson quipped, 'No, it's not true. I let them out a week later.' He went on, 'I think there was perhaps a change of emphasis when I arrived. We did perhaps work harder or longer because I thought that was the way to do it. There are many ways to skin a cat, it just happened to be my particular way.'

Lee Chapman recalled the manager's rigorous two-hour set-piece sessions every Friday morning. The players dreaded them, but Wilkinson was immovable. Any player not taking them as seriously would have hell to pay.

Chapman also highlighted Wilkinson's unwavering belief in his ability to mould average players into a team capable of competing with the best. He saw potential even in those whose careers had gone off track. It made sense given the club's financial constraints, which prevented Wilkinson from pursuing top players.

Having to shop in football's bargain basement led Wilkinson to adopt the teachings of Charles Reep. In came the long-ball football on which Wednesday thrived.

The approach is not pretty, and its success is entirely dependent on players' physical fitness, especially in midfield, where they spend the entire afternoon racing between the two penalty areas.

Wilkinson demonstrated at Notts County that he could put together a decent passing side with the right players, but he had been spoiled at Meadow Lane. At Hillsborough, he inherited a Jack Charlton squad devoid of the gorgeous touches and elegance of a Don Masson. Ever the pragmatist, he went with what he had, making the best use of the resources available to him. It wasn't beautiful football, but it was effective in a division that rewarded graft and percentage play. His name became synonymous with the style of football he played at Wednesday. But it was his obsession with the team, with cultivating the most wonderful team spirit, that left the most lasting legacy.

Wilkinson has always had a high level of loyalty from his players, the men who know him best, but this is a mystery to those outside his inner circle. Undoubtedly, that was down to Wilkinson's refusal to kowtow to the media, which always portrayed him as aloof and condescending.

That was exemplified by his first press conference at Hillsborough, which he fondly recalls. 'A gentleman called Peter Cooper who wrote for the *Daily Mirror*, who had a very, how shall we say, posh accent – not, you know, your usual run of the mill scribbler for a press man – he asked me in that superior way of his, "I believe you were a teacher?" So, I said, "Yes." He said, "And what did you teach?" And I said, "Children," and turned to the next man. Apparently, he took that personally, he thought I was being a smart a***. He bore that grudge for the rest of his life.

'To be honest, maybe I learned too much from [Jimmy Sirrel] because a lot of people have said to me, "You know your greatest problem, don't you? PR. You didn't court journalists, you weren't the best communicator with them" and so on.'

* * *

Charlton, never overly concerned with administrative affairs, had let many of the players' contracts lapse. When Wilkinson arrived, there were only 13 players registered with a surfeit of centre-backs. 'Because of what was at my disposal, for the first time possibly in England, we played with three at the back. We played with a very high line; offside was a big factor in what we did. We were very, very fit. We played a very, very high tempo, very high tempo, and we had a way of playing that suited what we'd got at the time.

'It took people until Christmas to work out what we were doing. These days they would suss it in two weeks. I was getting people to do what they did best and by doing what they did best we were winning, which is what footballers want.'

Wilkinson emphasised that playing with a high back line was risky, often suicidally so, but it was very effective when combined with a high tempo because the players knew their jobs and were so well drilled.

The clarity Wilkinson brought to everything made it easy to understand. It was all about routine and habit, muscle memory and Wilkinson's admonitions to 'trust your swing'. That maxim became legend in his time at Leeds, with players not having to think about what they had to do, like driving a car or playing golf. The more you practised, the better you got without even having to think about it – indeed, if you thought about things too much, you would mess it up.

The Wilko effect was palpable from the first whistle of the first match, a 1-0 victory at relegated Swansea. Wednesday tore through the opening weeks of the season, quickly moving to the head of the pack. They went unbeaten until the end of November, when they came a cropper at Crystal Palace.

Vince Hilaire, who would later 'serve' under Wilkinson at Leeds, was in the Palace side. 'I'd never played against a team with so much energy,' he recalled.

Unique features marked Wilkinson's approach. He assigned his goalkeeper to take all free kicks outside the area. Anticipating the massive punt forward, all the other players would race forward to manfully attack the dropping ball.

Wednesday never gave opponents a moment's break. They prided themselves on getting the ball in play quickly and were instantly at the other team.

So dominating was Wednesday's football that, even after the Palace defeat, they retained a three-point lead on second-placed Chelsea. The two teams were locked together all season.

Wilkinson had turned Wednesday into a force of nature. It didn't endear him to the London press, who castigated him as a long-ball merchant. Fleet Street smugly insisted that Chelsea played football while Wednesday were 'hoof it' hooligans.

Lyons retorted, 'Well it got us promoted! No one could have a go at us, really, because it was successful and if a way of playing is successful, why not play that way? We loved it if teams fannied about, passing around at the back. We'd press and press, get the ball off them and score!'

The other team in the promotion chase was Newcastle, whom Wednesday beat in November thanks to a brace from former Tyneside striker Imre Varadi.

Varadi had been replaced at St James' Park by Peter Beardsley, who formed a celebrated front line with Kevin Keegan and Chris Waddle.

The decision to release Varadi had always rankled with him and he was desperate to prove Newcastle wrong.

'I wanted to make sure that by the time I played Newcastle I was ready,' recalled Varadi. 'They came to Hillsborough with their big hitters and we won 4-2 – I scored two. I just made sure I rammed [the decision] back down their throats – in a nice way, you know, I didn't really celebrate my goals.'

Wednesday stuttered over Christmas with defeats to Grimsby and Middlesbrough. Undaunted, Wilkinson drove his men on and they quickly got back on track with three victories on the bounce in early January, including a 6-1 hammering of Swansea.

Wednesday made it through to the last eight of the League Cup, leading to several of Wednesday's Second Division fixtures being delayed. This exacerbated the problems of Christmas and Chelsea went top on New Year's Eve, having played two games more than the Owls.

Wednesday also made waves in the FA Cup, seeing off Barnsley, Coventry and Oxford before a quarter-final against Southampton. They drew 0-0 at Hillsborough in front of more than 43,000 fans, but Wednesday were swamped 5-1 in the replay.

Chelsea and Wednesday came head-to-head at Stamford Bridge on 21 January. Mickey Thomas, the Wales midfielder signed from Stoke, made his Blues debut and scored twice in a 3-2 victory. The victory took Chelsea top by dint of goals scored, with points and goal differences identical.

Despite Wednesday's outstanding form, Newcastle steadily gained ground on the top two. The last day of March saw the gap gone completely.

Wednesday had a local derby against Leeds at Elland Road. The home side were tenth in the table but Yorkshire pride was at stake and United rose to the occasion, scrambling a 1-1 draw.

With suspensions and injuries wiping out almost his entire defence, Wilkinson said it was a first outing for 'this' side. 'I thought the heroes today were the lads who came in. Up and down the country, people were secretly thinking we could get done here at Leeds.'

Wilkinson phlegmatically declared it a point won rather than two lost but, by virtue of Chelsea also dropping a point in a frenetic 3-3 draw at Cardiff, Newcastle drew level on points with their rivals.

Manchester City appeared to be the only side that could prevent the top three securing promotion but their chances were left looking slim after defeat at home to Huddersfield on 23 April. Wednesday needed one point from their final six games to reclaim their place in the First Division after a 14-year absence.

Their title chances were boosted when Chelsea blew a two-goal lead at Portsmouth to finish 2-2. That left Wednesday with a chance to clinch promotion the following day, but they squandered the moment, losing at Middlesbrough.

Wednesday's promotion was finally sealed on 28 April when Mel Sterland's cool-as-a-cucumber penalty, stroked into the corner, was enough to beat Palace.

Wednesday were accompanied into the First Division by Chelsea, who went up in style by beating Leeds 5-0.

The title's destination was still unknown as Wednesday's chairman and manager spoke to the media.

McGee's first thought was for the efforts of Charlton. The interviewer, taken slightly aback, countered with, 'But Howard has built on that and he's brought his own players in.'

McGee went on, 'He's spent more than £460,000 on new players and did well with them. You saw this season the result of a hell of a lot of hard work.

'Sheffield people, we've wanted success a long time, we've suffered in Sheffield. Yes, they want success in the First Division. We can't promise them the championship, but we'll promise them good results, a time to take stock, a time to build. We're not impatient in the sense that we will go out and think we can buy million-pound players and pay £2,000-a-week wages, that is a nonsense that is beating football. We want Sheffield people to enjoy Sheffield football at prices they can afford to pay at the turnstiles.'

Wilkinson: 'At the start of last July, if you'd said to me, will you settle for promotion and nothing else, six games from the end of the season, I think I … the chairman, the board, the spectators who've turned up week in and week out, I think they would have said yes.

'To be a Sheffield boy who supported them, who played for them, to come back with a hope of taking them to the First Division and to do it in your first season. Very, very emotional moment for me.'

Wednesday had a two-point advantage over Chelsea and a game in hand but the Londoners, with three matches left, could yet pip them.

That seemed unlikely when the Owls won their game in hand at Huddersfield on 1 May to open a five-point gap.

Against the odds, Chelsea maintained the tension with victory at Manchester City on Friday evening.

Wednesday could have all but wrapped things up the following day at mid-table Shrewsbury, but blew it again, going down 2-1.

When a further point was squandered on the Monday, in a goalless draw at home to Manchester City, Chelsea drew level after comfortably beating Barnsley. A goal difference superior by 13 meant that Chelsea needed to match Wednesday's result on the final day to wrap up the championship.

While Wilkinson's men did the business with a two-goal win at Cardiff, they were denied silverware when Chelsea inched home with a Kerry Dixon goal at Grimsby.

The tension had a lasting impact on Wilkinson. He was shocked when he saw photos of himself on the final day of the season. He said he looked like he'd escaped from a prison camp and vowed never to let a football season have that effect on him again.

Leading scorer Varadi attributed Wednesday's late slump to a loss of impetus.

'We got promoted six games from the end of the season,' he said. 'Mentally, we switched off as a group. It would have helped us had we gone to the second-last game to get promoted.'

Varadi attached no blame to Wilkinson, adding that he was never given the credit he deserved.

'Howard got us very fit. We must have been the fittest team in the land. We could go for 90 minutes and whoever played Sheffield Wednesday that season knew they were in for a tough game. We put teams under a lot of pressure, we created a lot of chances and Howard was one of the first managers at the time to play with three centre-halves and two wing-backs. He didn't get a lot of credit for that. Mel Sterland and Nigel Worthington got forward and put in crosses and it worked. He was ahead of his time back in the 1980s. Maybe that was because he wasn't a football purist type of person. He knew how to put a team together, get promotion and do a job.'

The team spirit at Hillsborough was exceptional, albeit moulded through unconventional methods.

Sterland recalls Wilkinson's dressing-room rages, when he threw all sorts of things around, even once lifting a bench in a threatening manner to prove a point. On another occasion, he smacked John Pearson round the face to get a reaction, only to be met by laughter from the amiable Pearson.

Wilkinson was content to allow the occasional scuffle between players, taking it as testament to their competitive spirit and will to win. Sterland and Imre Varadi were often at odds, and Varadi once came to blows with Chris Morris after they went for the same ball. Sterland remembers them 'knocking the sh*t out of each other'. Far from intervening, Wilkinson would normally leave players to slug it out.

Wilkinson spent the summer judiciously strengthening the squad. While selling Bannister, Megson and Cunningham netted him half a million, he spent less than half of that to bring in Hull winger Brian Marwood and Sunderland hitman Lee Chapman. Wednesday were undeniably stronger for the changes and had a new cutting edge.

Chapman had lost his way after a bright start to his career with Stoke City. A transfer to Arsenal was a disaster and a stay at Sunderland brought no redemption, but Wilkinson saw beyond the headlines.

The move came about almost by chance. Chapman was sat with Sunderland keeper Chris Turner as Turner tried to persuade Peter Eustace to give him a chance at Hillsborough. Eustace wouldn't budge on that one but fell into a conversation with Chapman, who agreed to take a pay cut to engineer a £110,000 move.

Chapman was a throwback to a different age, a towering centre-forward prepared to risk life and limb for a goal. He was exceptional in the air, big and powerful and always in the right place at the right time.

Wilkinson set up his team to play to Chapman's strengths and the striker repaid him a hundred times over. It was the beginning of a professional association that would last more than a decade.

While everybody knew that Chapman lacked finesse and touch on the ground, his height and superb aerial abilities made him a commanding presence. The country's top defenders grew to dread their encounters with Chapman. The secret to his success? Understanding his limitations.

'If I could, I would have a team of ten Bests or ten Beckenbauers,' admitted Wilkinson. 'But I can't. So, I try to get players performing at their peak, both individually and collectively.'

Wednesday were boosted by the changes, and they set about life in Division One with a resounding victory over Nottingham Forest at Hillsborough. But any notions that stepping up would be simple were dashed when they lost their next two games.

After that, they found their feet, progressing steadily. They emerged from a match at Anfield against reigning champions Liverpool in late September with a 2-0 victory to consolidate fifth position.

A month later, Wednesday beat Leicester 5-0 thanks to a Varadi hat-trick and climbed to second. They couldn't maintain such lofty heights as the teams around them sussed the Wednesday way, but they finished eighth. They reached the last eight of the League Cup, bowing out to Chelsea after an epic marathon.

The teams met at Stamford Bridge in the final days of the infamous miners' strike and during one of the coldest winters for years.

The match had to be rescheduled due to the freeze which caused an unplanned two-week midwinter break.

'As teams we were very close in the league but we were unbelievably different in styles,' remembers Chelsea winger Pat Nevin. 'They were big, strong, robust and we were more attack-minded and more skilful. I used to think of them almost as robots and that is how you ended up getting by them because they did the same things all the time.'

Wednesday took the lead but David Speedie equalised before the interval. Martin Hodge kept the Owls in the tie, saving a penalty from Kerry Dixon, the country's leading scorer at the time.

Hillsborough was packed to the rafters for the replay and Wednesday started emphatically, with Lyons powering home a header after eight minutes.

Andy Blair whipped a cross over to the back post for Chapman to head the second with Varadi following up to make sure the ball crossed the line. Chelsea were rattled and a string of yellow cards followed. They rallied and Peter

Shirtliff had to block Speedie's goalbound attempt, the post coming to the Owls' rescue.

Marwood drove a further nail into the Chelsea coffin in first-half injury time, curling a left-footed drive past Eddie Niedzwiecki. Hillsborough was rocking.

From the restart, Chelsea were right at it and half-time substitute Paul Canoville scored after ten seconds.

The Owls continued to press, and there seemed to be no immediate danger, but Chelsea were working their way back into contention in midfield. Midway through the second half, Dixon rounded Hodge to score. The tide was turning.

On 76 minutes, Pat Nevin burst into the Wednesday box, checked and played a perfect square ball for Thomas to side-foot home. A quarter of an hour to go, 3-3 and everything still up for grabs.

With four minutes remaining, Nevin produced the spark for Chelsea, releasing Dixon. Worthington and Lyons tried to close him down, but Dixon slipped the ball to Canoville, who found the net off the advancing Hodge.

It was Wilkinson's turn to be shocked.

Tony Gubba: 'Howard Wilkinson with his head in his hands … he can't believe it … the match all but won at half-time with Wednesday three up … and now it's all gone away and it's all gone wrong.'

Seconds remained. Fans streamed out of the exits. Nevin had possession and appeared to be safe in his own half but his clearance was blocked by Shirtliff, the ball falling to Sterland. The Wednesday man advanced into the box and slipped the ball around Doug Rougvie. Rougvie turned and felled Sterland. Penalty! Or was it?

The Wednesday full-back confessed to taking a dive. Rougvie never touched him. He also recalled how regular penalty-taker Andy Blair chickened out of taking the spot kick, leaving the unflappable Sterland to seize the moment. He confidently did so, shooting between the keeper's legs for the fourth goal.

The players had words afterwards, Rougvie calling Sterland a 'fat, lying, cheating bastard', but it was lost on the TV commentator who said, 'Isn't it nice to see two fellow professionals talking about the game.'

Neither side could settle the contest – the match finished 4-4.

A week later, the teams met again at Stamford Bridge for a rematch. Chelsea won 2-1, with Thomas' last-minute goal settling the outcome.

It had been a breathless episode, the most exciting part of a season in which Wilkinson was derided for his prosaic approach.

One match towards the end of the season, against Nottingham Forest, epitomised Wilkinson's tactics. His defence held a high line, repeatedly catching Forest players offside as they attempted to breach their ranks. After taking the lead, Wednesday preserved their advantage by safety-first defence as they closed out the game.

The approach was berated by many. Forest boss Brian Clough – 'I believe in fairies' – espoused an approach that contrasted sharply with Wilkinson's pragmatic style. After the match, he scolded his rival, warning, 'Howard, you'll get the game done away with playing football like that!'

Nonetheless, Wilkinson had his proponents, with *World Soccer* saying, 'He is a deep-thinking man, and the deeper he thinks, the more he becomes convinced by old-fashioned virtues. Those concepts are reflected in his commitment to the job, the commitment he demands from his players and the style of his team's play. So he remains undeterred by criticism. "I have a clear conscience about what I'm doing from the bottom to the top of this club," he says.

'Fortified with his beliefs, Wilkinson attempts – and usually succeeds – to coax the ultimate from his players by steering them along a straight, uncluttered path. He utilises their strengths and accepts their limitations.'

Wilkinson reflected, 'I expect to be a better manager in three years' time and better still in five years – provided I keep an open mind and stay fit and enthusiastic. You have to keep looking ahead and never be tempted to think you can afford to relax. Once you sit on your backside and get involved in all the claptrap, you're in trouble.

'The one certainty is that someday I'll get the sack. The important thing is to be yourself and not try to be anyone else. I'm not influenced by dress or speech. You have to be true to yourself, to your players, to your club and your profession. Nobody can ask more of himself than that.

'I'm employed to run this club in such a manner that when I leave it will be stronger and more successful in every way.'

Wilkinson had high hopes that Wednesday could build on their momentum and go even further.

There were changes in the squad.

He sold 21-goal Varadi to West Bromwich Albion for a club record fee of £285,000. Also on his way was first lieutenant Lyons, who had spent the previous season doubling up as youth-team coach and now moved to Grimsby to start his managerial career in earnest.

Their replacements were West Brom's Garry Thompson and former Blackpool, Leeds and Forest centre-back Paul Hart.

The Owls performed well again, second in the table in the early weeks of the season and seemingly offering the only challenge to runaway leaders Manchester United. Wednesday were the first team to lower the Red Devils' colours, winning 1-0 in front of over 48,000 on an unforgettable Hillsborough afternoon in November.

United came into the game on a 15-match unbeaten streak with many in the media tipping them to end their long title drought.

The decisive moment came five minutes from time when Chapman headed in from Mark Chamberlain's corner.

Wednesday were good value for the win after forcing 16 corners and numerous free kicks.

The season was best remembered for an exciting FA Cup run that saw Wednesday reach the semi-finals, where they faced Everton at Villa Park.

Wednesday couldn't handle a team contesting their third semi-final in a row. They failed to convert three golden chances – Everton won 2-1.

In the following programme, Wilkinson wrote, 'Footballers come in for some stick justifiably sometimes, for their lack of professional commitment and loyalty, but the uncontrolled and spontaneous tears shed after the end on Saturday were deep, sincere expressions of desperate and genuine disappointment.'

Wednesday finished fifth after winning five of their last seven games. The season would be remembered as Wednesday's best for decades.

It should have brought a return to European football after more than 20 years but the ban imposed on English clubs following the Heysel disaster a year earlier meant that there would be no place in the UEFA Cup to mark the achievement.

Wilkinson reflected ruefully on the matter but could be satisfied with the way that he had resurrected one of the game's giants. His success brought interest from other clubs.

Sunderland sacked Len Ashurst after being relegated from the First Division and losing in the Milk Cup Final. They needed a man who could get them up at the first time of asking and Wilkinson was on their shortlist.

Bert McGee announced he had agreed a new five-year contract to keep Wilkinson at Hillsborough, telling the press, 'Howard won't be leaving us. When you've got one of the best managers in the game you don't want to lose him. We aim to build on continuity and stability here. Sealing Howard's long-term future is a major move in that direction.'

Winds of Change

*I'm a firm believer that if you score one goal
the other team have to score two to win.*

12 APRIL 1987. The sun warmed the Hillsborough playing
enclosure as Coventry City and Leeds United came out to
contest the FA Cup semi-final.

A 50,000-strong crowd paid almost £400,000 for the
privilege of watching the game and the size of the purse
was a shot in the arm for Sheffield Wednesday chairman
Bert McGee.

McGee's tight housekeeping kept the club's finances on
an even keel. Wages were modest – Manchester United, who
finished one place above the Owls in 1986, had a payroll twice
as large. Since 1982, transfer spending had been frugal with
net outgoings of less than £400,000.

The investment in the stadium was just as cautious. Over
the same period, only £1.5m was spent, with at least £600,000
of the money coming from grants.

The club was profitable; there had been two years of six-
figure surpluses and the board refused to run up debt. One
could not fault McGee's stewardship. He had returned top-
flight football to the sleeping giant and considered 'steady as
you go' a sensible maxim.

The approach chimed with that of the local population.
Thousands of jobs were lost in South Yorkshire in the aftermath

of the miners' strike. Foreign competition threatened the city's metal and engineering industries, and unemployment stood at 16.3 per cent.

But McGee's approach put him at odds with Howard Wilkinson, who was desperate for funds to develop his overachieving squad. He was getting as much as he could out of the players and substantial investment would be needed to propel the team to the next level.

The budget set by McGee made it difficult to attract the calibre of players Wilkinson needed. Wednesday had gone off the boil after three years on an upward trajectory.

Wilkinson's pleas to McGee got him nowhere but he respected his chairman and the club too much to go public.

Wilkinson's men lost at home to Tottenham five days before the semi-final, dropping to 15th, far from the top-five finish he had hoped for.

With a blank weekend, Wilkinson decided to take in the Leeds–Coventry game. It was partly to witness what might have been – a month earlier, Wednesday had fallen victims to Coventry in the sixth round.

Wednesday had been expected to win despite Coventry being seven places higher in the table.

The 80s had brought good FA Cup memories for Wednesday – they reached the last four in 1983 and 1986. A crowd of 48,005 gathered to witness what they thought would be a 24th successive Cup victory for Wednesday at Hillsborough.

Wilkinson told the press, 'This is our tenth quarter-final match in three-and-a-half years and that's quite a record. Coventry have never been beyond the sixth round and that makes it a big psychological barrier for them to clear.'

Coventry weren't rattled by Wilkinson's remarks. Skipper Brian Kilcline pointed out that his team had 'faced enough tension in the past with their various relegation scraps, so an

FA Cup quarter-final held no fears'. Cheered on by 15,000 of their followers, Coventry were as good as Kilcline's word, winning 3-1 with two late Keith Houchen strikes.

Another reason for Wilkinson's presence at the semi-final was to watch Kilcline, whose career he had shaped at Notts County.

Kilcline joined County at the age of 16 and had made his senior debut before turning professional on his 18th birthday in 1980. He was an ever-present in the side that took Notts into the First Division in 1981.

Kilcline: 'I was taught by Howard about how to play centre-half. He totally changed the way we played. He was a space marker. All the other older lads had been brought up to mark players. I was taught to mark the space and that was fine because I was young but all the other senior players were kicking off about it. There was such an air of dislike for Howard when he first arrived. What used to drive the players mad was that everything he told us to do worked all the time.'

Wilkinson enthused about his protégé. 'He was a man at 17 in terms of his physicality and he was quick and nimble and decent with the ball. In fact, I'm sure I remember him maybe starting as a striker. I can't think of a game when he actually let you down or didn't come up to scratch.'

The rest of the country was eager to see how a revitalised Leeds United would handle their biggest game in years.

Leeds were even drowsier giants than Wednesday but were enjoying a memorable season under the management of Billy Bremner.

The Leeds legend's first year in charge had been poor, but the team started 1986/87 well enough to climb to second in October. But then the rot set in and their form deserted them; they hit a low point just before Christmas when they were thrashed 7-2 by Stoke.

Bremner gambled by selling midfield talisman Ian Snodin to Everton for £800,000 and used the money to rebuild, bringing in four new players. The move paid off handsomely: Leeds climbed the table and enjoyed a good run in the FA Cup, beating Telford, Swindon, First Division Queens Park Rangers and Wigan on the way to the clash with Coventry.

The semi-final was the first at Hillsborough in six years. Following incidents in 1981, in which 38 Tottenham fans were injured on the Leppings Lane terrace during the game with Wolves, the FA had ignored the venue.

After the 1981 game, Chief Constable Brownlow and Assistant Chief Constable Goslin of South Yorkshire Police met Bert McGee to discuss what had gone wrong. Things quickly became heated with McGee berating the police for failing to restore order. Goslin insisted that 'circumstances beyond our control had brought about the crushing situation and conventional methods of control had failed'. He ordered the opening of the perimeter fence gate and spectators were helped to evacuate the terrace to avoid serious injury. Fans were allowed to sit on the track against the perimeter fence wall. McGee described this as 'completely unnecessary and made the ground look untidy'. He said that it might lead to Hillsborough being overlooked for future semi-finals. When Goslin protested that there had been a 'real chance of fatalities', McGee snorted, 'Bollocks! No one would have been killed!'

The club's relationship with the police deteriorated in the weeks that followed. McGee criticised the police for turning away supporters wearing Tottenham colours but holding Wolves tickets from the Spion Kop end. They were directed to Leppings Lane to join Spurs supporters. This caused 'the congestion that resulted in the spill-over at the fence'.

The incident prompted the club to alter the ground's layout, dividing the open terrace into three separate pens to limit sideways movement and improve crowd control. This and other changes invalidated the stadium's safety certificate. Recommendations to feed fans directly into each pen from designated turnstiles were rejected on cost grounds.

The FA's all-ticket rule on all Leeds away fixtures was lifted for the game and tickets were on open sale. Thousands descended on Sheffield.

Leeds were allocated the Leppings Lane end while Coventry took the Kop. It was a recipe for trouble.

The ground opened at 9.30 for a 12.15 start. The Sunday staging and early kick-off were intended to prevent fans from drinking before the match.

Twenty minutes before kick-off, match commander Brian Mole delayed the start to accommodate spectators from both clubs who had been held up en route. Six thousand fans were still awaiting admission.

Leeds fan Steve Lawrence: 'We arrived about 11 o'clock. I wanted to make sure I had a good spot on the Leppings Lane terrace, directly behind the goal. I'd stood there in 1985 to watch Everton play Sheffield Wednesday in a league match so I knew it was a good position to see the game.

'It wasn't overly busy at first but as the next hour passed the pen became increasingly full, to the point where I literally couldn't move. I remember the hot sun shining on me and being unable to lift my arm to shield my eyes from the glare.

'There were crowd surges as people from behind tried to get into the pens, forcing their way in. The intensity wasn't something I'd experienced before. I was lifted off my feet and basically went wherever the crowd surge took me. I'd been used to standing on the Kop at Elland Road and I enjoyed the crowd surges that terrace football brought but this was something else, really scary.'

There were ticket inspections at checkpoints as supporters left the motorway but few at the stadium. The crowds streaming through the turnstiles instinctively headed for the tunnel leading to the central pens in the lower tier of the Leppings Lane end.

Ferenc Morath told the Hillsborough Inquiry that police checked his ticket before he disembarked from the coach and again as he approached the ground. There was a mass of people in front of the turnstiles, with no orderly queues.

By the time he got in, the match had started. 'There was no direction being given by police officers or stewards inside the ground and everyone like myself headed for the tunnel under the West Stand. As I entered the tunnel, I noted that the crowd was back up the tunnel. I believed this was the only way on to the terraces, not having seen any other signs directing otherwise. I therefore pushed my way through the tunnel not knowing what was ahead of me. I noted that people, generally fathers with young lads or girls, were pushing back out of the tunnel, away from the pitch. At this point there was what I would describe as a bad crush.'

The crowd was tightly packed. Morath saw fans climbing the fencing and others being helped up into the West Stand. He said that 'outside the turnstiles and inside the ground there was a total lack of organisation'.

South Yorkshire Police told the Hillsborough Independent Panel that the delayed kick-off was caused by fans arriving late. 'This may be related to the restricted access to alcohol in grounds.'

Fans in the central pens experienced some of what Liverpool supporters would suffer in 1989: surges, crushing and little chance of escape; of 'everyone squeezing the life out of each other' and of 'nowhere to go unless you were willing to climb over the fences'.

Steve Lawrence recalls supporters at the back of the pens 'taking the option to climb up into the seating [in the upper tier], helped by supporters who could see the mass below. I often look back and wonder what the difference was between Leeds in '87 and Liverpool in '89. A very fine margin … It was a tragedy waiting to happen.'

Despite the chaos, it could have been a glorious afternoon for Leeds United, who did everything they could to bridge the gap between the two clubs. It was they who had the early momentum.

'Leeds, resembling a roaring bush fire, burned alarming holes in Coventry's security,' wrote Stuart Jones in *The Times*. After 15 minutes, David Rennie headed in at the near post from Micky Adams' corner.

Leeds kept pushing and should have extended their lead. They seemed set to secure a memorable victory until City manager John Sillett called Micky Gynn from the bench.

When a Coventry through ball pierced Leeds' half, Brendon Ormsby appeared to have things under control, but he misjudged it, thinking he could shepherd it out for a goal kick. It was a fatal error – he was wrong-footed when Bennett stole the ball and instantly centred. Gynn was on it in a flash to fire home.

Leeds' momentum had gone and it was no surprise when Houchen rounded Mervyn Day before netting.

Shoulders sank down the Leeds end, but Bremner chanced his arm, bringing on Peter Haddock and Keith Edwards for the tiring John Stiles and Pearson.

He reaped an instant reward – Edwards' second touch of the ball saw him head home from Ritchie's cross, forcing the game into extra time.

The adrenaline rush was intense but it soon became clear that Leeds were running on empty. Bennett made it 3-2 to Coventry in the first half of the extra 30 minutes after Day could only parry a Houchen effort.

Leeds could not come again and gave way gracefully, their race run.

'Leeds United players hobbled off, some in tears, to a standing ovation from their own and Coventry's followers after an extra special FA Cup semi-final,' reported the *Yorkshire Evening Post.* 'Right to the last minute, Leeds might have forced the game into a replay the following Wednesday, Steve Ogrizovic smothering Keith Edwards' dash on to a Neil Aspin shot to complete Coventry's day. None of the 51,372 spectators who composed the wall of sound inside the stadium would be able to forget this titanic battle ... The tie will go down as being among the best semi-finals in the history of the tournament.'

'I thought they looked half-decent,' remarked Wilkinson when asked years later what he thought of Leeds' display, though he remembered little of the detail. 'Beyond that, I couldn't say. I remember the day. For some reason, sunshine is in my head. I remember the game, but I couldn't make an accurate assessment of what I thought at the time, other than my memory is telling me it wasn't a disaster.'

Damned by faint praise!

The glorious defeat became legend in United folklore, fans revelling in the spirit shown rather than lamenting the bad luck. There was still a path to glory; United's league form pushed them into the promotion shake-up.

There was an additional option in 1987 with the introduction of end-of-season play-offs.

In December 1985, a ten-point plan was agreed to revitalise the Football League's finances. The 'Heathrow Agreement' included a structural reorganisation, reducing the top tier from 22 clubs to 20, while increasing numbers in the other divisions, resulting in three groups of 24. The play-offs were introduced to facilitate the transition.

The initial arrangements were different from later years – they included not only the teams that ended just below the automatic promotion places, but also the one that avoided automatic relegation.

Only when the play-offs began did the realisation sink in that a team could finish sixth in the table and be promoted at the expense of a club that had finished way ahead of them.

The excitement of that first year overshadowed those concerns and the play-offs, originally intended as a temporary addition to the football calendar, were here to stay.

Bremner's men squeezed past Joe Royle's Oldham Athletic in the semi-final on away goals with the sides level on aggregate after two enthralling legs.

'We finished seven points clear of Leeds, so to go out on away goals to them means there is something unjust,' Royle complained.

First Division Charlton defeated Ipswich in the other semi. They won through at Selhurst Park thanks to a brace from Jim Melrose.

Melrose also scored the winner in the first leg of the final against Leeds, his 88th-minute strike at Selhurst Park giving the Addicks a slim advantage going into the second leg.

The biggest crowd of the season gathered at Elland Road to witness an epic encounter.

Charlton weathered the early onslaught but could not prevent Ormsby equalising at the start of the second half. That meant a third instalment as the two sides met again four days later in a replay at St Andrew's, home of Birmingham City.

The police limited the attendance to 18,000 with Leeds fans making up three-quarters of that number.

When the game drifted into extra time, it looked for all the world that the outcome would be decided on penalties but up stepped John Sheridan to send his team and supporters into raptures.

In the 99th minute, Leeds won a free kick when Paul Miller handled the ball 30 yards out to halt Edwards' drive towards the area. Sheridan strode up purposefully and effortlessly floated the ball over a five-man wall and into the top right-hand corner, seemingly condemning Charlton to the most agonising of defeats.

But the Addicks started the second period like men possessed, tying the game with seven minutes remaining when former Sheffield Wednesday defender Peter Shirtliff calmly slotted home. Four minutes later, he found the net again and United's world crashed about them.

Bremner struggled to build on the progress made. He had to sheepishly go along with Bill Fotherby's madcap assertion that Leeds were about to sign Diego Maradona in the summer and he was completely deflated when the team slumped into the bottom half of the table. The nadir was a 6-3 defeat at Plymouth in mid-October that left Leeds in 16th position after just three victories from the first 14 games.

It was as if the players were suffering a hangover after the elation of the spring.

Leeds' season was rescued by the signing of Bobby Davison and the emergence of teenage midfielder David Batty, who helped the team break into the top ten after Christmas. It was enough for Bremner to be voted Manager of the Month for December.

Unfortunately, every time they threatened to crash the promotion party, they faltered: three consecutive defeats in January, one win in four February games.

Leeds' third successive victory, a 5-0 hammering of Sheffield United in March, moved them within two points of the play-off positions, but it was five games before the next win. That left a mathematically unbridgeable gap.

Bremner could only splutter and moan about points thrown away as he contemplated a seventh straight season in the Second Division for Leeds.

Bremner, as in previous summers, looked to shake things up in the off-season, making a double raid on recently relegated Portsmouth to sign Noel Blake and Vince Hilaire.

He had already brought Ian Baird back from Pompey in the spring, hoping that the influx of new men would spark a revival. Few shared his optimism.

The club directors gathered at Leslie Silver's house to discuss the upcoming season. A faction, including Peter Ridsdale, wanted a fresh start without Bremner. 'I don't think Billy Bremner is good enough,' opined Ridsdale. The decision hung in the balance, with a split in opinion. Silver's casting vote tipped the scales in Bremner's favour. Bremner's reprieve heralded no new dawn. Leeds failed to win any of their first four games, including a humiliating 4-0 loss at Portsmouth.

The first victory, against Barnsley on 21 September, saw them edge up to 17th. Bremner insisted before the game that his players were confident and ready to launch their season. He got the response he needed with a strong performance and a 2-0 win.

For Bremner, there were too many scares in the game, and Leeds struggled to convert their dominance into goals.

The breakthrough came after 62 minutes, Davison heading home after Batty's shot bounced up off a defender. It was not until three minutes from time that United could relax when Hilaire coolly added a second.

The relief was short-lived. Leeds lost at home to Chelsea, and it was clear that Bremner's number was up.

Outside the stadium, there was a brawl between rival fans and thousands of pounds' worth of damage to the Fletchers Motor Group showroom a mile away. Rocks and rubble were thrown through showroom windows and at the cars on display. Police officers were stoned as they attempted to stop the trouble.

The chairman of Fletchers demanded that Elland Road be closed, and local Labour MP Derek Fatchett asked the club to compensate local residents and businesses for the damage.

Ridsdale later recounted the tense atmosphere in the boardroom, how subdued the directors were. The silence was punctuated by shrill cries of 'Bremner out!' from outside. They rang loud and clear, 'Bremner out!' The final straw came with the brick that hurtled through the window, disrupting their deliberations. The axe came the following day for the manager.

The decision to part ways was revealed on 28 September, the day after a narrow League Cup victory over Fourth Division Peterborough. It left a question hanging – what comes next?

When asked why the club fired Bremner, Silver confessed that the board had lost faith in him, that 'if we were going to have to bring someone new in at some time then the sooner the better. I've worked well with him on a personal basis, but it hasn't worked, and therefore it's better to change.'

The Man with a Plan

I laughed, said I'd think about it, and
put the phone down. I thought, yeah,
absolutely no chance.

'YOU'VE GOT to be joking. Aren't they in the Second Division?'

Howard Wilkinson's wife's reaction to the news mirrored feelings across the country as the identity of the man that Leeds United wanted as their manager was confirmed.

'She said I was crazy,' Wilkinson recalled. 'A few others said the same and, to be fair, they had a point. My first reaction when asked if I was interested in Leeds was to reply, "You must be joking." But I soon saw it as a chance to, not so much start with a clean sheet of paper, but rub the bad off the paper and keep the good.'

Leeds were in the depths of the division below Sheffield Wednesday and everything was against them – poor form, aimless players and a fan base notorious for both its racism and a propensity for hooliganism.

Few could comprehend why a manager as highly regarded as Wilkinson would be interested in the most poisonous of chalices. He had previously turned down lucrative job offers from Ipswich Town and Saudi Arabian club Al-Ittihad but his love affair with Sheffield Wednesday had soured. 'Wednesday became known as the big-city club with the small-town mentality. By the end of my third season there, it was clear we needed to invest in better players. We'd finished 13th in the league, eight places lower than the previous season.

'I had an excellent relationship with Bert McGee. He was a gentleman, but at the end of my fifth season I had gone to the board and said, "Look, we have gone as far as we can go with some of these players and to bring about the change required to push us on will take money." I gave them a figure.

'The board wouldn't budge. The club had been in deep trouble a few years earlier, nearly going to the wall. The board, all Wednesdayites, didn't want to ever be in that position again. I understood that.

'I started to realise we had probably gone as far as we could. The policy of investment would not change dramatically. My thinking was the club would only stagnate with that policy and I didn't want that.

'After the final game, I found Nigel Worthington sitting alone in the dressing room. "Gaffer," he said, "you need to leave here. You can only squeeze so much juice out of a lemon."'

Players can smell a lack of ambition at a club and the sales of Brian Marwood and Lee Chapman confirmed it. Wilkinson was powerless – he could not match the wages offered by other clubs for those he wanted to sign or persuade to stay. He wanted to push on, to invest, to take his team to the next level, but he was frustrated by the directors' caution.

'I would have dearly loved Sheffield Wednesday to have gone all the way and with me leading them. It was on, it was unfortunate that when we finished fifth we didn't get in Europe and when we got to the semi-final we didn't get to the final. It's little things like that that can make all the difference.'

Wilkinson braced himself to get back to work, but a new, unsolicited challenge beckoned.

Over in West Yorkshire, Leeds United had sacked Billy Bremner and were in the market for a new manager. The board initially approached former Everton boss Howard Kendall, then in charge of Athletic Bilbao in Spain.

Flattered by Leeds' interest, Kendall found himself sitting across from Bill Fotherby, 'one of the most persuasive men I have ever met in my life'. Fotherby was a force of nature, pushing the benefits of joining Leeds. Captivated by the power of Fotherby's hard-sell approach, Kendall was forced to listen to the terms of the contract on offer. He had doubts, however, when asked to guarantee Leeds United's promotion. There was no way on earth that he could promise such an outcome.

Kendall remained in Spain and the thwarted Leeds board turned to England manager Bobby Robson, but he also rejected the notion.

'All right then, tell me,' a frustrated Fotherby asked Robson, 'who would you recommend if you was in my place?'

The Geordie was unequivocal. 'There's only one person and he's down the road from you. Get Howard Wilkinson.'

One of the directors, Jack Marjason, fuelled the fire by recounting a rumour that Wilkinson was unhappy at Hillsborough.

Fotherby and Leslie Silver, pessimistic to say the least, enquired of Robson, 'Why on earth would he come here?'

'If you don't ask, you will never know.'

Wilkinson was tipped off to Leeds' interest by David Walker, a football journalist, 'probably the person who knows me best amongst the media. We became quite friendly when I was at Sheffield Wednesday, not in a totally football sense but we just seemed to hit it off, you know. It finished up with him being more than that. On occasion he was an advisor and good friend.

'To all intents and purposes, it was a rusty old Rolls-Royce. It was a tatty old car in need of a new engine. It needed a heck of a lot of bodywork, I can tell you.

'They were second from bottom; they hadn't won a game for God knows how long; they didn't own the ground and they had debts up to their eyeballs.

'I said no and I said no about five times.

'I then got another phone call from David saying, "I've been asked to ring you again. They are very, very serious about this. They'd just like the chance to speak to you."

'I eventually gave in. What followed was a series of conversations, first with Bill Fotherby, and then, and most importantly, with Leslie Silver.'

Wilkinson, in a moment of stern counsel, told Silver, 'You've got to change. The Revie era has gone, but you're clinging to its memories. You haven't got Revie players. You've succeeded in the paint business, and you haven't done that by making the same paint the same way you were when you started.'

Fotherby recalled, 'I'd arranged with Howard, I'd meet him on the motorway. They were playing at Blackpool, Sheffield Wednesday. I took this contract down. I took my pen out and I wrote down his salary, and I said, how's that? Well, he says, give us your pen, Bill. I said, here, peace in our time. We've got a manager.'

'Bill was a salesman,' says Wilkinson, 'the ideal foil for Leslie. He was a salesman and he sold off the pitch as well as on it. He could walk into a car showroom and be told after a quarter of an hour, "No, no, not interested. No, sorry, go on, away you go," and then three hours later come out of there with a deal. And the owner of the car shop's scratching his head, thinking, "Why have I just said ... I must be crazy."'

'That were Bill and to a certain extent, that's how I finished up there. I got a phone call and he eventually finished up going down and round to our house more than once.

'Yeah, him and Leslie were totally different characters superficially.

'Leslie was quiet, somewhat shy, actually. But a good bloke. Nothing about Leslie said, "Look at me, I'm worth all this." He was a genuine Leeds supporter. He wasn't in it for stardom and it was his money. He was supplying the coal for the fire.

'I walked out of his office with both of us agreeing to a long-term future for Leeds United which would see Leeds United out of the division the next season. We could then look at winning the title maybe four years after that, after we consolidated.

'We talked from top to bottom, from first team to youth team, talked about and agreed to a new training ground. The reason I wanted to agree strategy was I believed Leeds were, at the time, one of only a few clubs who could challenge again at the top of the First Division.

'By the time we had six meetings, I'd gone through what you'd need to do over the next ten years to be the top team in Britain and stay there. And it was a very comprehensive discussion because I also mentioned at that time the thought that one of the things a good club will have will be a good academy. Already in my mind I had this idea of, as it were, a school, so when we built the new training ground, we had accommodation built and we were bringing the boys in at 14. We had a link with the local secondary school, so they were getting more coaching but at the same time that was being combined with school, so school wasn't losing out.'

Wilkinson grew more impressed by Silver with every meeting. He saw him as 'the ideal chairman. When you needed him, he was there, but never ever was he in your hair. He managed to remain one of Leeds United's biggest, most enthusiastic fans.

'By the time I'm finished talking to Leslie on the occasions that we talked, I came home knowing that I'd met a gentleman who had basically said, "I've listened to what it is you said we need to do and I agree with it. The only thing is, I want you to come and do it."'

There was one crucial exchange towards the end of Wilkinson's discussions with Silver, one that shaped the future of the club for the next five years.

'Before I go,' said Wilkinson, 'you've got a decision to make. Do you want this the quick way or the slow way?'

'What's the difference?'

'About three to four million pound ... I know that's going to be your money because I know we don't own the ground and I know that the club is subsisting on you at the moment. That's what you've got to do.'

Wilkinson outlined his preferred option, an ambitious strategy of investment in transfer fees, salaries and long-term planning. He presented a ten-year plan for transforming Leeds United into a club that could compete with the best by producing its own players to star in a rebuilt stadium.

Silver pledged himself to the fast route. Fotherby was tasked with raising funds through commercial deals, pushing through his plans for corporate hospitality and merchandising. Wilkinson signed the contract, satisfied with the assurances given by his new colleagues.

Years later, he was asked, 'Was it important to you, knowing where Leeds United were, to have that sort of influence from top to bottom and look at the whole club, not just the playing side, but the whole club?'

Quick as a flash, Wilkinson responded, 'Yes it was. The concept was quite modern in the sense that the club would have a plan going forward and there would be stages in that plan, that it would be comprehensive, it would be understandable and that it would require consistency. It would require good staff in place and good staff who would be in place for as long as it took. It required Leslie's intelligence and faith to have sat through all these meetings, listened to all of our discussions and thought, "Wow, this is different to the way football works as I've experienced it." What he had experienced was a thing that basically focused on the first team, the results and the manager and the chairman really not having any real understanding of this thing, this mystery called football.

'And what I tried to show him was that football has differences but fundamentally it's very similar to business and that a good business needs a good leader and the good leader needs good staff and the leader and the staff need to understand what they're doing and where they're going and how they're going to get there and feel part of it. And so that was new to him and he liked that, having made a business himself.'

Wilkinson handed in his resignation and went to inform his staff and players at Hillsborough. His farewells were tearful as he spoke of his feelings for Wednesday. When he was done, he went down to the South Stand's empty boot room to collect his thoughts.

Suddenly, he was overcome with grief, sobbing unashamedly into a Wednesday towel, the realisation that he was leaving his spiritual home hurting far more than he had anticipated.

The outpouring of grief allowed him to clear his mind, to put his old club behind him and focus on the job at hand.

Turning his thoughts to the future, Wilkinson told the press, 'My main job now is to get Leeds United away from the foot of the Second Division and eventually get them into the First Division. I have no timescale on that because I don't know what the task at hand is, but obviously the supporters will set a timescale on it. Whether it's a reasonable one doesn't matter. Just as when I went to Sheffield Wednesday, they have been in the Second Division now a long time, too long for them, they feel, and they'll be looking for me to work a miracle.'

Asked whether he felt any added pressure taking over from a legend like Billy Bremner, Wilkinson said, 'No, not really. Billy was a great player, a legend whose achievements were absolutely unbelievable, a world-class player at that time and a leader. But that was Billy on the pitch. I was not taking over from Billy on the pitch, I was taking over from Billy in the office and those are two different jobs. Very early on in my coaching career I asked Don Howe, "Don, what difference does it make having been a great player when you start coaching and managing?" Don had had a great career and he said, "About eight to ten games."'

Wilkinson and Bremner were like chalk and cheese, according to physio Alan Sutton.

'Anybody will tell you who worked there with Billy Bremner – what a special time! But football was changing. Billy was like still from the Revie era, playing five-a-sides every day, doing this, doing that and really to them it was the shirt. Wearing that shirt, you know, wearing that shirt, kissing that badge had to be everything and that's what it was with Billy.

'Then Howard Wilkinson came in and I think he was the new type of thing. He realised that everything was changing. I remember talking to Gary McAllister one time. He said the reason he played until he was 38, 39, same as Gary Speed, Gordon Strachan was the first person to play as a 40-year-old and he put it down to all them pre-seasons under Howard Wilkinson that got him that fitness that maintained him all the time.'

Sutton was shocked that Wilkinson decided to keep him on, especially after seeing Norman Hunter receive his P45 after his services as a coach were dispensed with.

'I'm still scratching my head how I ended up working eight years with Howard Wilkinson … I wasn't chartered or anything. I would have thought I'd have been one of the first people to be shown the door. Like Norman was, which I was really sad at, because I was working with Norman Hunter at that time as well and Norman was great to work with.

'I understand from Mick Hennigan later on, that Sunday when [Wilkinson] left Sheffield Wednesday to go to Leeds, he said to everybody in the backroom staff, "Anybody who wants to come with me tomorrow to Leeds United, just show up at lunchtime tomorrow and you've got a job." And there was only Mick who came.

'There's a physio at that time at Sheffield Wednesday, a great, great friend of mine, Alan Smith, and he sent word through Glynn Snodin some weeks after that he wouldn't be moving up. And, as I said, I'm still scratching my head today.'

Mick Hennigan – always 'Michael' to Wilkinson – was the second-in-command so typical in the military, the man who would ensure the boss's requirements were followed to the letter, no questions asked.

Wilkinson invited assistant manager Peter Eustace to accompany him to Leeds, but he declined and took the job at Hillsborough, though he lasted just three months.

Wilkinson was disappointed by the rejection and, as a result, leaned even more heavily on Hennigan, who thrived in the new environment.

He kept order in the camp, ensured there was no dissent among the ranks and made life as easy as possible for Wilkinson, who gave him the opportunity to coach the youth team at Sheffield Wednesday. The promotion enabled him to resign his position with the Central Electricity Generating Board and earned his eternal gratitude. 'I could only ever pay Wilkinson back by working my bollocks off for him, and I tried to.'

There was no way Hennigan would not accompany Wilkinson to Elland Road, where he became the scourge of any slackers and a constant support for the boss.

Not everybody in the United camp took to Hennigan's methods. The free-spirited Vince Hilaire proved to be a constant challenge to Hennigan and Wilkinson. Hilaire's autobiography revealed a prank involving a set of toy daffodils that, when triggered by a loud noise, would dance. Hilaire hid them from sight in the dressing room, ready to ambush an unsuspecting Hennigan.

Wilkinson's assistant regularly tore a strip off some of the old lags who weren't in Wilkinson's first-team plans. Their patience was wearing thin. As half-time arrived, Hennigan launched into a furious tirade about their lack of commitment. The conspirators creased up as the daffodils danced to their heart's content above the bemused Hennigan.

Wilkinson was relieved to have a loyal servant with him as he walked into Elland Road, determined to stamp his character on Leeds United. Fourteen years earlier, Brian Clough had tried the same trick but was quickly shown the door. Wilkinson was less abrasive but just as firm, ordering that the images of Don Revie's famous squad should be removed. 'It was bad, bad enough for me to take the major risk in my first month of removing all the pictures and memorabilia. That caused Richter-scale vibrations, but my reason for it was that when we'd made a team and a club worthy of those achievements, we'd put them back. Leeds had lingered too long in that era.'

There was none of the antagonism associated with Clough. Everyone knew that something different was needed at Leeds and all accepted that Wilkinson was the man to bring it.

Wilkinson was bothered by other issues. A staunch advocate of strong leadership, he felt there were too many directors eager to offer a view, including four city council nominees.

'You couldn't run an organisation with a board that big,' scoffed Wilkinson, 'where everyone has a say and an opinion. I don't disagree with that, all I'm saying is that in football it doesn't work, because sometimes you have to make quick decisions so it's essential the chain of command is kept as small as possible.'

Wilkinson laughed off the idea that this made it difficult to get what he needed. 'It was very easy to get decisions made because of my relationship with Leslie. The reason I went to Leeds was Leslie Silver and the fact that I trusted him to be true to his word with regard to what we'd agreed for, over first of all, the next five years and beyond that, even to ten years. And so, when we got to actually doing that, it wasn't a problem for me, because whatever I wanted I got, but maybe Leslie was finding it more difficult than it should be in the boardroom. Because if you're sitting at a table, you think you're entitled to a view, which is fair enough. But in the ideal situation, you have a plan and that's the plan. And people will afterwards want to do this, that and the other. You have to say, "Well, look, we've agreed what we're going to do, so that's what we're going to do."

'And if there's going to be a change, then the change will have to be me talking to the influential people on the board which is Leslie, and two others and, you know, that's it. There's not a lot to discuss, when it comes to talking about how we play, what we do, who's playing well and who's not playing well and who might be a good player if we got him and who we might sell if we got a chance to. The fewer people involved in that line of communication, the better.'

The Wilko–Silver–Fotherby axis ran the show, providing the single-mindedness that success demanded. If it was important, it was decided by the trio, end of chat.

The hierarchy was formalised at an extraordinary general meeting when Fotherby, Silver and vice-chairman

Peter Gilman pushed through the formation of a holding company that sat above the board. The three men persuaded shareholders to accept a simple executive structure to improve decision-making efficiency. At a stroke, the triumvirate gained absolute control, freezing out the other directors.

Wilkinson's concerns about the board and the way that the club was run were exacerbated when he was summoned to appear at the annual general meeting in January 1989.

When word spread that Wilko had a 'prior engagement' and would not be present, Silver was warned that there would be trouble.

Silver came up with a solution. He changed the agenda so that shareholders could question Wilkinson at the start of the meeting before the accounts were agreed. Even that compromise left Wilkinson in a foul mood.

Silver attempted to start the meeting before the scheduled time of 7pm, so that 'Mr Wilkinson could answer questions from shareholders before any other business. Unfortunately, Mr Wilkinson would have to leave the meeting early to fulfil a prior engagement.'

It went down like a lead balloon. Some shareholders considered it a slight, others thought it inconsiderate and a dozen or so gave the board a good deal of grief after Wilkinson left.

Wilkinson was also rubbed up the wrong way by some of the fans, including Neale Sheldon. He travelled everywhere, home and away, and attended as many reserve and youth matches as possible, as well as friendlies. If any Leeds team was playing, Sheldon would be there.

'I can remember taking Wilko to task,' recalls Sheldon, 'over the club not informing the youth players about who they would be awarding pro contracts to and who they were releasing.

'The vast majority of clubs have usually informed young players around Easter time regarding their football future.

Unfortunately, Wilko hadn't got round to that at Leeds and players and parents alike were worried that time was running out for them to get trials at other clubs.

'After an away first-team match, I waited for Wilko, before he boarded the team bus. I asked him when he was going to tell the players whether they were going to be kept on.

'"What do you want to know for?" was his reply. I explained that time was running out for released players to get trials for other clubs. "I'll tell everybody when I think fit," was Wilko's curt response.

'Luckily for me, another supporter sensed that things were getting heated and grabbed hold of me before I could follow Wilko up the steps and on to the team bus.'

Wilkinson had dealt with difficult situations before and wasn't fazed. He recognised, however, the significance of an early statement of intent.

'We needed to change things. It's important to know what needs changing and then it's important to say what kind of change quickly. Quick wins help you at the beginning so it's not necessarily the most important thing that needs changing that you try to change first. Because you think, "That's going to take me eight months and eight months is a long time from this first month when I'm trying to create a different mindset. That's the most important change I need to make but it's not necessarily the one I can make quickest," and when you start it's the quick ones that you try to deal with.'

The Crusade

Spiritually, we were like close brothers.

SOME OF the raw materials Howard Wilkinson needed were already on hand. There were good, reliable pros like Mervyn Day, Peter Haddock, Noel Blake, Ian Baird and Micky Adams, some flair with John Sheridan and Vince Hilaire and the promise of David Batty.

Wilkinson was under no illusions that there were problems with the attitudes of some players, particularly the chaotic Sheridan and the pig-headed Batty, but he was confident that he could improve what he had with a little bit of organisation.

'They hadn't had a good start,' recalls Wilkinson. 'I'd seen them play a few times. I'd been able to get hold of video … the players were better than the results. If you looked at the players individually and you looked at the performances and the results, there was no comparison. Some of the ability of the players would allow you to think that they should be doing better than this. So changing that round was not difficult and you come with the benefit of you're new and everybody thinks we've all got a chance.

'The first thing I said to them when I met them was, "There's a passenger jet on the runway and it will take off next summer and everybody in this dressing room can be on that plane. There's a seat for everyone but you have to earn that seat." There was enough there to do better than they were doing and that's what we did.

'We went on quite a run. It was double figures unbeaten and that was just giving people the big picture about the team and then individuals knowing their jobs, what the team expects of you. So that made a difference and that start gave me the opportunity, because things had changed for the better, to look around but not in any panicky way at what we need for next season and where we might get it and who would be the best.

'Basically, going in there, given where we were, it was just about structure. What are we going to do when we lose the ball and what we're going to do when we get the ball. I said the same three things that I've said everywhere. I said, look, we can be the fittest team in the league, and we can be the best at defending set pieces and we can be the best at attacking set pieces.

'There were lots of things that I had to do but one of them I thought, having watched them, was we needed to get fitter. And then it was basic things about when we lose the ball, what are we going to do? When we win the ball back, what are we going to do?

'I was always a great proponent of the value of set pieces for and against. I said to them, you know, if we do our job right here, up to 25 per cent of the goals we score can be got from set pieces.

'Now then you see them go, "What?" So, yeah, yeah, if you get organised on our set pieces, 25 per cent of the goals we finish up with at the end of the season, or at least 20 per cent, can come from set pieces. What we're not gonna do is concede 25 per cent of the goals we concede to set pieces. Because if we know the value of them and we know how to organise to score from them, we should know how to defend them properly better.

'On top of that, we could be the best organised in terms of individuals knowing their jobs within the set-up. So there'd be a structure to the things we do. That's not to say that they are robots but that's what a team needs. It needs structure.'

That structure had real impact – United went 11 games unbeaten after Wilkinson arrived, taking them from 21st in the table to 11th. And this was all with Bremner's existing squad.

It began with a League Cup victory at Peterborough. 'As far as we're concerned,' Wilkinson told the press, 'tonight's the start of our season. It's always nice at the start of the season to score your first goal and get your first win.'

He was asked how much influence he thought he'd had in his first few days in the job.

'Absolutely none. None, not really, I mean, minimal. I did say before the game that I had no bearing on tonight's result, other than someone had arrived and they had someone who was the manager.'

'Did it seem a bit strange tonight, here at Elland Road after so many years at Hillsborough?'

'Absolutely; really very, very bewildering. There were times even tonight when I sort of thought to myself, where am I? It was like an away game. Before the game, I got changed in a different place, different strip. It had a sort of dream-like quality to it. It was as if I was standing outside it, looking in at times.'

Alan Sutton remembers the first time Wilkinson addressed his troops.

'He had got all the players in. He said, "Right, as from now, I am the third-worst manager, I'm virtually the worst manager in this league until we put it right and we start winning matches and get us up that league."

'It hit home with the players. In that first week or second week we had a training session in the morning, a training session in the afternoon and then that night the same players had to go play against Blackburn in the reserves ... They were back in again the next day, training again the next day.'

Wilkinson recalls his first few days vividly. 'What I found was a club in depression. Even at that age, I knew it didn't take long for that sort of decline to become terminal. So, we needed to take action and we needed to take action quickly and in some cases it might shock.'

Batty, Mark Aizlewood and Sheridan had all been regulars in midfield, but Wilkinson had had enough of Batty's simmering resentment.

Batty's ego took a battering when he was dropped from the team – not even a spot on the bench. He had initially retained his place under Wilkinson, but after a few weeks, he was suddenly out.

Batty, the apple of Billy Bremner's eye, was a shadow of his former self, his mentor's influence gone. He found Wilkinson's training system stifling and monotonous, and the playing style, reminiscent of the Wednesday model, uninspiring.

Bremner's words still echoed in his mind, urging him to assert his dominance, impose himself on opponents. Yet, Wilkinson seemed determined to curb his natural aggression, leading to a battle of wills, a test of endurance between two unyielding characters.

Batty reflected on the experience. 'Wilkinson's mission in life was to take me down a peg or two, to make me conform to his rules.' Batty had no argument with his logic; it was his manner he could never come to terms with. He rebelled against the new man's autocratic ways.

Batty found it difficult to get back in the side, something he found particularly galling given that the man who took his No 7 shirt was the unassuming Mike Whitlow, signed from Witton Albion. Leeds rose to sixth by February, so he couldn't complain. When he did return, a run of nine games was ended by the arrival of a man who could never be accused of being unassuming.

Wilkinson wasn't desperate for immediate promotion, though he would have taken it if it had fallen into his lap. He knew he needed time to lay sound foundations. The first goal – eradicating any chance of relegation – had been met and Wilkinson now embarked on the next stage of his transformation of Leeds United.

'Both at Notts County and Sheffield, I tasted immediate success,' recalled Wilkinson. 'In my first full season at both clubs, we won promotion, and the board backed me. Leeds were safe from the drop, and I had a vision of a team that could win promotion the following season.'

He stressed the need for experienced players. 'We needed guys who'd been in the limelight, who'd played for big clubs like Arsenal or Man U, players who wouldn't buckle under pressure. That meant spending money. It was a risk, but one we all agreed was worth taking.'

The chairman pushed back. 'Talk to Bill, he does all the ins and outs of the club, he does all the deals, transfers, players' wages, contracts.'

'No, no, I only deal with the chairman, I do not deal with the managing director. No, I won't do that.'

Silver was adamant. 'Well, I'm afraid I don't deal with the manager.'

Fotherby intervened, telling Wilkinson, 'Howard, just let's you and me go in the next room for ten minutes, that's all I ask of you.'

That conversation paved the way to a meeting of minds.

Fotherby reassured Wilkinson. 'Howard, trust me. You don't know Leslie like I do. He's different from the other chairmen you've worked for. For this to work, you and I need to be in harmony, move together, speak as one. Just give it a month. That's all I ask.'

Wilkinson bit his lip. He remained cautious but began to appreciate the wheeler-dealer's worth.

Wilkinson found Fotherby's help invaluable in some areas, especially dealing with agents. 'If we're considering selling a player, I'll give you my valuation, then you take the reins. I don't want to spend hours on phone calls. I'd rather you handle the negotiations. I don't want to be spending hours on telephone calls doing this.'

Fotherby's knack for solving problems complemented Wilkinson perfectly. He never had to ask Fotherby anything twice, and Fotherby always found a way to sort things out. One day, Wilkinson came up with a brainwave to improve the atmosphere at Elland Road, of having microphones suspended from the roof of the stand to pick up the noise of the crowd. He hadn't a clue how to do it, but he mentioned it once to Fotherby.

'Leave it with me, I'll have a word with a few people.' Days later, it was done.

It was hard persuading players of the required calibre to join a Second Division side, but Fotherby was a man who simply refused to take no for an answer.

'Howard Wilkinson gave me a list of players he wanted and the top one was Chrissy Fairclough,' Fotherby recalled. 'I went down to Tottenham to see Terry Venables, I had a chat and he said, "You won't be able to sign him, Bill, the deadline's at 5pm and his wife is expecting a baby at any time."

'I said, "Just find out where he is." He did and I went to see Chris. I gave him the sales pitch and he said, "I'd love to sign for you, Mr Fotherby, but my wife's having a baby." I said, "People in Leeds have babies too, you know," and that was that.'

The purchase of Fairclough was massive news, but it paled when set next to Wilkinson's statement signing.

'I had a lucky break,' Wilkinson admitted. 'What played a massive part, and which I couldn't have predicted, was getting

Gordon Strachan to come in so quickly, because he had great respect and by the time he'd been there a month, the players respected him even more. To have someone as respected as he was when he arrived is a great help in terms of getting the message across.

'What was I looking for? Well, first and foremost, I was looking for a leader. It wasn't a centre-half, or a midfield player or a striker … I wanted someone to come in who immediately could reflect my values on the football pitch. And having seen Gordon, having seen his career up in Scotland and later down at Man U, I thought that he might be that person.'

Strachan was 32 years old and available when Alex Ferguson decided he was no longer part of Old Trafford's future.

Manchester United were going through a rough patch in the league, but Ferguson had high hopes that Strachan could lead them to the FA Cup Final. Despite how much they had achieved together at Aberdeen, and how much Ferguson did to reignite that success, Strachan failed to recreate his magic. He was a shadow of his former self during United's quarter-final against Nottingham Forest. He was bullied off his game by Stuart Pearce, and when he suggested that he had become bored with life at Old Trafford under Ferguson, it spelled the end.

Strachan recalled the moment when it all came crashing down. 'One morning, around 7.30, I had a knock on my door. There he was standing there, Sir Alex, telling me in no uncertain terms that I'd never play another game for the club. It was still early, so I went back to my bed. I woke up about half past nine and I thought it was all a dream.

'People believed that once you left Manchester United, you faded away, curled up and died. I didn't fancy that, dying a death at 32. My stamina and fitness were still good, but my passion for the game had gone.'

Ferguson didn't have to wait long for interest in Strachan. 'The Monday following our defeat to Forest, I took a call from Ron Atkinson. He was now at Sheffield Wednesday and had an interest in Strachan.'

However, a complication arose. Howard Wilkinson had previously inquired about Strachan's availability. He was told that there was no chance, but Fergie had promised to notify him if the situation changed. Honouring his word, Ferguson reached out to Wilkinson, suggesting a deal could be done for £300,000. It was considerably more than what Atkinson had in mind, but Wilkinson was ready to pay. It put him in the driving seat.

Ferguson was delighted, feeling it was a good price for a 32-year-old who was running down his contract. When Atkinson matched Wilkinson's figure, Ferguson told Strachan that the choice was down to him. He appreciated Strachan's rapport with Atkinson, the man who had signed him from Aberdeen, but encouraged Strachan to have a conversation with Wilkinson.

'After hearing what Wilkinson had to say, Gordon could not wait to sign,' recalled Fergie. 'It was a coming together that neither Leeds United nor the player ever regretted.'

Strachan had enjoyed working with Atkinson at Old Trafford and knew that Big Ron believed in him. He was certain his future lay at Hillsborough but agreed to meet Wilkinson out of politeness, all ready to give a pat 'Thanks, but no thanks' response. He told Wilkinson that he had the option of moving into a coaching role at Wednesday.

'No, no, no,' blurted out Wilkinson when he heard that one. 'You're too young, too fit, too good, to even start thinking about coaching. You aren't in the twilight of your career, your career hasn't even started. What I am offering you is a crusade, as a player and a skipper. Come to Leeds and help me get this club back to where it belongs.'

Strachan, listening to this man's passionate discourse about his ambitions for Leeds United, found himself captivated. 'Gordon saw the potential in my vision for Leeds,' Wilkinson reflected. 'He could see the pivotal role he could play in our future success.'

Strachan was in line for a lucrative pay increase, yet it was Wilkinson's skilful massaging of his ego that ultimately settled his mind, even before he had spoken to Atkinson.

Strachan's visit to Leeds delayed his arrival at Hillsborough, yet Atkinson laughed off the concerns of his colleagues. Strachan's tardiness was notorious. 'He'll be here, don't worry. He never lets me down.'

However, this time, Atkinson's faith was misplaced. 'I'm sorry, Boss,' said Strachan. 'I want to go to Leeds.'

'Leeds were standing still, I was standing still,' reflects Strachan. 'When I met Howard, I thought, "Alright. They're trusting me with a crusade here." I was tasked with leading the team to promotion, getting them into the top league. It was like a new start after a couple of stagnant years. I believed them, because I could tell they also had a real sense of responsibility.'

'Ron claimed that I accused him of tapping Gordon up,' recalls Wilkinson, 'and added that he had given me a rocket over the phone, letting me know in no uncertain terms that I wasn't dealing with any stupid footballer. I find the idea of me staying quiet to take a roasting from Ron Atkinson totally hilarious.'

Wilkinson and Fotherby worked their magic on Strachan, convincing him of the merits of going to Elland Road. 'After we'd spoken, I was convinced,' said Strachan. 'They knew where they wanted to go; there was a long-term plan.'

They outlined the job they wanted him to do, to lead their club to the First Division. 'These guys really trusted me to do a job here. It was the first time for a long time that I felt someone really believed in me as a player. I got a great buzz from that. And I was offered a lot of money!'

One of the best bits of business that Wilkinson and Fotherby ever did was completed for the princely sum of £300,000. The history of Leeds United was changed forever the day when Strachan walked into Elland Road and told Fotherby, 'I'd like to come and join you. I think you're going places.'

Both Wilkinson and Fotherby contributed to Strachan's conviction. While he found common ground with Wilkinson, it was Fotherby who clinched the deal. 'I don't think I'd ever have come to Leeds if it wasn't for Bill.'

Their conversation flowed freely without the stifling presence of an agent. Fotherby, as always, worked his magic. 'After negotiations with Bill Fotherby,' said a deadpan Strachan, 'I ended up buying a box and ten season tickets off him! There was no negotiating when I signed. Bill told me the money I'd be getting and that was that.

'I vividly remember when Howard told me to discuss my contract with Bill, and I came out having agreed to sponsor a match. I'm still not sure how that happened. But Bill had a knack for dealing with people. He was happy making tough calls or ruffling feathers when he had to, but he did it with a smile.'

'If you are going to spend money,' smiled Fotherby, 'you have to pick the right men. And he was certainly the right man.'

Wilkinson had no Plan B, no backup strategy. 'If I hadn't got Gordon,' he admitted, 'it would have been a question of doing what we did when Gordon arrived, but there would have been no Gordon Strachan.

'You want people who represent what it is you're trying to get them to do and think like, because they're important. Because you will also have terrorists in a group, and the terrorist, as we all know, loves company. The terrorist on his own is harmless, but if he can get one or two with him, he feels he's succeeding. So having the Strachans, that sort of person is very important because they represent what it is you want to see and it's a better message if Gordon Strachan's giving the message to another player. It's a better way to deliver the message than to have me say it. And on top of which you then get reinforcement for your views within the group.

'Gordon was key. He helped me gel together the new group of players and in him I had someone amongst the staff who shared my values. We had the same thoughts on how the game should be played, on how people should live and what discipline should be enforced to make sure that was realised.'

Strachan was as much part of the solution to Leeds' problems as Wilkinson. He made his debut on 25 March 1989 when Leeds beat Portsmouth and was declared man of the match.

Yorkshire Evening Post: 'Portsmouth were firing on all cylinders, but they could not match the agile mind of Gordon Strachan in the 69th minute. He was sent flying by a heavy tackle from Mike Fillery on the right touchline and while others were catching their breath, Strachan was bouncing to his feet demanding the loose ball from the ball boy 20 yards away. The former Manchester United winger lifted the free kick into John Sheridan's path and though he had hitherto had a wretched afternoon, the Eire international took the ball coolly on his chest before lobbing the ball to the far post in one sweet movement. The rest was easy for the unmarked Ian Baird ten yards out, the striker heading his 13th goal of the campaign.'

Fairclough was also an instant hit, less obtrusively, but bringing confidence and elegance to the Leeds defence.

When asked to identify his best ever signing, Wilkinson pauses before replying. 'It would be easy to say Gordon Strachan but there were also unsung heroes – Chrissy Fairclough. Chrissy Fairclough played when he shouldn't play.

'Chrissy Fairclough was a centre-half who wasn't big enough to be a centre-half but dominated that position. Chrissy Fairclough had a dodgy knee for the whole time he played, Chrissy Fairclough was a leader, he lived the life properly, he said the right things in terms of he wasn't afraid to speak his mind but he wasn't a shouter.

'On four or five occasions I got Chrissy to go and man-to-man mark someone. Peter Beardsley was probably the one that comes to mind and because of that we got results and that's not easy because the instruction is, "I don't mind if you come off the pitch not having kicked a ball as long as he hasn't." Because if you said to the team, "Do we want to win this game Saturday or do we want to play an enjoyable game?" then Chrissy Fairclough's answer might be the second. Yeah, but what if we've got a better chance of doing it if he does that … changing from what he's doing to doing this job which is a job for the team which the experts will pick on but nobody else. But afterwards, everybody knows.

'The silent assassin, Chrissy. He had a real sense of the responsibility every member of the team had to each other. He would be the first to point that out.'

Strachan and Fairclough played every minute of every match, through to the end of the season, their quality shining out.

Carl Shutt, a striker who worked for a couple of years under Wilkinson at Hillsborough, also arrived in a £250,000 swap deal. Bob Taylor made the reverse journey to Bristol City.

Shutt had a dream debut, scoring all three goals in the victory over Bournemouth on 1 April. His promising start was cut short in his third game, a defeat at Plymouth. After wasting two fabulous openings before the break, he was taken off at half-time with a knee injury. No worries, Shutt would be back.

The rebuilding of Leeds United had begun.

Separating the Wheat from the Chaff

You've disappointed me a bit. I've just been down to the players' lounge. Can't find one speck of blood in there.

1 May 1989.

With ten minutes remaining, a cross soars towards the Walsall goal. Mark Aizlewood powers a header in, almost through the keeper, to give Leeds the lead.

The supporters in the Kop pour forward but they suddenly notice something untoward.

A furious Aizlewood is striding towards the crowd and before Vince Hilaire or Gordon Strachan can reach him, the Leeds captain flashes V signs at the crowd.

Aizlewood has been booed by the crowd for months and has had enough. Aizlewood was jeered every time he touched the ball that afternoon, and he is furious. When the boo boys applaud his goal, he completely loses it.

'Look at Wilko,' one fan exclaims. 'He'll never stand for that. He's told 'em to get him off.'

True enough, David Batty is on the way as the curly finger beckons Aizlewood. It comes as no surprise to the Welshman, who tears off the captain's armband and stomps off, face like thunder. Wilkinson orders him to sit down.

'Go f*** yourself,' comes the reply as Aizlewood storms down the tunnel.

He will never play again for Leeds United.

Eight weeks later, the players are in a pre-season gathering. There is an unmistakable atmosphere of tension in the air, with players in separate groups, emphasising the cliques that have emerged.

Aizelwood's resentment has spread to others, those who are uncertain that they figure in Wilkinson's plans. They are huddled in one corner, conspiratorially chatting amongst themselves, sparing no words for the rest of the squad.

The young guns, the most prominent of whom are Batty and Gary Speed, laugh and joke easily, as if unaware of the simmering unease.

Wilkinson's signings represent a third faction, surrounding Strachan and earnestly discussing the future. The rest, owing no allegiance to any of these groups, are silent, wondering what the coming weeks will bring.

Slowly, a door creaks open, drawing all eyes to it as a lean, mean-looking man, his head shaven at the sides, enters the room. He is frowning darkly, eyes blazing, his jaw set with determination.

'Right, you lot. Who wants some?'

Vincent Peter Jones has arrived at Leeds United.

For months, things had been building up. Aizlewood was one of several players whom Wilkinson had written out of the future. He'd allowed him to keep the captaincy, but his indiscipline was the final straw – Aizlewood was shipped off to Bradford City in a £200,000 deal.

No other player was as blatantly provocative as Aizlewood, although Vince Hilaire and Micky Adams ran him close.

Adams had been suffering with tendonitis in one of his knees, using painkillers and injections to see him through games. He would rest up during the week to save himself for matches.

When Bremner left, Adams knew that his approach wouldn't cut it with the new manager and agreed to an operation to fix the problem.

'If anyone was injured,' recalled Adams, 'they would go into the canteen, have a bacon sandwich and a cuppa until they were called in for treatment. To be honest, it was a jolly-up. It all changed when Howard came in. The new manager's big thing was team meetings. We'd have hundreds of them. His No 2 was a fella called Mick Hennigan. It was the classic good cop, bad cop routine; although, in Howard's case, it was more bastard cop.'

Injured players were required to report for assessment and were expected to do circuits to show that being injured was no cushy option.

Alan Sutton confronted Adams. 'Where have you been?'

'What do you mean, where have I been? Having my breakfast.'

'You don't do that anymore. The manager will be after me.'

'Well, it's not as if I can do anything anyway. I'm in plaster.'

'Yes, you can. You can go on one of those little trampolines. And with your good foot, you can bounce up and down on it to keep your muscle strength up.'

'You're f***ing mad. I'm not doing it.'

'Listen, you'll do as I'm f***ing telling you.'

Sutton squared up to Adams as the situation threatened to get out of control.

'Look, Sutty, get out of my face, because if you don't, I'm going to do something about it.'

'Micky, get on that trampoline.'

Adams smacked Sutton in the mouth. His false teeth went flying, his mouth bloodied. Adams told him to back off when he rose to retaliate, but on he came. Sutton wouldn't back down and Adams hit him again.

A few minutes later, Hennigan shouted, 'Micky Adams – manager wants to see you.'

When Adams got to the office, Wilkinson asked, 'Is this right, what I've been hearing?'

'I dunno what you've been hearing, boss.'

'That you have assaulted one of my staff.'

'Well, if he says I've done it, I can't deny it. There was a confrontation.'

'I'm not having that.'

'Can I just say something, gaffer? He asked me to do something I didn't agree with. He got in my face and I defended myself.'

'Did you throw the first punch?'

'Yes.'

'Well, I'm not having that. I can't have that. You're fined two weeks' wages.'

The transition from the old regime to Wilkinson's was also a rocky one for Vince Hilaire. In reflecting on the period, Hilaire was frank, 'I'm not sure that I gave up on Leeds, but I did give up with Howard Wilkinson. He was organised and professional, sure, but his manner was so grim, so stereotypically Yorkshire, that he was difficult to connect with.' He was abrupt, dour, and lacked the warmth Hilaire needed. 'You couldn't joke with him. The players eventually stopped playing for him.'

Wilkinson's coaching style was equally hard-nosed. Hilaire, a winger, not known for his work rate, was taken aback when Wilkinson introduced a style of football that was all about hard running, high tempo, and physicality. He was shocked when Wilkinson told the players that if ever they couldn't actually win a header, they should be prepared to get kicked or headbutted to prevent an opponent getting in a clean contact. Hilaire thought he was talking to Ian Baird and John Pearson but turned round to see Wilkinson pointing at him. 'Yes, I'm talking to you!'

Wilkinson's philosophy was simple: run, fight for the ball, and then run some more. His training sessions were gruelling, with players expected to sprint everywhere. He told them before one training session, 'When I blow the whistle, I'll shout something, and I want you all to sprint to that position.' After about 10 to 15 seconds, he blew and shouted, 'Corner for.' It didn't matter where the players were on the pitch, they all had to sprint and get into their positions for a corner in their favour. They'd set off again, and he'd shout, 'Corner against,' and they'd all have to sprint again. They weren't allowed to walk – they even had to sprint to throw-ins. There was no room for leisurely walks in Wilkinson's world.

Some of the more rebellious souls in the squad dreaded the inevitable half-time lectures after they ran off the field 'just to show how fit we were'. In one home game, Aizlewood whispered to Hilaire, 'That was a nightmare. Look how long I'm going to spend in the toilet at half-time.' He locked himself in there for the whole break just so he could avoid Wilko.

The arduous training sessions were one thing, but it was Wilkinson's monotonous lectures that truly tested the players' patience. Hilaire remembers these sessions as a one-way street, with Wilkinson droning on and on, boring them silly. He wasn't looking for feedback, it was just a monologue.

Hilaire acknowledged the importance of working hard, giving 100 per cent, earning their money, but he also believed that there was more to football than just being fit. He felt that when fans looked at professional footballers, they should see individuals performing feats that they couldn't. They should think, 'I couldn't do this or that, and that's why he's a pro and I'm not.' They shouldn't think, 'They're a fit side. If I was fit, I could play for this team.' Talent should be what separates professional footballers from the public.

In the Leeds dressing room, a game of silent musical chairs was often at play. Every player, Hilaire included, vied for a spot where they were hidden from Wilko's piercing gaze.

One day, he was in one of his moods. His voice, gravelly and obviously frustrated, echoed off the walls. 'How many more times do I have to tell you about going offside when there's no pressure on the ball?' he growled.

A tray of teas sat precariously on the edge of the treatment table, steam dancing into the air. With a sharp movement, Wilkinson sent the tray flying. The players watched in wide-eyed silence as a cascade of scalding liquid flew across the room.

One cup found its mark on David Rennie's shoulder. The hot tea soaked through his shirt, leaving a dark, wet patch. Steam rose from the spot, yet Rennie remained still as a statue. He didn't dare move, not even to wipe away the burning liquid. His fear of Wilkinson, it seemed, was greater than any physical discomfort.

Wilkinson knew that not all the players bought into his ethos. 'You get leaders who create energy within the dressing room, within the training. They create energy themselves, their leadership spreads and they take responsibility not only for their performance but other people's performances. Then you've got the people who are the followers who are good guys and just latch on to this and say: "Hey you know, this is for me, I like this."

'And then there are those who drain energy and they are there in every workplace. They drain energy from the place.

And the trouble with those is that the old saying is, "misery loves company", so they're not happy being miserable on their own. They want to make sure that you are miserable so rather than pat you on the back and say, "Come on, it'll get better," they'll tell you it's his fault.'

Wilkinson knew that something meaningful had to be done to clear the decks, to show them he was in charge and to draw a line in the sand. And he knew just the man for the job.

The news that Wimbledon midfielder Vinnie Jones was on his way to Leeds sent eyebrows skyward.

'What's he thinking of? Jones is trouble.'

Wilkinson knew exactly what he was doing, certain about what Jones would bring to Leeds. He attended Wimbledon's match at Highbury, accompanied by Mick Hennigan.

Dons boss Bobby Gould had just signed an overseas player, Detzi Kruszynski. He was the antithesis of what Jones stood for: he was not a team player, focusing only on doing his stuff when he had possession of the ball and he frequently neglected defensive responsibilities. This infuriated Jones, who was the most committed of team men. He detested such dilletantes, and he didn't hesitate to say so. Kruszynski's arrogant stare provoked an assault by Jones. A full-blown confrontation had to be halted physically by the referee.

Wilkinson, initially in London to watch Arsenal, found himself beaming at the unfolding scene. He turned to Hennigan, remarking, 'There you go, Michael, that's what we need. That is the man I want, someone who cares.'

'I talked at length to Dave Bassett, who had become, by then, a friend,' recalled Wilkinson. 'I talked to Dave and got the real Vinnie story.' He quickly learned that his reputation obscured the real Vinnie Jones. His antics were for show, he was a leader, a man willing to shoulder responsibility. He was intelligent, a team player, and someone who galvanised people.

'Vinnie came in, was unbelievable and of course the good thing with that is he's unbelievable because they expect *this*, but they don't get *this*, they get *that*.'

Jones was disillusioned with life on £500 a week at Wimbledon, and fell out with Bobby Gould, with whom he'd had a 'pushing match' at Luton. He told owner Sam Hammam he wanted out.

There were two clubs interested: Aston Villa and Leeds. Jones remembers Bill Fotherby calling him.

Fotherby gave him 'the full nine yards. Charlie big bananas. He was more like a market trader than a chairman. Fotherby was first on the phone, so when [Villa manager Graham] Taylor rings up, I tell him I've already spoken to Leeds.'

Jones was desperate to sign but kept a poker face during talks with Fotherby and Peter Ridsdale. He remembers seeing a bottle of champagne on the table and thinking, 'I've got him. I was on £500 a week and asked for two-and-a-half grand, plus a BMW. With side skirts. He never even twitched. I remember thinking, "F***, I could have doubled it."'

Jones could see the depth of the schisms in the dressing room. He singled out Baird, Davison, Aizlewood, Sheridan and Ormsby as a clique. When Wilkinson announced his squad for the new season he told the rest, 'You're over there. Do what you want. And you can get yourselves another club.'

Remarks were made, particularly about the signing of Jones. Why buy him when you had someone like Sheridan?

'Listen, pal, it's a case of us against them,' said Strachan, pulling Jones aside.

Jones had had enough of the snide whispering. He rose from his seat in the players' restaurant and took Davison to task.

'No, no, you've got the wrong end of the stick,' tried a shaking Davison.

Jones was having none of that – he gave Davison a fat lip and announced to the room, 'This all stops, right here and now. If any of you want to say anything or do anything, here I am.'

Jones stomped off to the dressing room to collect his kit.

Strachan raced after him. 'You all right, big man? Come on, calm down.'

'F*** them. I've not been brought up with this kind of situation. I'm used to everyone being together, I can't handle this, I want out of this place.'

Another voice cut in. 'The gaffer wants to see you,' came the command from Hennigan. 'Come on, son. He wants to see you in the office.'

Jones feared the worst but was caught unawares by Wilkinson's admission that Jones' actions were exactly what he had been looking for when he sought him out.

'From that moment in the manager's office, the problem was sorted and I was far happier,' recalled Jones. 'I felt wanted and needed and gradually, as a lot of the other players started going to the restaurant – Lee Chapman, Strachan, Batty, Gary Speed – we were becoming a close-knit force. It was like the early Wimbledon days.'

Wilkinson saw Jones as the ideal foil to Strachan, 'a footballer waiting to happen, a misunderstood individual' who might just be perfect for Leeds.

Jones had hoped to be named captain but that honour was reserved for Strachan, whom Wilkinson felt was best suited to deal with the slings and arrows that United would face.

Jones remarked that, when he first came to Leeds, Strachan thought he was 'crap'. 'Actually,' Strachan said later, 'I didn't think he was as good as that.' Then something odd happened. The ex-hod carrier from Watford began to grow on Strachan.

'They very quickly developed a healthy respect for each other,' says Wilkinson. 'Gordon respected what Vinnie was trying to do and how much he was trying to change his game. With time, he kept telling Vinnie that he was a much better player than he had previously thought.'

'It was like chalk and cheese,' recalls Strachan, 'the way our lifestyle was, but when we met on the football field or at the training ground, we were exactly the same. He wanted to beat me at every running session and I wanted to beat him, which dragged everybody else along. He's infectious, that's what I love so much about people like him, everything he does is 100 per cent.'

Jones' arrival had an immediate impact, especially on David Batty, who had found a new mentor.

Batty had been unimpressed by the news of Wilkinson's appointment, claiming that 'a shudder of apprehension ran through the first-team squad'. He was sold on the media description of Wilkinson's long-ball football and fearsome training runs. Batty was a fan of slick passing football, something which belied his own public persona, and declared his disaffection for Wilkinson's style. Already grappling with the departure of Billy Bremner, he never gave Wilkinson a genuine chance.

The relationship between Wilkinson and Batty was strained. Batty acknowledges that the manager's approach was intended to improve him as a player, but 'it would be hypocritical to claim that I enjoyed working for him or that I admired his methods and the way he had us play ... I never came to terms with Wilko's management style.'

In later years, Batty would berate Wilkinson, branding him 'boring, authoritarian, unimaginative and inflexible ... Howard's team talks were so boring. They went on for so long that, by the end, I had forgotten how they had started.'

Wilkinson was moved to consider legal action after hearing the remark. The issue that irked him was Batty's claim that Wilkinson told him that Bremner 'may have been a great player but he wasn't such a good manager'.

Wilkinson told *The Guardian*, 'The comments made by David Batty are extremely disappointing. I wish to make it public that at no time whatsoever have I either written or spoken any implied criticism of Billy's managerial skills at Leeds United or anywhere else. It is alarming that David Batty has chosen to make these public allegations he wrongly claims I've made about a man sadly no longer with us.'

Batty was a constant rebel at training, especially during Wilkinson's mandatory dead-ball practice. 'I was never involved in taking free kicks, anyway, so being forced to participate in the mind-numbing exercises on the training ground was just a bind as far as I was concerned.'

The majority of the team dutifully followed Wilkinson's orders, but there was one notable exception, as Tony Dorigo recalled. 'One time, the manager decided on a drill with no opposition and no football. So, Howard rolls this imaginary ball to Mel Sterland at right-back. He controls it and passes to the centre-halves. Everyone is going along with it.

'The "ball" then ends up in midfield with David Batty. He wasn't having it. He chipped it up and booted it straight out of play. That was the end of that.'

His sullen attitude almost spelled the end for Batty, but the manager saw too much in the young midfielder to write him off, unlike Sheridan, his partner in crime.

The difference between the two was that Batty's contribution was integrated into the team in a way that the shining skills of Sheridan never were.

When asked directly about Batty, Wilkinson refused to openly criticise.

After mentioning that 'I quickly realised the strengths of this youngster,' Wilkinson added, 'It's important at a football club if you're a player that you be yourself but being yourself cannot be at the expense of the group. So, be as far right or as far left as you want to be, but recognise that there's a structure here and there are some basic principles here, and it's important that we all pull together.'

Batty revealed later, 'I would aimlessly blast balls all over the pitch. Wilko brought the situation to an end when he walked up to me one day and presented me with a ball, on which he had written "Batty's Ball".'

'Go to a quiet part of the ground and amuse yourself until we've finished,' Wilkinson said. 'I'll call you over when I'm ready.'

Batty requested a transfer, but Wilko refused to consider it. Jones was tasked with taking Batty under his wing, in a way that Batty would never have allowed Strachan to do.

'Dave Batty became my best mate,' recalled Jones. 'I used to go to his house for tea even when he wasn't in because he lived with his mum and dad. His dad was a dustman and his mum a supermarket worker and they were both very down to earth, smashing people. I suppose it was the family involvement that I wanted. They made me feel so welcome.

'I took Batts under my wing big time … we hit it off straight away. I could make him laugh in a second. I know people don't believe that, but I mean he could look at me and I could make him laugh, you know.

'Batts was like me, a little psycho when he ran across the line, you know what I mean. When the whistle went, we were both little psychos, I think, and I was like the older brother, very much so. And we grew thicker and thicker as well, stronger and stronger.'

The kinship was crucial in convincing Batty that it was worth persevering, that if Jones rated Wilkinson, he must have something.

By the start of the season, Aizlewood, Adams, Sheridan, Peter Swan, Bob Taylor, Neil Aspin, John Stiles and David Rennie were all gone. Davison stuck around to be part of United's future.

Only the departure of Sheridan elicited a reaction from the fans, distraught at the loss of a man who had been the symbol of Leeds in the 80s.

Sheridan had expected to spend his entire career at Leeds but knew it was unlikely to work out for him under Wilko. So did Wilkinson.

'I just didn't like the way he played and his training,' says Sheridan. 'I think it was time for me to leave, even though I'd have stayed. The style of play didn't suit me. I think Howard had made his mind up more or less about me.'

Alan Sutton: 'Shez would never ever be a Howard Wilkinson kind of person. The day Howard Wilkinson walked in here on the Monday, Shez didn't even bother turning up for training. He probably still had a few over the weekend and Billy could handle that whereas Howard Wilkinson wasn't having that kind of culture. Shez didn't bother turning in, he was in bed, I think, in Manchester from a weekend out.'

The state of the Elland Road pitch was also a factor in Sheridan's departure. Wilkinson feared that the stadium's use for rugby league games would render it unsuitable by each spring for Sheridan's smooth passing style, making him an expensive luxury.

The players for whom Wilkinson didn't see a future were banished to the reserves. There was no open discussion, but they soon worked out they were not part of the future and leaving the club was in their best interest.

If Jones was the key signing, there were others, the most crucial being Mel Sterland and John Hendrie.

Wilkinson and Sterland had built a rapport in their Hillsborough days. When Wilkinson moved to Leeds,

Sterland left for a doomed stint at Rangers. A major falling-out with manager Graeme Souness followed. Souness had promised Sterland a position as right-back, with Gary Stevens playing centre-back. That never happened. Souness stationed Sterland out on the right wing – a position Sterland loathed. Despite his feelings, Sterland complied, driven by his desire to represent Rangers.

Just weeks into his contract with Rangers, Sterland bought a house north of the border on the back of reassurances from Souness. Sterland was taking a few days back in Sheffield to visit his wife's sick mother when there was a telephone call.

'It's Ron Atkinson.'

'F*** off, Ron Atkinson, who's messing about?'

'It's Ron Atkinson at Sheffield Wednesday.'

'Come on, stop messing about, tell me who it is or I'll put the f***ing phone down.'

'Mel, it's Ron Atkinson.'

'Oh, sorry Ron, what can I do for you?'

'Do you want to come back to Sheffield Wednesday?'

'What do you mean? I've signed a four-year contract up here, I've got a nice house and I'm happy.'

'Well, let me just tell you something, you're for sale and I'd like to bring you back to Hillsborough. We'll look after you and give you a sponsored car.'

'I'm not interested. I can't be for sale because I've been assured by Graeme that I'm going nowhere.'

'Well, I think you'll find out that you'll be on your way.'

Sterland regarded the whole thing as nonsense. Until he received another call …

It was QPR manager Trevor Francis, asking if Sterland was interested in going to Loftus Road. Hours later, there was a call from Bill Fotherby and Sterland knew that something was up.

'When I managed to get hold of Souness, who was in an Italian restaurant, I wasn't prepared for what he told me,' recalls Sterland.

'Look, son, I'm going to let you go because I'm looking to bring Trevor Steven back. I've spent too much money and you're the only player I can get my money back on pretty quickly.'

'Does that mean I can talk to anybody I want to?'

'Yes, and I wish you luck, wherever you go to. We'll hopefully get back the money we paid for you.'

Sterland didn't fancy a move to London and Atkinson was offering less money than he had been on previously at Hillsborough, but Sterland started to worry he might not get anything.

As Sterland travelled south for talks with QPR, a call from Howard Wilkinson interrupted his journey. 'Don't sign for QPR,' the Leeds manager implored. 'On your way back up, come and talk to us. I'm going to sign some good players and win promotion with Leeds United.'

QPR offered Sterland a three-year contract, but it failed to pique his interest. Heading back north, he made a detour to a Nottingham hotel to meet Wilkinson and his chief scout, Ian MacFarlane. Their words resonated with Sterland, and he promptly signed. 'We'll win the league this year,' promised Wilkinson.

When asked whether he signed for the club or the man, Sterland responded, 'Both. Leeds were a big, big club, and as I'd worked with Howard before, I knew he wasn't messing around. He wouldn't have taken the job if he didn't think he would be successful.

'He had definitely mellowed — there were none of those bloody cross-country runs! I think he was just that bit more experienced. He'd got better players around him to work with, and a chairman who was backing him all the way. He was generally a lot more relaxed.'

Rangers took a £200,000 loss on the deal as Wilkinson secured a force of nature.

John Hendrie had long been admired by Billy Bremner but he had lost his way at Newcastle. Wilkinson was convinced he could rebuild his career and was only too pleased to sign him, looking for drive and goals from the right flank.

Other signings were made, but none had the impact of Jones, Sterland and Hendrie. As Wilkinson admitted privately, 'If you get three out of every five signings right, you've done a good job.'

The signing of Mickey Thomas was bizarre, an early example of the aberrations that would come to characterise Wilkinson's transfer dealings. The midfielder had a half-century of Welsh caps but was 35 years old and past it, with Wilkinson's interest down to a few bright showings for a relegated Shrewsbury side.

The deal was almost scuppered when Thomas told Wilkinson, 'You can f*** off. You slaughtered me in my Chelsea days. You said I would sod off and fall out with the boss. You did me in.'

Wilkinson didn't bat an eyelid, merely assuring Thomas that he had admired him throughout his career. 'You are the type of player we want at Elland Road.'

Thomas agreed the move but then received a call from Tranmere. Thomas confessed that he had signed a contract, but secretary Norman Wilson persisted, saying that he could get out of it if he wanted. Thomas agreed to go to Tranmere to discuss the matter, taking his contract with him. Wilson had to admit that he could not match Leeds' terms.

That was that, thought Thomas, but he was wrong.

'Two days later I got another phone call. Mick Hennigan was on the other end of the line. "Mickey, son, we have a problem," he told me. "We're not very happy with you. You have been talking with Tranmere. We know all about it."'

The situation was quickly resolved, but Thomas' card was indelibly marked.

Wilkinson worked his men like dogs in pre-season to get fitness levels up and integrate the newcomers. Former Ipswich defender Chris O'Donnell struggled. According to Jones, he 'looked several stones overweight and couldn't run'. O'Donnell was six laps behind the rest on a testing cross-country run. Jones couldn't bear to see him out there alone, so he ran alongside him for another six laps to get him round.

Jim Beglin was another player who struggled pre-season. The Irish left-back had a stellar pedigree. A member of Liverpool's Double-winning side in 1986, he suffered a severe leg fracture in a Merseyside derby in January 1987 and there were fears that he might never play again. He turned down Ipswich and Middlesbrough before committing to Leeds.

'Howard knew he was taking a risk with me, and he arranged a session on Fullerton Park. We played a five-a-side in which I showed I was comfortable on the ball and I even chipped in with a few goals. Afterwards, he held me back for a vigorous routine of running. I was absolutely knackered. My legs and lungs had gone. He told me to pop into the referee's room, have a shower, then report to his office to continue the negotiations.

'He had worked me so hard in that session that I thought I was going to black out. I had to have a lie down and pray I wouldn't get caught – luckily I didn't and I was delighted to eventually put pen to paper and sign for Leeds.'

Another newcomer was veteran Watford defender John McClelland, who holds the distinction of being the first player to play professionally for clubs in all four home nations.

'My contract had a clause in it saying they would let me go for a minimal fee but there was no agreement what that fee actually was. Nigel Worthington said that Howard Wilkinson was interested, so I phoned Howard up. I said, "If you phone Watford they will tell you I have got a three-year contract, but what they won't tell you is that I have a clause to leave."

'So, Leeds rang Watford and the deal was on. At the last minute, Graham Taylor tried to get me to go to Aston Villa. He was offering me a two-year deal with a free transfer at the end. Leeds offered me three years. I said to GT that I'd get a free at that age anyway. Leeds were paying more and Graham said, "Well, we can't pay that."

'I overdid the training initially and ended up in plaster and I played only four games in two years. It took Leeds a while to let me do my own training. At Watford, I was joining in with the full training only a couple of times a week. At Leeds they thought I was lazy but when they let me do my own training I got fit and I played a part. I played until I was 40.'

The big pre-season test came on 30 July with a high-profile friendly against Anderlecht. Wilkinson selected a team that many people expected to be his first choice: Day, Sterland, Snodin, Jones, Blake, Fairclough, Strachan, Batty, Baird, Thomas, Hendrie.

Beglin was absent after injuring his knee in a training challenge, so Glynn Snodin stepped in at the last moment.

Leeds had stuck five goals past Chesterfield five days earlier, with Davison scoring twice, but Anderlecht was the big one and the striker was left out as Wilkinson packed his midfield.

Leeds held their own until Noel Blake was sent off after 64 minutes for elbowing Marc Van Der Linden. Anderlecht ran riot after that, running in five goals.

Blake's baser instincts let him down but Jones got away with a transgression of his own. Strachan heard a crack that suggested fist on face. Jones winked as he trotted past his captain. 'First of the season,' he smirked, as a Belgian lay spark out, blood streaming from his nose.

Strachan was horrified, confronting Jones in the dressing room. Wilkinson made Jones aware of exactly what was and was not allowed.

It worked. Jones' discipline improved noticeably under the leadership of Wilkinson and Strachan. He received only three yellow cards all year.

An injury to Chris Fairclough and Blake's dismissal meant both would miss the first league game, away to Newcastle.

Jones was also missing. 'I was the fittest I'd been in my life … I played a stupid little five-a-side on the Friday night when we travelled up. I went up for a header and I came down on my toe and went over on my ankle. I was absolutely gutted.'

Wilkinson had to shuffle his pack. Gary Williams was expected to fill in at left-back, but he suffered a knock in training the day before the game. Wilkinson gambled on Beglin, even though the Irishman knew he wasn't ready.

The week after the Anderlecht debacle, a centre-back pairing of John McClelland and Peter Haddock looked solid against Doncaster. Wilkinson stuck with the pairing at St James' Park and handed out four other first-team debuts.

Leeds led 2-1 at the break with goals from Davison and Baird, but McClelland and Beglin were struggling. The left-back conceded the penalty that allowed tubby Newcastle debutant Micky Quinn to score for the Geordies.

Leeds fell apart in the second half with John Gallacher giving Beglin nightmares. Quinn notched a second-half hat-trick as Newcastle scored four without reply.

Wilkinson defended his team publicly, reminding critics that it was a marathon not a sprint.

'The second-half goals were a joke from our point of view,' he added. 'The players know what I think and they think the same themselves. We defended very generously.'

Leeds had been overrun in midfield and the entire afternoon had been a sobering experience for Wilkinson. He took immediate remedial action.

McClelland only played twice more, while Beglin was sent on loan to Plymouth to recover fitness. Fairclough was recalled and formed a decent partnership with Haddock, relegating McClelland and Blake to bit parts. Mike Whitlow filled in so well at left-back that he was ever-present until January.

Jones was not yet fit to start and was used from the bench in the next two games but he quickly became a fixture with Thomas unceremoniously dropped. Before the end of the season, he was farmed out to Stoke.

Wilkinson could have been excused for a moment of self-doubt with some of his buys looking like expensive mistakes, but not a bit of it. He simply sighed heavily, cleared his head and set about the rest of the season.

There was a chance to right the wrongs of Newcastle with Middlesbrough visiting Elland Road four days later. Leeds duly did the business.

'The atmosphere that night was electric and we got off to a perfect start with a Bobby Davison goal and I flashed a volley just over the bar,' recalled Hendrie. 'I'll never forget Vinnie coming on for his debut. With the scores level at 1-1, Vinnie entered the field of play like Hulk Hogan. He was pumped up and got us and the crowd going.'

With three minutes remaining, Jones replaced Baird. Describing his entry into the fray as 'a great managerial decision', Vinnie added, 'The manager told me to go out and go for it and it paid off.'

'As the clock ticked down, Vinnie played the worst through ball ever,' remarked Hendrie. 'Gary Parkinson attempted to play the ball back to the keeper. However, the ball hit a divot and bounced into the back of the net. We were obviously ecstatic but the lads were in hysterics when Vinnie tried to claim the goal.'

Jones remembers the game as the one that cemented his standing with the fans.

'I just turned and ran to the Kop – I was going f***ing mental and overcome with joy and the Kop just kind of all stepped back and went "whooooa" – it was like they looked at me and said, "You'll do for us." I think the fans saw in my eyes what it meant to me.'

Confidence remained high even with the next three games finishing in 1-1 draws.

The final fixture in that sequence was at home to Ipswich. Leeds were boosted by Jones' first goal for the club after 12 minutes, diving to head home after Baird flicked on a Strachan corner, but they could not add to the score. Ipswich dominated and Leeds were indebted to Mervyn Day for an outstanding goalkeeping performance. He couldn't stop the 77th-minute equaliser, deflected in off Fairclough's head after the ball came off the bar.

Wilkinson was enraged by the slackness, slapping his knee in exasperation, but recognised that Day saved the points by denying Ipswich twice in the final two minutes.

Leeds snapped back to form with victory at Hull on 16 September, the only goal of the game coming from Baird.

United were ninth after six games. Dave Bassett's unbeaten Sheffield United side looked like they were going to run away with the title. The Blades posed a significant threat to Wilkinson's ambitions with the striking duo of Brian Deane and Tony Agana scoring by the bagful.

Wilkinson remained confident that Leeds would come through, having settled upon a successful formation and combination almost by chance – midfield was their strength with Batty and Jones acting as enforcers down the middle while Strachan and Hendrie showed creativity out wide.

The striking partnership of Baird and Davison was doing well with the former's bludgeoning force earning the latter time and space to exploit.

Leeds found a rhythm that saw them safely through the winter.

Victory at West Ham in October was crucial, Jones smartly flicking home the only goal from a Whitlow cross. The London press pilloried what the *Mail On Sunday*'s Patrick Collins termed 'a quite disgraceful exhibition of all that is indefensible in the English game'. He mocked Leeds as 'cynical scufflers who won three points, 15 offside decisions and the contempt of the neutrals'.

Wilkinson was furious. 'Ever since I came here that one keeps being thrown up. You only have to commit a foul and on Monday morning it's the old, cynical Leeds.

'If you do something well, nobody ever writes about the old, terrific Leeds.

'I wouldn't mind if Trevor Brooking had come up to me and said, "I've got to tell you I feel that strongly about that, that was rubbish." But I get a handshake, I get a nice smile and "Can we have Vinnie?" Nah, nah, I ask you … these are the things the general public don't see.'

Leeds' form at Elland Road was excellent, but they slipped away from home in November, losing at Leicester and West Brom.

The latter defeat increased the significance of Newcastle's subsequent visit to Elland Road. Leeds still owed the Geordies one for their earlier mauling.

Newcastle were serious promotion rivals, trailing Leeds by a slim two points. Another defeat was unthinkable – it would have dealt a severe blow to Leeds' promotion credentials.

The fiercely competitive nature of the fixture was evidenced pre-match by a confrontation recalled by Baird.

Jones was 'being Vinnie', the aggressive, manic character whom Leeds fans by now adored, and Newcastle goalkeeper John Burridge was no shrinking violet. The pair did their best to gee up their colleagues pre-match.

'To get to the changing rooms,' recounts Baird, 'the players had to go through a multi-gym first. Vinnie made sure he was in there when the lads from Newcastle arrived and he started doing what Vinnie did, shouting and screaming, trying to intimidate them and wind them all up.

'Burridge walked in, saw what was happening, went straight over to the bench press and benched 100kg ten times, just like that. The tone was set and it left you thinking, "Yeah. This is a big one."'

The game itself was just as competitive, settled in the second half when Baird headed the only goal.

'I hadn't scored in a while,' said Baird. 'It wasn't that my performance had been bad, that wasn't the problem, but the goals had not been coming.

'It was a nice move. Gordon Strachan sent all 15 stone of Mel Sterland flying down the right wing and he put a cross right on my head.'

A diving Burridge got a hand to Baird's header but could only push it into the side of his net.

It was a massive three points, confirming that Leeds meant business, that there would be no collapse, no limp surrender.

Sterland embodied the United spirit, playing manfully on despite damaging his ribs when Newcastle striker Mark McGhee fell on him heavily. 'It was very painful,' admitted Sterland, 'but there was no way I wanted to come off.'

Davison and Baird were also injured and missed the game at Middlesbrough. With Hendrie still out, Wilkinson was forced to rely on his reserve front two, big John Pearson and Carl Shutt, giving each man his first start of the season.

Shutt got the first goal and Fairclough the other in a 2-0 victory that was Leeds' ninth from 12 games. The result moved the Whites above Sheffield United in the table.

Howard Wilkinson's Leeds United had found their mojo.

Bournemouth

One of the saddest aspects about the events in Bournemouth was that until that juncture we had been winning the battle to improve our public relations image.

AS CHRISTMAS 1989 approached, Howard Wilkinson was locked in battle for the Second Division title with old friend Dave Bassett as Leeds United and Sheffield United were neck-and-neck.

Leeds trailed the Blades by a point after 21 games but had seven in hand on third-placed Sunderland. The Yorkshire clubs appeared certainties to clinch the two automatic promotion spots, but Wilkinson was determined to leave nothing to chance.

He demanded victory when Brighton visited Elland Road on 16 December. John Hendrie had made a couple of reserve appearances after 17 games out, but Wilkinson had no qualms about starting him.

The 3-0 win was routine, built on goals from Gordon Strachan and Hendrie, and was capped by one of Vinnie Jones' finest goals in a Leeds shirt. Like the smartest of inside-forwards, he side-stepped a defender before slickly curling the ball inside the right-hand post. He gleefully milked the Elland Road applause.

With Sheffield United held at Port Vale, Leeds slipped into top spot – it was the ideal preparation for the two sides' Boxing Day clash.

The game was already a big one for Mel Sterland, a diehard Wednesday fan with a deep dislike of their Steel City rivals.

In the week leading up to the game, Sterland engaged in playful banter with some Blades fans he knew. He bet one of them a fiver that he would score in the game.

When Leeds were awarded a free kick 30 yards from goal, Sterland approached Gordon Strachan. 'Gordon, I'm going to hit it.'

'Nae, big man, you'll not score from here,' countered Strachan.

'Just leave it, Gordon,' Sterland insisted.

He caught the ball perfectly. It sailed into the top corner, and Sterland, unable to contain his joy, galloped towards his mate in the crowd, dancing an impromptu jig.

'He still owes me the fiver, because I haven't seen him since then. I got loads of abuse from the Blades fans after the goal. They were singing, "You fat bastard" and "Have you ever seen a salad?"'

The Blades responded with goals from Wilf Rostron and Tony Agana, both poor from the Leeds perspective, but Leeds earned a point thanks to a Carl Shutt equaliser.

Their steady progress was undermined by defeat at Barnsley. Leeds thought they'd earned a point but Jones' spectacular late goal was disallowed.

Leeds had appeared one-dimensional and blunt, relying on high balls to Baird and Shutt up front. Barnsley coped easily with such lack of imagination. United seemed to have lost their way.

When they could only draw at home to Oldham on New Year's Day and then went out of the FA Cup at the same venue, the criticism became pointed.

Wilkinson conceded his concern at his side's inability to convert their territorial advantage into goals and Leeds were quickly linked with a number of big-name strikers – Arsenal's Niall Quinn, Graeme Sharp of Everton and Paul Stewart of Tottenham.

Wilkinson maintained his faith in Baird, but he was struggling, having scored just once since the middle of November. Determined to give Leeds a boost, Wilkinson sought out a known quantity.

Wilkinson's goalscoring totem at Sheffield Wednesday was Lee Chapman, whom he knew could be trusted.

Leslie Silver's cash paved the way and an offer of £400,000 persuaded Nottingham Forest to release the striker. It was an astute piece of business by Wilkinson.

Chapman scored on his debut at Blackburn on 13 January, diverting a shot from Strachan, but Rovers had the upper hand. They took an early lead and threatened to overrun United, but a second goal was denied by the woodwork.

Leeds weathered the storm and equalised through Chapman, who then set up Strachan for the winner. Blackburn deserved a point but squandered a late penalty.

Chapman had provided a powerful focal point, dominant in the air and with the happy knack of being in the right place at the right time. His style was similar to Baird's, but he brought a more potent goal threat.

A home game against bottom club Stoke promised to be a gimme. Leeds created numerous chances but couldn't apply the killer touch and the game remained goalless at the break.

At the start of the second period, David Batty's last-ditch challenge on Carl Beeston was deemed a penalty but Mervyn Day saved Batty's blushes by blocking Wayne Biggins' poor spot kick.

Strachan made no such mistake when Leeds were awarded a penalty for a foul on Chapman by Stoke keeper Peter Fox.

The custodian went the right way but Strachan's cool finish was right in the corner.

Hendrie added a crucial second as the clock ran down and another three points were in the bag, though Sheffield United kept pace with victory at home to Middlesbrough. A 12-point gap was opened over third-placed Swindon.

Behind the scenes there was trouble – Baird saw red over the purchase of Chapman and gave Wilkinson a piece of his mind.

Later, he reflected, 'Me being the way I was then, which was very impatient, cost me. I was playing well but not scoring. Bobby Davison was and we felt it was a good partnership. Stupidly – and it's a big regret of mine now – I went storming in to see Howard.'

'I'm not having this … why have you signed him?'

'I've signed him to strengthen the squad.'

'I want to leave.'

'What do you want to leave for?'

'I'm not playing second fiddle to anybody.'

Wilkinson asked Baird to extend his contract, but within 30 minutes, Middlesbrough manager Bruce Rioch was on the phone and Baird was gone.

Wilkinson filled the void by bringing in another former Wednesday player, Imre Varadi. He bolstered further by luring utility player Chris Kamara away from Stoke City.

Kamara was already in talks with Middlesbrough, whose chairman, Steve Gibson, he had been at school with. A good deal was on the table and Kamara was ready to go.

Wilkinson confidant David Walker called Kamara to tell him that Leeds were interested and asked him to meet Wilkinson before he travelled to Middlesbrough.

The Leeds manager, flanked by Bill Fotherby, made a lucrative offer to Kamara. The contract would triple his pay, included a substantial signing fee, and a promotion bonus.

Kamara, eyes wide with disbelief, was quick to accept, promising Wilkinson that he would sign the very next day. However, he felt it was only right to inform Middlesbrough's manager and their chairman face-to-face.

Wilkinson, his brow furrowed, was reluctant to allow the player to depart without signing, the thought of Kamara reconsidering overnight worrying him. Wilkinson gestured to Fotherby that they should have another talk. They returned moments later with another £10,000 on the salary.

'I'd still like to sign it on my way home from the Boro tomorrow,' persisted Kamara.

Fotherby and Wilkinson withdrew for yet another private chat, leaving Kamara in a state of amused bewilderment. Despite his assertions of commitment, they suspected he was holding out for more money.

After a lengthy discussion, they returned. Fotherby, his voice firm, rapped, 'This is our final offer. Take it or leave it, because it won't be there tomorrow.'

Kamara's gaze landed on the contract laid out before him, its value now inflated beyond his wildest dreams. With a sheepish grin of thanks, he signed off his allegiance to Leeds.

Both Varadi and Kamara were given debuts on 10 February against Hull, with the latter covering for Sterland, who had missed three games due to an injury sustained at Blackburn. United's injury problems were so severe that Vince Hilaire and Chris O'Donnell were added to the matchday squad for the first time.

Leeds had lost their previous game at Swindon and needed a win to get their promotion push back on track.

Bottom-five side Hull looked like cannon fodder, but United's history is littered with examples of opponents raising their game. The game epitomised the phenomenon.

Things were on track after 18 minutes – Hendrie sent a remarkable header from outside the box looping into the

Hull goal. Tigers keeper Iain Hesford, who had worked for Wilkinson at Wednesday, had come out to challenge for Strachan's corner and Hendrie saw the opportunity early. His header was inch-perfect, dropping precisely under the bar.

On the half-hour mark, Hull snapped back with an unexpected equaliser. With Jones down and in need of treatment at the Hull end, the Tigers stormed into the Leeds area. Dave Bamber made to take Day on but was felled by Haddock. Penalty!

Leeds did their best to psych out young striker Andy Payton as he prepared to take the kick. There was massed jeering from the crowd and Bamber was quick to draw the attention of referee David Axcell to in-yer-face barracking from Day and Chapman as they sought to unnerve Payton. He held his nerve and smashed the ball into the roof of the net.

Restored to health, Jones quickly took a hand, restoring United's lead with a wonderful goal. Haddock's long free kick arrowed towards the opposition area. It looked like there was no danger as the ball was headed clear, but Jones had other ideas. He swung into an instant volley from 30 yards that flew as precisely as Hendrie's header just under the Hull bar. 2-1, and the crowd went wild as Jones went into his best psycho celebration.

Wilkinson laid down the law at the break, insisting that his men push on. But the best-laid plans of mice and men and all that – Hull were level six minutes into the second half.

Leeds had all the early pressure and Chapman netted. His effort was disallowed because the ball had gone out before Varadi nodded it back to his strike partner.

Leeds pushed on, sometimes leaving one lone defender to deal with Hull's sporadic forays. They paid the price when Bamber drove into the Leeds area. Fairclough's challenge from behind was poorly timed and sent the front man sprawling to concede another penalty. Payton again kept his cool to tie the scores.

Hull's tenacity had been mildly irritating at first, but now it was embarrassing, and they were not yet done.

With 12 minutes left, Steve Doyle produced a pale imitation of Jones' wonder strike. It was neither as far out nor as powerful, but it was just as accurate as it soared inside the top corner to put Hull ahead for the first time.

When the going gets tough, the tough get going – and at that moment Strachan showed exactly how tough he was.

Strachan danced his way to the byline as Hull ran the clock down. He cut it back for Varadi, but the first shot was poor. Strachan retrieved it and set up Varadi again – this time he couldn't miss. 3-3, and it was game on.

Jones did wonders to keep the ball alive 30 yards out and dutifully obeyed Strachan's signal to slip a pass into the space in front of the Scot. The ball was despatched unerringly into the top corner for a superb winner.

Strachan lay prone, soaking up his team-mates' adoration.

It was an incredible afternoon, the kind that gets the blood racing, as Wilkinson acknowledged. 'No matter what might happen, Vinnie doesn't give in and that's something money can't buy. Strachan is the same. He too doesn't give in. They make an odd couple really, but they are an ideal pair.'

It was glorious, but Leeds' form abruptly collapsed – they went four games without a win, despite Chapman finding his scoring boots.

Somehow, they retained top spot and a two-point lead, though Sheffield United's run through to the last eight of the FA Cup left them with two matches in hand. The Blades had gone unbeaten since the first week of January and momentum was with them.

Sheffield hosted Manchester United in an FA Cup quarter-final on Sunday, 11 March, meaning Leeds could extend their lead with victory at Oxford on Saturday.

Oxford were in form and closing on a play-off spot. Wilkinson took nothing for granted and was proven correct as Oxford took a 2-0 lead, giving United's once impervious defence the jitters.

Knowing he could not afford another defeat, Wilkinson threw caution to the wind, summoning Hendrie from the bench to replace Beglin.

Hendrie terrorised Oxford, but Sterland, a constant threat from the right, was equally important.

When Sterland pumped a ball towards Fairclough, just before the hour, he opened the way. The centre-back flicked it on to the back post and Chapman took the ball down before driving it into the corner. Oxford heads dropped as Leeds got the bit between their teeth.

After 73 minutes, Varadi applied the finish to Hendrie's cutback to level the scores.

Fairclough was a fixture up front now and was rewarded for his efforts two minutes later when he looped a header into the net following an overhead kick from Hendrie.

Chapman touched home a fourth from Speed's low cross.

When Hendrie was sent flying in the area in the final minute, Chapman insisted on taking the penalty to complete his hat-trick but he hammered the ball straight at the keeper.

Wilkinson was enraged, claiming that in a tight promotion chase, the fifth goal could have been vital. He tore a strip off Chapman.

Sheffield United, who were knocked out of the FA Cup by Manchester United, played one of their three games in hand on the Wednesday, but had to settle for a draw at Brighton. They remained third behind Swindon but cut the gap to Leeds to four points.

The Whites' weekend clash with West Ham was crucial; it was essential that they did not give the Blades a sniff of a chance.

Elland Road was packed with a crowd of 32,536, the day's largest in the Second Division and Leeds' highest attendance in four years.

Chapman scored two more goals, bringing his total to eight in nine games. At half-time, the brace separated the sides.

The Hammers pulled one back, but Strachan restored the two-goal lead. Chapman's own goal in the 68th minute offered the visitors hope, but Leeds held on for the three points.

It was just as well, because Sheffield United thrashed Wolves 3-0 to glide past Swindon.

United's victory at Sunderland on Tuesday was massive, with Sheffield losing by five the following day at West Ham – Leeds had 70 points, seven more than the Blades.

Dave Bassett was devastated, saying, 'They simply tore us apart. We came second in just about every aspect of the game and I willingly concede that there was very little that we could do about it. It wasn't so much the five-goal drubbing that we received that worried me so much, it was the mental effect that the game would have on my team.'

Bassett's men retained two games in hand, but the fate of the title was in Leeds' hands. They enjoyed a ten-point advantage over third-placed Swindon with ten games left.

Things looked even more positive at the weekend with Leeds beating Portsmouth 2-0 while Sheffield United lost at home to Barnsley and Swindon drew at Oxford.

Suddenly there was a stumble with Sheffield United winning two away games during the following week while Leeds succumbed to nerves in more ways than one at Wolves.

Leeds fell behind when Batty's poor pass let Wolves in. He didn't seem himself and it soon became evident why.

The young midfielder ran gingerly off to the dressing room, much to Wilkinson's confusion. He despatched Alan Sutton to investigate.

'What the f***'s going on?' screamed Sutton at Batty. 'What's up?'

'I've sh*t myself,' was Batty's succinct response, cringing with embarrassment as he sorted himself out.

Leeds drew their next two games, against Bradford City and Plymouth, but Bassett was even more concerned about Sheffield's sudden inconsistency. The Blades lost twice before bouncing back to thrash Watford 4-1.

By the second week of April, both sides had six games left, with Leeds three points to the good. Newcastle had established themselves atop the chasing pack and were closing rapidly on the top two. They were nine points behind Leeds, but with a game in hand and playing so well that anything seemed possible. Wilkinson, for one, would not discount them.

The Geordies won two more games on the bounce and Leeds' defeat at Oldham, combined with the Blades' victory at Oxford on 14 April, left the top two tied on 75 points with Newcastle three points back having won their games in hand. Only Leeds' superior goal difference kept their noses in front, their ten-point advantage squandered.

The Easter Monday showdown between Leeds and the Blades at Elland Road became doubly critical – defeat for either side might prove fatal.

Wilkinson's column in the matchday programme was more succinct than his normal rambling prose. 'What can I say about today's game that has not already been said or appeared in print? Including this afternoon's encounter, we have five matches to go in what can turn out to be Leeds United's most important season for a decade. So let's get on with it.'

Wilkinson called up Kamara to replace the fading Batty. If the column and the line-up screamed 'Up and at 'em', they belied Wilkinson's thoughtful planning. It was designed to lull Bassett into thinking it would be all blood and thunder.

Wilkinson had watched Sheffield and devised a strategy to blunt them. Leeds were criticised for long-ball play, but the Blades were even more direct. With Brian Deane and Billy Whitehurst such aerial threats, goalkeeper Simon Tracey's huge kicks were an important part of their arsenal. Wilkinson knew that Tracey was prone to temper and that he could be got at. He directed his front men to apply pressure to Tracey but 'to stand four yards off him so there could be no possibility of the referee deeming that they were deliberately trying to obstruct his kicks'.

The tactic had failed at Bramall Lane on Boxing Day. Undaunted, Wilkinson ordered, 'Same again, lads.'

It took some time for Leeds to reap the full benefit, but Tracey fell apart in the second half.

There was an early hint when the keeper's clearance out of his hands cannoned off Davison's back and into touch.

Tracey was on pins for the rest of the game, dropping Jones' cross under pressure only to be let off by Davison and Chapman.

The inevitable Leeds goal came after 17 minutes. Gary Speed's clever header allowed Strachan to race clear into the area. Tracey blocked his shot, but it fell to Kamara, who fired goalwards. When Paul Stanicliffe blocked it on the line, Strachan reacted faster than anyone else and poked the ball home.

Kamara, Jones and Strachan dominated midfield as Leeds piled pressure on Tracey. He was fortunate when he came out to deny Davison, but the game remained 1-0 at the break. Leeds' failure to finish things off tore at their nerves and it was the final 20 minutes before their persistence paid off.

They began to carve out openings and Strachan and Kamara contrived to send Speed away down the left. Kamara skewed wide from his cutback, but pressure was building, with Speed enjoying plenty of the ball and his crosses a constant threat.

Now it was that the pressure told on Tracey. He was furious when another of his kicks went into touch off Chapman and he remonstrated at length with the referee.

The throw was deep inside the Blades' half and Leeds regained possession, freeing Speed once more. He hit the byline and his driven cross went under Tracey's dive, allowing Chapman to touch home at the back post.

Tracey was then guilty of the most colossal f*** up. After fielding a long shot, he made to punt downfield, only for his kick to strike Davison and run wide. He lost out in a foot race with the striker and when Davison slipped past him, Tracey dragged him to the turf. It could be nothing but a penalty despite Tracey's protests and sharp words in Davison's direction.

A nerveless Strachan sent the spot kick effortlessly into the top corner for 3-0.

Speed's contribution had been massive and he got his reward in the closing seconds. As Leeds broke out from a corner, Kamara drove the ball down the left wing and Speed ran on to it from inside his own half. He advanced on the Sheffield area and clipped a shot across Tracey and inside the right-hand post, a gorgeous way to cap a match-winning performance.

The 4-0 victory was emphatic, giving Leeds' goal difference a massive boost. The Blades fell to third place after Newcastle defeated Stoke 3-0, the Geordies' sixth successive victory.

Leeds seemed home and dry with four games left, but nerves took them as they drew at Brighton.

With 20 minutes to go and Leeds shading it at 2-1, Wilkinson hauled off Kamara and replaced him with Batty.

Kamara was furious that Jones, 'who hadn't kicked a ball all game', remained on the pitch. He berated Wilkinson. 'What have you brought me off for?'

'Because I'm the manager, that's why.'

'I know you're the manager, but I'm doing all right. Vinnie's not doing anything out there.'

Wilkinson pointed his finger and told Kamara to 'Shut it.'

Mick Hennigan stepped in to cool things down, pulling Kamara away. 'Come on, sit down, Chris. You'd better keep your mouth shut.'

'No, I won't. There's one rule for one and one rule for the other here. I've worked my socks off to get in this team and I'm playing well and now you've dragged me off.'

Now it was Wilkinson who lost it. 'You better shut it now, or you won't be at this football club tomorrow.'

Brighton netted at the death through John Crumplin's inch-perfect back-post header. Kamara seethed with righteous indignation while Wilkinson angrily bit his lip – Leeds' cushion shrank to a point after Sheffield's fortunate victory over Port Vale.

Leeds then suffered a more costly and unexpected result, at home to relegation-threatened Barnsley. When Fairclough nodded home just before the interval the outcome appeared to be a formality.

The centre-back had been off for 13 minutes to get ten stitches in a head wound but showed no fear when he rose to meet the ball.

Leeds had numerous chances to wrap up the three points but were undone in the closing minutes when Barnsley manager Mel Machin threw caution to the wind. In a desperate attempt to get something from the game, he replaced his central defenders.

His gamble paid off, as both substitutes, Brendan O'Connell and Owen Archdeacon, scored in the space of eight minutes.

The first came when Day botched a clearance, leaving O'Connell to slide the ball into an open net. Then Archdeacon was left unmarked at the back post to smash home from a throw that flew across the goalmouth.

Leeds men had their heads in their hands – their promotion chances hung by a thread.

Wilkinson: 'I was worried, obviously. I recognised that if you're in professional football long enough, you'll discover and have to get used to not winning games you should have.'

The upcoming fixtures were suddenly massive – Leeds at home to Leicester, Sheffield United hosting struggling Bournemouth and Newcastle paired with West Ham.

Wilkinson was upbeat before the Leicester game, insisting that he'd rather be in Leeds' position, with points in the bag. Nonetheless, even after Sterland brought the roof off with a stunning driven goal after 13 minutes, there was a fatalistic feel about Elland Road.

Strangely, the strike failed to settle the nerves as Leeds squandered chance after chance. Leicester fought back to equalise midway through the second half. Gary McAllister's glorious shot was greeted by a deathly silence from a tense stadium.

McAllister came close again as Leeds fans feared the worst, and it looked like the wheels had come off.

But cometh the hour, cometh the man – Gordon Strachan stepped forward for his moment of destiny.

A Sterland throw deep inside Leicester's half unsettled their defence, but they scrambled the ball to the edge of their area. There was Strachan, waiting as if time was standing still, to put his left foot through the ball. It flew into the top corner.

Strachan later admitted that it was a lucky, aimless swing, but he added, 'Every now and then I get a feeling in my left foot that is the same feeling I had when I scored that goal. Every training session, every run I had to school, every time I threw up and had been sick because of training, every knock-back I got, every horrible game I played in, it was all kind of destined for that one moment. It made it all worthwhile. Just for that one moment. I can always live off that for the rest of my life.'

Elland Road erupted as fans poured on to the pitch to dance a conga as word spread like wildfire – Leeds were up!

A story went round that Newcastle had drawn and Jones was quick to propagate the fake news.

Alan Sutton: 'Vinnie Jones all of a sudden comes in. "Lads, Newcastle have drawn, we're up." At that point some of the lads were actually half-crying, you know, you could see tears coming down. I've got out of the dressing room, I'm going down the corridor, I've seen John Helm.'

'Oh John, have you seen, we've done it.'

'Nah, Newcastle are still playing.'

'What? But Vinnie's come in and ...'

'As the final whistle blew,' explains Jones, 'all these fans poured on to the pitch. I bumped into a guy I knew near the tunnel who said, "Newcastle have lost, we're promoted and have won the league."

'I went into the dressing room and told all the lads. I also told a few fans, but then it turned out this fella had got it wrong. By then, though, it was too late and everyone was celebrating on the pitch. It was a right cock-up and I felt awful.'

Newcastle had conjured a late winner against West Ham and the war was not yet done.

Leeds were left in the promotion box seat when Sheffield United could only draw at Blackburn during the week. Victory in their final-day fixture at Bournemouth would secure the championship if one dismissed the improbability of a ten-goal victory for Sheffield at Leicester. A draw would leave a loophole for both the Blades and Newcastle to exploit. Leeds might yet have to settle for the unthinkable lottery of the play-offs.

It seemed that everyone in Leeds wanted to get to the game. Fans had been queuing for four hours by the time the ticket office opened at 9.15am. The area heaved with people desperate to get a ticket – the 4,000 tickets were gone in two hours. Thousands were disappointed, but it came as no surprise to the board. Fearing what a Bank Holiday invasion of Bournemouth might mean, the directors did everything they could to discourage ticketless supporters from travelling to the south coast. Four venues in Leeds were set aside for live broadcasts: Roundhay's Astoria Ballroom, the Colosseum on Cookridge Street, Leeds University's Refectory and Armley Sports Centre.

'We want a turning point in this club's history, in two things,' said Jones, whom the club put forward as spokesman. 'One, to say Leeds United fans can behave themselves. The other to say Leeds United are back in the First Division. We just want to have a good day – let's not have any problems. I've got faith in these fans, they've been superb this season.'

For all the good it did, Jones might as well have been baying at the moon. No self-respecting Leeds fan would pass up such an opportunity. Thousands descended on Dorset, determined to be there, even if they couldn't make it into the stadium.

There were complaints about a lack of tickets and fury that 'We've watched Leeds all year, we should be able to go to this game.' The fortunate few who were able to buy tickets knew that they risked the wrath of their ticketless fellows and that there could be trouble with people trying to pinch their tickets.

For months, there had been dire predictions that the staging of the game over the Bank Holiday weekend would cause havoc. Local police had strongly advocated for the fixture to be rescheduled and Leslie Silver had done everything he could to persuade the Football League to reconsider the game's timing.

The authorities would have none of it; the integrity of the competition demanded that all clubs play the last game at the same time and hang the consequences.

It was Leeds' biggest game in years, the most important since the European Cup Final in 1975.

The intervening period had been unkind to Leeds. The club was unlovely and unloved and their followers yearned for payback.

As the unwashed hordes made their various journeys south for the day of reckoning, mob mentality took over.

Wilkinson knew that he needed to keep the camp relaxed and isolated from the feverish atmosphere in West Yorkshire. On the Thursday, he took the squad away to the New Forest.

'For the first time in my reign at Leeds, we took all the players to dine together at an Italian restaurant,' recalls Wilkinson. 'Sat around the table were virtually all the people, players and staff, who had contributed to our promotion campaign. The players were told they could have whatever they wanted to eat and, to a degree, whatever they wanted to drink … I had no fears of anybody abusing the hospitality.'

One man who was missing was Andy Williams.

Wilkinson had decided to relieve the tension with, of all things, a gentle game of baseball.

He enlisted Sutton's assistance in arranging things, knowing that the physio lived in a neighbourhood teeming with Americans. They explained how it worked and provided the equipment.

Sutton recalls, 'The game's going all right, game's going fine, until Vinnie Jones goes in. You knew that it wasn't going to be a simple thing from there. Sure enough, Vinnie, he gets the first pitch, miss. He got the second pitch, miss. Then on the third pitch, he smashes it, and off he's run but, you know, Vinnie, thinking he's at Yankee Stadium or somewhere like that, as he's setting off, he throws the bat behind him and hits Andy Williams and fractured his cheekbone. So that's it. Here we are going to Bournemouth, poor old Andy, who thinks he's going to be maybe on the bench, I'm taking him to hospital to get it confirmed. Sure enough, I've had to leave him at hospital to get an operation while I get back.'

In reality, Williams was nowhere near making the squad – he had been pushed down the pecking order by the emergence of Gary Speed – but there was a bigger issue when Bobby Davison injured his knee in training.

That would mean a call-up for Carl Shutt, but Wilkinson knew how nervous he would be if he knew he was starting. The manager decided to keep Davison's problems under wraps, telling only Strachan and Hennigan and warning them, 'Do not tell anybody about this.'

He told Davison, 'You will start the game. You might come off after a minute, it might be three, it might be five, but you will start the game.'

* * *

Bournemouth had been taken over by Leeds fans, the pubs and clubs packed out and drink flowing freely. There was no holding back, behaviour was getting more difficult by the second, shop windows and cars parked in the town centre used for target practice. There were arrests and running battles, the trouble still going at 3am. Suspicions were voiced later that fans of rival clubs had swollen the ranks coming to Bournemouth in search of a ruck. Alcohol had its victims and many supporters crashed out on the beaches to sleep it off.

Two hours before kick-off the next day, trouble reared its head again. Local pubs had been closed down as a precaution, but alcohol was easy to obtain from supermarkets across the town. Tension was heightened when some holders of genuine tickets were excluded because others with forgeries had got in first. There were more scraps with police outside the stadium, thousands of fans being confronted by officers in riot gear. A BBC Radio car was overturned.

The police advised Wilkinson to leave early for the game, warning that Leeds fans had blocked the road to the stadium.

'The coppers told us we had to leave three-quarters of an hour before I wanted to leave,' recalled Wilkinson. 'I said we would leave at the same time, and he said he could not be held responsible for us being there late because the road was crammed with Leeds fans. I said that was all right, if we have to walk, we have to walk.

'We get there and the crowd is a bit packed, so I tell the players, "Off we get, we'll walk now." The crowd parted and they were cheering us and everything else.

'When we got in the dressing room, what had just happened with the walk had taken everyone's mind off everything.'

Second Division football had only arrived at Dean Court three years before and the humble old stadium still smacked of lower-league football with supporters crammed right up against the edges of the pitch. The crowd was less than 10,000, but Dean Court was bursting at the seams. Nobody could believe that such a tiny enclosure had held 28,799 when Manchester United came to town in 1957.

John Helm parroted the party line that 'Bobby Davison's come through a fitness test okay' as Bournemouth kicked off, intent on taking the game to Leeds in the hope of alleviating their own relegation worries.

United, however, were the more confident starters in their sunshine-yellow away kit. Speed intercepted a ball deep in Leeds territory before turning away from Bournemouth players and storming forward, putting his side on the offensive. He created a promising position before momentum was lost when Jones fouled a defender.

Bournemouth responded immediately with some route-one football, and Kamara's attempted pass back to Day fell to Luther Blissett. The former England striker missed a golden opportunity, but the whistle had gone for an infringement.

When Davison inevitably broke down after six minutes, the call came: 'On you go, Shutty.' With no time to develop nerves, Shutt ran out determined to do his bit in the Leeds cause.

After some decent build-up play by Strachan and Speed, Shutt had a chance to become an instant hero, but keeper Gerry Peyton denied him with his feet and Leeds' wait for a breakthrough went on.

They came again, driven forward by Beglin's diagonal dash, but Peyton was alert once more, denying Kamara from inside the six-yard area.

Bournemouth were awarded a free kick in a dangerous position on the corner of United's area, and Trevor Aylott was given a free header, but the ball was smuggled away by the Leeds defence.

When Jones prepared to put the ball back in from the left, the Bournemouth players expected a long throw. Instead, Jones astutely opted for a short throw, setting Beglin free on the byline. Kamara, seizing the opportunity from outside the area, unleashed a shot, only to see it thwarted by Peyton.

A high, searching pass caught Kevin Bond off guard, allowing Shutt to intercept his pass back to Peyton. The keeper was rapidly out from his line, rescuing Bond from the blunder.

When Strachan was brutally taken out, there were calls for a penalty, but referee Roger Gifford would have none of it and the game reached the interval without a goal.

Sheffield United were 4-2 up at Leicester with Newcastle goalless at Middlesbrough – if results stayed as they were, Leeds would be promoted but the Blades would take the title.

'Keep it going, lads,' urged Wilkinson. 'Keep it nice and tight, they're blowing.'

He pointed at Kamara. 'And you just sit there in the middle, none of your wandering forward.'

Just after the break, Leeds came as close as they had all afternoon when the ball came back off the inside of Peyton's post after Bond misjudged his clearance.

For the most part, Kamara obeyed Wilkinson's orders, but he could not resist the occasional surge forward. It provoked another shouting match with Wilkinson.

The call came from the sidelines with 20 minutes to go, 'Sit in midfield and hold your ground.'

Kamara appeared not to have heard and pushed forward.

'Sit in midfield and hold your ground. If you don't, I am bringing you off.'

Wilkinson's brow furrowed. 'Damned fool.' He gestured to Batty to get warmed up.

'If you make one more run, I am bringing you off!'

An unconcerned Kamara blanked Wilkinson. He said later, 'At that point I made a burst down the right wing from a pass from Chris Fairclough. I looked up and saw Lee Chapman on the far post.'

Kamara raced on to the ball, and his controlled cross was perfectly placed for a towering Chapman to head powerfully home at the back post.

'Marching On Together' blared down from the terraces as Kamara beamed a huge grin at Wilkinson. The celebrations began, but they were premature. Haddock was forced to take Blissett out as he threatened to breach the Leeds defence. The booking was just reward for Haddock's professional foul.

Beglin took a Bournemouth shot full in the face and stayed down, prompting fears that he had swallowed his tongue. His colleagues anxiously rolled him on to his side. As Leeds continued to attack down the other end of the field, the referee rushed over to assess the damage but forgot to whistle. There were moments of genuine concern for Beglin as Wilkinson and the St John's Ambulancemen arrived to assist but there was no lasting harm done.

Batty was brought on for a brief cameo, as recalled by author Daniel Chapman. 'With seconds remaining, he was brought from the subs' bench to the touchline, ready to take Carl Shutt's place. Bobby Davison walked over to Batty and pounded him encouragingly on the back. With a start Batty stopped adjusting his socks and spun round to identify and glare out the perpetrator of this assault. Davison, looking chastened, translated the back-smacks into a thumbs-up and retreated to a safe distance. Batty turned to face the pitch again, grinning. I can't be sure, but I think David Batty punctuated the most agonising seconds of football Leeds United had known in years by punking Bobby Davison.'

Chapman was played clear at the death but fluffed his opportunity to finish in style – Gifford's whistle sounded seconds later to confirm the outcome as thousands of supporters flooded on to the pitch.

Sheffield United had won at Leicester, but Newcastle had taken a battering at Middlesbrough, confirming promotion for Leeds, who took the title on goal difference.

They had done it, ending eight years in the Second Division wilderness. Howard Wilkinson had led Leeds back to the Promised Land and the players partied like there was no tomorrow.

'I was pissed for about four or five days,' said Mel Sterland. 'The trip on the way back was great, there was champagne and booze and it was never-ending, knowing that we were playing the big boys the season after.'

Leslie Silver, Bill Fotherby, Peter Gilman and Peter Ridsdale were drenched in champagne from head to toe as Kamara serenaded them with a chorus of 'Champ-eee-o-nes!'

Away from the glee in the dressing room, the occasion took on a more solemn tone as the full extent of the damage done to the town became clear. The bill was estimated at more than £1m and 120 arrests were made.

Dorset Chief Constable Brian Weight turned his anger on the football authorities for failing to heed his repeated warnings, the first of which dated back to the previous June. He asked the Association of Chief Police Officers to push for a power of 'veto on particular fixtures where, in the police view, there is a high risk of disorder'.

There were questions in the House of Commons, with Home Secretary David Waddington making a statement on 'the scenes of violent disorder', which he described as 'absolutely disgraceful'.

He demanded that 'the football authorities must be made to face up to their responsibilities right now to prevent any repetition of the deplorable scenes of this Bank Holiday weekend ... I have called in both the Football League and the Football Association to discuss the matter. It is high time that the football authorities heeded rather than ignored sensible advice.'

Leeds West MP John Battle, a United fan, responded to Waddington's statement by defending the club, claiming that the board had done what they could.

'The impression I was getting in Parliament,' said Battle, 'was that many of the MPs, particularly on the Conservative side of the house, had this image of Leeds fans as animals and hooligans. I felt more consideration needed to be given to looking into what had actually gone on.'

He rose to ask, 'Is the Home Secretary aware that the club pleaded with its genuine fans, via the local media, television and radio, not to travel to Bournemouth, and that 5,000 of them remained behind in Leeds to watch the event on cinema screens at venues throughout the city? The genuine fans without tickets remained behind. It is others, who have hitched a ride on the club's good name this season, who have brought ignominy on the city of Leeds, which should not bear that shame.'

Waddington countered by saying, 'The fact remains that Leeds United fans have acquired for themselves a very bad reputation and that people are most fearful of what will happen next season unless something serious is done.'

He announced a select committee inquiry into police tactics, numbers and costs as well as the roles of football clubs and government. Anti-hooligan legislation was rushed through, adding to the revolution in train following the Taylor Report into the Hillsborough disaster.

Football League chief executive Arthur Sandford admitted, 'With hindsight I think we made a mistake.' He promised they would heed police advice before future fixture lists were finalised.

Bournemouth petitioned the FA to fine Leeds, while others demanded that their promotion be revoked. The football authorities were sensitive to UEFA's forthcoming decision on whether to readmit English clubs to European competition. Despite their reservations, UEFA were lenient and allowed clubs back in from 1991.

Over the previous few years, United had done much to reduce the incidence of hooliganism and violence at their games, and Bournemouth was seen as an aberration. But it was clear that momentum was building in favour of a heavy sanction.

Leslie Silver apologised profusely and reminded critics of the club's warnings against the game going ahead as planned. 'Encouraging Leeds supporters to travel down the motorway on a Bank Holiday was always a risky move,' said Silver, before adding that the League had insisted. 'What can we do?'

A huge banner declaring, 'Bournemouth We're Sorry' was strung across the front of Leeds Civic Hall. The directors rejected calls to fund repairs, claiming that the violence was beyond their control.

The FA decided that voiding Leeds' promotion was going too far, but they needed to be seen to act. They ordered that if there were any more disturbances at United matches, the club would have to play four games behind closed doors. Any further violations would result in the club's membership of the FA being scrapped – this would effectively mean that Leeds United would be thrown out of professional football.

Things were even grimmer for Bournemouth – they were relegated to the Third Division by the result, the town was devastated, and the club was barred from staging future Bank Holiday fixtures, a sanction lifted only in 2003.

Freshmen

*If resolve and courage matter at all
in determining success, then we start
with fair prospects.*

ENGLAND MANAGER Bobby Robson was preparing his squad for Italia 90 when he heard Football Association chairman Sir Bert Millichip warn that he either had to win the World Cup or go.

Robson took Millichip at his word and negotiated a position at PSV. Robson informed Millichip but agreed to keep the matter under wraps until after England's first training session.

When the press reported that Robson had resigned due to a personal scandal, the FA were bounced into a hasty press conference.

A week later Aston Villa chairman Doug Ellis gave the FA permission to interview Graham Taylor for the job. Howard Wilkinson was also reported to be in the running along with Tottenham's Terry Venables, Howard Kendall of Manchester City and Joe Royle of Oldham.

Taylor and Wilkinson went back a long way.

'Graham and I had known each other since we were 16,' said Wilkinson. 'He and I played for England Grammar Schools. As we left school and started playing and so on, we both also got very interested in coaching around the same age. Graham took his preliminary award, which is now a B licence, a year before me in our early 20s. Then we took our A licence within a year of that. He and I were A licensed coaches probably by the time we were 24.'

The two men worked their way up through the ranks in a similar manner, with Wilkinson managing non-league clubs and Taylor starting with Fourth Division Lincoln City.

Taylor worked as an ITV World Cup pundit while Wilkinson assisted Robson, scouting future opponents. His most memorable contribution was telling the England team that 'they had a bye, basically', against Cameroon in the round of 16. Only two nerveless penalties by Gary Lineker allowed England to scrape past their plucky opponents.

Taylor was widely expected to succeed Robson, but an impasse over compensation between the FA and Villa delayed the announcement until mid-July.

Leslie Silver blocked any designs Wilkinson had on the job, something the United manager fully understood.

Wilkinson was delighted when his old pal was appointed – the two were like peas in a pod, both branded long-ball merchants, who valued effort over flair and had difficult relationships with the media.

Wilkinson's plans for the First Division were laid long before the finals. He admitted: 'I brought in players who aspired to be in the First Division and others who were only meant to get us there.' A number of squad members were to be moved on when Wilkinson could upgrade.

Bill Fotherby stalked Leicester's Gary McAllister, who promised to sign after the finals. Fotherby refused to wait, even throwing in the Mercedes that he was driving as a sweetener, despite it not being his to give. The fee, determined by tribunal, was a cool million, a new United record.

McAllister was expected to join Nottingham Forest, but he rejected the opportunity after a meeting with Brian Clough.

The Forest boss, looking at the player's cowboy boots, asked with heavy sarcasm if he was related to John Wayne. He then trotted out a litany of McAllister's flaws. 'You can't head the ball, you can't tackle and you can't chase back. But you can control the ball and you can pass to one of your team-mates.'

Gee, thanks! McAllister was enraged by the encounter and Clough's rudeness to a waiter clinched the rejection.

After that, Fotherby's fawning attentions made the decision to join Leeds simple.

A £1m fee also landed Arsenal's John Lukic, who left Elland Road for Highbury in 1983. He was a multiple trophy-winner under George Graham, including the championship in 1989. It was his clean sheet in the final game of the season at Anfield that set things up for Michael Thomas' vital goal deep into injury time to seal the deal.

But on transfer deadline day, March 1990, Graham told Lukic, 'I've signed David Seaman and I'm happy for you to go on loan to QPR until the end of the season.'

Ironically, Seaman left Leeds at the age of 18 because United manager Eddie Gray preferred Lukic and wanted a more experienced deputy.

When Leeds came in for him, it was an easy decision for Lukic, dubbed 'the tightest man in football' by Mel Sterland. He was not the showiest of keepers but was regarded as an improvement on Mervyn Day.

The other new signing was centre-back Chris Whyte, for whom West Brom demanded £450,000.

'West Brom went to the States and we played a couple of exhibition games out there in LA,' recalls Whyte. 'I roomed with Don Goodman and one night I was nodding off to sleep and the phone went. Don answered it and he said, "Whytey, it's for you." So I took the phone and the person on the other end said, "Chris, it's Mick Hennigan, I'm Howard Wilkinson's assistant and he's asked me to contact you."

'No word of a lie, I put the phone down as I thought it was a wind-up! No word of a lie, I put the phone down, ha ha! I'd just dropped off to sleep and the phone went again. Don answered it and again said, "Whytey, it's for you." I took the phone and as quick as you like it was, "Chris, it's Mick Hennigan, please don't put the phone down." Basically, he explained how Howard had asked him to contact me and the rest is history. I ended up meeting Howard and Bill Fotherby and I couldn't wait to get going.

'[Fotherby] knew how to sell the club to a player, but of course I knew the size of the club and what it means to Yorkshire and the Leeds fans. I couldn't wait to get going once I knew Howard wanted me and I saw the players that were at the club.

'When I spoke to people, certain people said it doesn't seem like Howard has any charisma and is dour and this, that and the other. But when you work with him, he was very organised and you knew that he wanted to get the best out of you and I really enjoyed playing for him. Yeah, he may not have had the flamboyancy of a Ron Atkinson, for example, but in his own way he'd get the best out of his players.'

The investment in new men was a major show of faith by the board, made easier by the £3m received in season ticket sales.

The strengthening of the squad made perfect sense, but it brought a falling-out with United's cult hero.

There was no way that McAllister would play second fiddle to anyone, so a decision had to be made. Some thought Gary Speed would be the odd one out in midfield.

It never occurred to the super-confident Vinnie Jones that he would be the one to miss out – he reported back sporting a Leeds tattoo and brimming with excitement for the new season.

Wilkinson assured Jones that he wanted him to stay, that he was important to the squad, but the damage had been done. Jones was off.

'That wasn't an easy decision,' admits Wilkinson. 'I didn't really want him to go. He would tell you today that his time at Leeds was his best time in football. He had a huge impact and could have developed further. I honestly think if he had stayed with me, he would have probably gone on to be a football manager by now.'

Despite Jones' feelings about his future, he allowed none of that to show to McAllister, who recalled, 'Vinnie was great. I arrived and was on my own in a hotel room when I got a call. Outside was Vinnie, in a limo, and he took me around the town, showing me the right bars and introducing me to the right people. That was big of him.'

Wilkinson was unequivocal about his line-up. Always a man who valued stability and consistency, every week it was the same. There were two exceptions: left-back and up front, partnering Lee Chapman.

This was the year that the myth of Leeds' left-back curse began.

Jim Beglin was the preferred option, but he injured his knee representing Ireland in a World Cup warm-up game. Glynn Snodin struggled with glandular fever, Mike Whitlow had a blood clot behind his brain and Chris Kamara was ruled out with Achilles problems.

It was Peter Haddock who suffered the most grievous blow. A disgraceful foul by Sunderland's John Kay crippled him and he lost his place to Snodin. The latter lasted a month before giving way to Haddock, who had a good run until he suffered a knee injury in the Rumbelows Cup which would eventually end his career.

Wilkinson was left with no obvious partner for Chapman after a move for Peter Beardsley was rejected – Carl Shutt played the most games, but was a limited presence, never quite sure what to do or having the capability of executing it if he did. Imre Varadi, Bobby Davison and John Pearson had strictly bit parts.

Otherwise, Wilkinson's preferred selection was remarkably consistent: Lukic, Sterland, Fairclough, Whyte, Whatsisname, Strachan, Batty, McAllister, Speed, Thingummybob, Chapman.

Lukic and Whyte brought quality at the back. Alongside them, Sterland and Fairclough relished their First Division returns, one a rampaging demon up and down the right flank, the other a cool head who understood exactly where he needed to be at any given time.

United's best feature was undoubtedly midfield, where McAllister gelled wonderfully with Strachan, Batty and Speed. Wilkinson saw it as a match made in heaven, the best midfield he had ever worked with. The combination was lauded as the finest in the country.

McAllister took time to settle. 'Verbally, he used to abuse players quite a lot,' says Strachan. 'That had to be put right. And it was – it was a simple thing. Once he did that, he got all the respect from the players that he wanted. But to begin with, he couldn't understand why people couldn't read his flick round the corner, pass or one-two. All he could do to be a good pro was to try to teach them to come to the same level as him.'

Sterland had a similar recollection. He acknowledged the talent of the newcomer but admitted to several disagreements with him.

During one match against Southampton, Sterland's decision not to pass the ball to a heavily marked McAllister resulted in a display of petulance from the Scot. Much to the chagrin of Sterland, McAllister threw his hands to the skies in disgust, right under Wilkinson's nose. Sterland's scowl of annoyance was plain for all to see.

As they exited the field, Sterland confronted McAllister. 'Macca, don't f***ing show me up in front of the manager.'

'I'm sorry, I was just frustrated that you didn't give me the ball.'

McAllister struggled to match up to Wilkinson's fitness demands. He had thought himself in good nick but 'on the first few runs under Wilkinson's watchful eye even the goalkeepers were beating me. I was fighting fit all right – fighting for breath and fit for the bucket. I was well off the pace in those runs and the only consolation – minor though it was – was that Whyte was back there alongside me. I thought I had signed for Leeds Harriers or a local athletics team of some sort.

'I had a lot of catching up to do to get to the same level of fitness as the lads who had been through a Wilkinson pre-season before, but at least it let me know quickly – very quickly – what I had to do. It was a bit of a shock to my system. But that also applied to just about everything to do with the club.

'Some people seem to think Howard Wilkinson has an obsession about fitness, almost to the exclusion of all else. But that is simply not true – unless, of course, you call getting his players fit enough to play through an entire season an obsession.'

As he acclimatised, McAllister became what Wilkinson knew he could be, the missing piece in the jigsaw.

And at the business end was Chapman, who returned to the top flight with such gusto that one wondered why his stints at Arsenal and Sunderland had been so disastrous. Chappy plundered goals at will, brave as a lion and a constant out ball for stretched defenders.

Wilkinson's first matchday column was cautiously optimistic. 'We have strained every sinew in the last 20 months at every level in this club in an effort to put Leeds United back where it belongs. Now we're there, we've got to stay there and that will be no mean feat. The financial gamble in which we've involved ourselves is almost too frightening to think about. However, we've kept our nerve so far and at the moment our decisions look like good investments in a sound football future.'

Bill Fotherby struck a confident tone after the opening-day victory at Everton.

'I have sensed the excitement surrounding Leeds United in the city for the past eight years and all that was needed was a little success. Once that was achieved, I knew the whole place would explode.

'We decided the people of Leeds had waited long enough and decided to go for experienced professionals and splashed out for them. Of course, we all know that spending money is not a guarantee of success, but we have the advantage of having someone like Howard Wilkinson at the helm. He is so professional in his approach and a great thinker.'

The words came from the programme for Elland Road's first sniff of First Division football in eight years. It was a huge game, against the detested Manchester United.

This was the moment that Vinnie Jones and Elland Road had yearned for. The crowd roared in anticipation, spitting venom at their reviled visitors. They had gathered under the cold, unyielding lights, their hearts ablaze with the hope of seeing Jones stamp his mark on the opposition midfield. But their hopes were brutally crushed. Jones was not merely overlooked; he was not even listed among the substitutes.

One faithful fan, his face etched with shock, cornered Jones. 'After all you have done for this club, I can't believe you're not even sub.'

Jones, a mix of emotions raging within him, hastily excused himself. He could make no sense of it, and a chilling realisation began to creep in – his time at Leeds might be at an end. He turned away; his face contorted into a scowl so dark it could have curdled milk.

Curiously, there wasn't a full house in a stadium with a reduced capacity for the new season, lush new turf and a new family area in the South Stand.

To counter its suspended death sentence, the club introduced a membership scheme and some members neglected to collect their tickets. There was also a gap at the front of the Lowfields, segregating home supporters from travelling fans.

Alex Ferguson was angered by Leeds' forthright approach to the game, complaining so vigorously that he had to be spoken to by police officers. He was enraged by Whyte's agricultural foul on Mark Hughes and by challenges that got Sterland and Batty booked.

A dour first half produced few chances, other than one limply missed by Mike Phelan for the visitors. Wilkinson ripped into his men at the break, telling them that they could handle 'this lot'. They threw themselves into the contest with a will, launching wave after wave of attacks.

The aimless hoofs downfield were ditched for a passing game, as McAllister dictated the flow. Leeds played their way out of defence with a slick 12-pass move that culminated with a shot from Sterland as he and Strachan targeted an anxious Mal Donaghy.

Batty blotted out Paul Ince to such an extent that he was subbed off. Batty took it as a personal triumph, proof that he could succeed at this level. 'When the United bench signalled for Ince to be substituted, I got a surge of satisfaction. I remember looking up into the stand and motioning at my dad with a gesture that said, "Yes, I've seen him off."'

Leeds had their chances after the break, with Varadi firing across goal after capitalising on a poor Gary Pallister pass back to Les Sealey.

McAllister curled a beautiful pass into the penalty area only for Varadi to misfire. The ball bounced nicely for Chapman, but he betrayed his rustiness, blaming his appalling miss on the pitch.

The game ended level and Leeds added more points with a 3-0 thumping of Norwich.

Driven by his fear of rejection, Jones pushed himself to the limit in training. His muscles screamed in protest, but he achieved his goal. As he readied himself to board the coach for the following game at Luton, he wandered over to Wilkinson. 'Will I need my boots today?'

His question was met with a cool glare, but Jones decided to push things a bit further. He had a brainwave that would quickly become part of Leeds United folklore.

He had been doing some shooting in Leeds and decided to take his kit with him on the coach, planning to spend the weekend down south with his father.

Wilkinson was just settling down for the journey when he felt something cold and metallic against the side of his head. Turning, he found Jones at the other end of a 12-bore shotgun, his finger wrapped around the trigger. His voice was steady, his eyes burning as he asked, 'Now, are you going to bloody play me at Luton?'

The gun was empty, the safety lock in place, but Wilkinson's face blanched as he took in the sight.

He later reflected, 'Anyone who saw that without knowing the back story would think, there he goes again, look, that's him reverting to type. In fact, it's not at all, it's him being personally in a very, very bad place in terms of disappointment and yet managing to turn it into something funny.

'I thought we needed to bring added quality to midfield and by that I don't mean quality as a person, I mean quality as a player. And in bringing Gary McAllister in, I thought that I'd done that.

'I did not appreciate fully what it would do to Vinnie, that not being first choice would kill him. With hindsight, I was wrong on that one. If only he'd have just bounced back and given it a go – to have kept him at the club would have been … I think he'd have been a huge asset.'

Whether Jones' actions on the coach made any difference or not, he was in the side at Luton. He marked his return by committing the game's first foul within 40 seconds but failed to see the match out after being replaced in the second half by Imre Varadi.

'We played well, we played three in midfield, Batts, me and McAllister,' recalled Jones. 'McAllister should have scored a couple of goals. He was one-on-one with the keeper. So, me and Batts were there grinding it and McAllister had the licence to bomb forward. I think he had two or three one-on-ones. If he'd scored them, we'd have won five- or six-nil, it could have all been different. A lot of things Gary McAllister did could have changed my life at Leeds but Gary's a fantastic player, and I knew that. I knew I could do a job alongside him or alongside Batts or the three of us or something.'

Jones went to find his usual shirt but had a nasty shock when Mick Hennigan told him, 'Er, Vin, you're not No 4 today, Batty's got the 4.'

'You're joking, I've worn the 4 shirt all my life, even as a kid. I'm not stopping now.'

'You put the No 8 on and Batty wears the No 4,' responded Wilkinson.

Jones was gutted and being taken off in the second half didn't help his mood, although he thought he was back in the picture.

He trained like a Trojan on the Monday, only to be told by Wilkinson, 'I don't know whether you're interested or not, but I've had Dave Bassett on the phone.'

For once, Jones was speechless. His immediate thought was, 'Right, sod you, I'll go.'

Wilkinson protested, 'Look, I don't want you to go. I want you to stay here but it's up to you. You've been great for this club and I'll support you in whatever you decide.'

It was no good. Jones' mind was made up and even cautionary words from his father could not shift him. 'Sleep on it, sleep on it. Do you realise where Sheffield United are? They're at the bottom of the First Division.'

'It was only after I'd signed that I looked at the league table and realised that what the old man had said was a fact,' recalls Jones. 'Sheffield United had got off to a rotten start. Bassett wanted me in as captain but … in footballing terms I was going backwards.'

It was as if the heart of the club had been torn out.

The rough patch that began with a single-goal defeat on Luton's derided plastic pitch included three defeats in six games. Many critics predicted that Leeds would struggle once the adrenaline rush faded, but they caught fire as Chapman found his scoring boots. It took him a while to get going, but he closed November with goals in six successive games.

Leeds were suddenly a fixture in the top five and launched an exciting assault on the Rumbelows Cup, efficient and emphatic in despatching Leicester, Oldham and QPR.

Some critics remained unimpressed, dismissing it as a flash in the pan. Looking haughtily down their noses, they proclaimed, 'Typical Wilkinson side, long-ball merchants.'

Leeds were undoubtedly direct, but the criticism was unfounded – United had brought vivacious, ebullient football to the First Division and few teams could live with them when they were on form. Their performances through November were outstanding, energetic and unforgiving.

McAllister's vision and passing range transformed Leeds. Strachan had someone of real quality to play with, and the skipper rose to even higher standards.

Sterland's blood and thunder approach up and down the right made him an ideal partner for Strachan, combining cleverly, each capable of creating and scoring goals.

United were undeniably back, and Wilkinson revelled in it. He was voted Barclays Manager of the Month for November.

Leeds' sixth victory in seven games, 2-1 at home to Southampton on 1 December, set them up nicely for their rematch with Manchester United at Old Trafford.

In a contest as competitive and breathless as their first, the Red Devils took the lead with a speculative effort from Neil Webb that was deflected past Lukic.

Leeds equalised when Sterland's 30-yard daisy-cutter free kick flew past Les Sealey into the corner. Didn't Zico love that one!

Leeds won their next four league games, conceding a single goal in the process, the highlight coming on a rain-soaked Boxing Day when they hammered Chelsea for four.

With Leeds preoccupied by knockout football, the New Year brought complications.

First came the FA Cup – a replay was required against Barnsley in the third round, but Leeds hammered the Tykes 4-0 at Elland Road to book a fourth-round clash with Arsenal.

Leeds advanced to the last four of the Rumbelows Cup after another four-goal showing against Aston Villa. They would face Manchester United over two legs.

The unlamented Full Members' Cup also became a factor. This obscure competition, branded for the season as the Zenith Data Systems Cup, was introduced to fill the void in the fixture schedule with English clubs banned from Europe. There was little substance to the reasoning – the clubs that would have been in Europe turned up their noses at the FMC.

The competition was open only to full members of the Football League, the clubs in the top two divisions. Four of the self-styled 'Big Five' – Arsenal, Liverpool, Manchester United and Tottenham – refused to compete, while the fifth, Everton, took part three times and were twice beaten finalists.

Leeds were regular contestants, and in 1991 they made it to the Northern final against Everton – the average attendance at their five games barely topped 11,000 with the third round against Derby drawing only 6,334.

It was those five games that did for Leeds, coming on top of their run in the Rumbelows Cup and the 420 minutes over four games it took Arsenal to put Leeds out of the FA Cup. Wilkinson's team had to deal with the kind of fixture congestion that plagued Don Revie in the 1970s.

After defeating Luton in the First Division on 19 January, they played a single league game in the next 41 days, so ravenous were the cup competitions. The game in question came on 2 February at Tottenham.

Leeds desperately needed points from the game after losing twice on the road post-Christmas, at Liverpool and Norwich. The goalless draw at White Hart Lane left Leeds marooned in fourth.

Leeds went into the Spurs game without Batty (suspended), Shutt and Varadi and soon lost another front man.

Chapman and Steve Sedgeley tangled on the touchline after barely two minutes. Sedgeley's challenge appeared innocuous, but Chapman, bending to head the ball, took the Spurs man's boot square in the face. His momentum took him tumbling face-first into the cinder track surrounding the pitch. Unable to use his arms to cushion the fall, he was out cold.

Chapman's face was ripped to shreds, his nose broken in two places and a tooth cracked after ripping open his top lip. His mouth was full of gravel and he had not a clue where he was.

Mervyn Day and Alan Sutton accompanied him to hospital for urgent treatment. He was operated on the next day, a plastic surgeon cleaning his wounds before restitching them to minimise scarring. His nose was devoid of skin, but the surgeon solved that one by cutting an inverted V shape between Chapman's eyebrows and pulling down the skin on his forehead to cover the missing area.

Shortly after the operation, Chapman was shown his face in a mirror. 'It was hard to recognise my bloodied and swollen features. I looked so horrific that my two-year-old son, Joseph, was afraid to come near me!'

Yet Chapman had thoughts only for the Rumbelows Cup semi-final against Manchester United, due to be played a week later. There had been no neurological damage, but the wounds were still some way from being strong enough to take the punishment of a competitive match.

Chapman was taken to see boxing trainer Brendan Ingle, who had worked for many years with middleweight champion Herol 'Bomber' Graham.

Ingle was one of the best cuts men in the business. He advised Chapman to bathe his injuries with surgical spirit to harden the skin. For matches, he was told to paint on plastic skin, a resin-like fluid that sets hard when applied, to form a second skin.

Eight days after the Tottenham game, Leeds found themselves facing off against Manchester United at Old Trafford. Against all expectations, Chapman, his face held together by 30 stitches and coated with plastic skin, took the field with the rest of the team. He resembled something out of a horror film. Bryan Robson, himself one of the bravest and hardest men in football, could only stare in disbelief at Chapman and shake his head. 'He must be mad,' he whispered to a colleague.

'It was the kind of match that every professional dreams of playing in, and I could not bear the thought of missing out,' admitted Chapman. 'I decided, after that game, never to make the same error again.'

Leeds lost 2-1 and went down by a single goal in the Elland Road return.

The end of March brought the peak of the congestion – Leeds lost 2-0 at Arsenal on Sunday, 17 March, drew 3-3 with Everton in the first leg of the FMC Area final on Tuesday, lost 3-1 after extra time in the second leg on the Thursday and then by 3-1 at home to Crystal Palace in the First Division on Saturday.

Eight players – Lukic, Sterland, Fairclough, Whyte, Whitlow, Strachan, Batty and Chapman – played every minute of the four games. McAllister, Speed and Shutt featured in all four but were spared some minutes by substitutions. Such exertions sapped mind and body, but the men in white seemed unfazed, sustained by Wilko's conditioning.

Leeds hung on resolutely with three straight victories, including a five-goal thrashing of Sunderland. They trailed runaway leaders and eventual champions Arsenal by 16 points but maintained clear blue water between themselves and the two Manchester clubs, in close order behind them.

There was only one UEFA Cup place available, and Liverpool took that as a consolation prize after being relentlessly hauled in by the Gunners.

Leeds had the opportunity to close the nine-point gap to Liverpool on 13 April when the Reds were the visitors to Elland Road. Following Kenny Dalglish's surprise resignation in February, Ronnie Moran was installed as caretaker manager.

Leeds got off to a good start, with a Shutt effort saved by goalkeeper Mike Hooper and Sterland nodding wide, but then the Reds took control. John Barnes pulled the strings; he was involved in everything as his side built a 4-0 lead by the break, sliding home the fourth himself on the half-hour mark. The Leeds defence looked flat-footed and naïve, playing far too high a line and allowing Liverpool to exploit acres of space in behind.

At the break, the game looked done and dusted, but Wilkinson found the words to make a difference. The second half featured classic waves of blood and thunder as Leeds poured forward in search of the unlikeliest of recoveries.

They forced Liverpool on to the defensive and got the goal their momentum merited after 68 minutes.

On the right, Strachan and Sterland combined nicely to set up McAllister for a shot that Hooper could only parry. A lurking Chapman pounced, untidily clipping home off the underside of the crossbar.

It looked a mere consolation, and there was no racing after the ball to restart. Something much greater appeared to be on nine minutes later. Chapman had already been denied a second goal after being adjudged to have fouled Hooper as he rose above him to head home Batty's high ball. Shutt found time to turn and slip the ball home when Speed's throw caused panic in the Reds' defence – 4-2.

At that point, Liverpool woke up to the danger, and Barnes scored after being set up by a Rush back-heel.

That should have been that, but not a bit of it. Leeds pulled another goal back after 81 minutes, Chapman beating his man to head home from Batty's chipped pass.

Leeds, scenting blood, pushed on.

Two minutes more and Chapman made it 5-4, rising to nod home imperiously at the back post after Strachan weaved his way to the byline.

The fans were ecstatic, but they had seen all they were going to see – the Whites could not find a fifth. Their supporters hardly cared, they had seen Leeds at their rip-roaring best and went home hoarse and happy.

'The manner of our fightback, the quality of our fightback, those things gave great promise for the future,' Wilkinson told the media, 'but as I said last week, as I said yesterday, as I said again this morning, today showed what we are good at, and it showed what we've still to get good at.'

Leeds won three of the next four games to cement fourth place. They were in with a shout of beating Crystal Palace to third as they went into the final game. That would need Leeds to win at FA Cup finalists Nottingham Forest and Palace failing to beat Manchester United at Selhurst Park.

Forest boss Brian Clough could have been excused for resting players a week before the final but went for it with a full-strength selection. Forest raced to a two-goal lead courtesy of goals from Garry Parker and Nigel Clough. Leeds briefly rallied when Strachan released Chapman to score his 30th of the season.

Forest extended their lead in the second half, but Leeds came again. Chapman made it 3-2 with his 200th career goal before Carl Shutt equalised after some shoddy Forest defending.

The game took a final twist with four minutes remaining. Clough Junior was on hand to stab a late winner to keep the final three points of the season in the East Midlands.

Wilko: 'Overall, you've got to be satisfied with what we've got and what we've achieved. Massive disappointments relative to the cups, to go with Arsenal all those minutes and hours, to lose out in the Zenith semi-finals, to lose out in the Rumbelows semi-finals. At the time, you think you'll never get over it, but you do. And better to lose in the semi than lose in the first round.

'The players can take great, great credit in their first season in the First Division. They might have a word with themselves and smack themselves on the back of the wrists for maybe not doing slightly better, but overall they've done all that could be asked of them.'

Chapman finished as the top scorer in the country with 31 goals, his 21 in the league bettered only by the 22 notched by Alan Smith of champions Arsenal.

Batty rounded off a remarkable personal season by making his England debut against Argentina at Wembley in May. He was the first Leeds player to make it into the international side since Trevor Cherry in 1980. Within a month, he had won a further three caps under Graham Taylor.

Strachan was the pick of the bunch, the catalyst for everything. His remarkable consistency saw him add the Footballer of the Year trophy to the Scottish equivalent he lifted in 1980.

'I am so happy to pick this award up,' he said. 'I accept it as an award for the team. It gives me hope that the efforts we have all made to give Leeds United a better image are working.'

That Difficult Second Season

A number of things need to be done to keep a club progressing after one decent year in the top division. There is momentum after, if you like, having gone on to bigger and better things.

HOWARD WILKINSON'S reflections on Leeds' return to the First Division were that he needed a decent forward to partner Lee Chapman and had to sort out his problem left-back position. In both areas, the Whites had been found wanting.

Five different men had worn the No 3 shirt: Glynn Snodin's 19 appearances were the most, though the man whose main claim to fame was being Ian Snodin's younger brother never fully convinced Wilkinson. Long-term injuries forced Jim Beglin and Peter Haddock to retire, and a specialist replacement was needed.

Imre Varadi, Carl Shutt, John Pearson and Bobby Davison had all been given a chance up front, but none had impressed. Shutt's seven goals in his last ten appearances marked him out as the best option, but Wilkinson needed more than a nearly man if Leeds were to progress.

Bill Fotherby did Wilkinson's bidding well in splashing out almost £3m to bring in Chelsea's Australian-born England international Tony Dorigo and Southampton forward Rodney

Wallace. For the next five years, the pair would be stalwarts of the side.

Wilkinson chose the little-known Wallace, a busy player, ahead of other rumoured targets. He and his twin brother, Ray, were at Southampton with older brother Danny, who left for Manchester United in 1989. While Danny was the best-known of the three, Rod was no slouch and had been a regular with the England Under-21s.

Ray was included in the deal, though he would never be more than a bit-part player. Fotherby revealed as much when he said, 'I think Rod's got an exciting future ahead of him because he's only 21. As for Ray, I don't know how old he is, so I really couldn't say ...'

Dorigo was one of the best left-backs in the country. He had six England appearances to his name and was a non-playing member of the Italia 90 squad. He had made over 250 league appearances for Chelsea and Aston Villa.

Perpetual motion up and down the flank, Dorigo had outstanding pace and a magical left foot. With a defensive game that could not be faulted, he was the ideal left-back. Certainly, he was all that Wilkinson could wish for.

Dorigo's move came only after he had submitted and withdrawn a transfer request at Stamford Bridge after falling out with manager Bobby Campbell over a contract dispute.

He met Chelsea chairman Ken Bates to try and reach a resolution. The response was blunt.

'I remember going to see Mr Bates because I actually wrote a transfer request,' recalls Dorigo. 'I sent it and he called for me and said: "Come in and let's discuss it."

'I'm thinking uh, okay, let's get in there and say how I feel. So, I went in there. He was very polite, he sat me down and I explained why I wanted to move. He said, "Okay, Tony, let me just get your contract out of the filing cabinet and let me turn it over."

'Now on the back of football players' contracts is the amount of years you have left. On the front is a lot of details, but on the back is the years that you have left. And he said, "Tony, it does seem like you have two years left. There's the f***ing door."'

Dorigo eventually got his move via a tribunal, but not before an odd meeting with Wilkinson, who used an unusual tactic to convince him he should move to Leeds.

'He started talking about golf holes,' says Dorigo. 'What I liked was he'd done a bit of research into me and knew that I liked to play golf. We then verbally started playing golf. He said: "Right, we're on the first tee." In reality, we're in a hotel talking in Leeds. This is our first meeting and he's trying to convince me to join Leeds United. And we're now going through golf holes. And we verbally played two holes.

'"You tee off and, listen, there's a lake 200 yards away," he tells me. "You may be able to hit it 300 yards but let's ramp it down and take a three wood and hit it down, so you don't go in the water. So, when you get there …"

'And I'm thinking, "My god, this guy's nuts, what's going on? I'll sign, get me out of here!"

'He was trying to say we use the right club for the right opportunity, in that, whatever tools you've got, use them in the best way. I thought if you'd just said that you'd have saved half an hour!'

Dorigo also fell victim to Wilkinson's wit.

'It's buried deep, but he has a dry sense of humour,' recalls Dorigo. 'When I signed, I went away with England on tour. I came back needing a double hernia operation. It was going to take six weeks to recover.

'Howard pulled me into his office. "Wow, I think I've signed the softest Aussie ever." I'm thinking, "Is he serious?" He went on, "I had another left-back at Sheffield Wednesday,

Nigel Worthington. He had the same operation as you. Doctor said six weeks, he was back in five.'"

Dorigo snapped, 'Nigel Worthington? F*** me. If he was back in five, I'll be back in four.' He was duly fit in time for pre-season.

During United's pre-season friendly in Cork, Dorigo found himself christened 'Tommy'.

The Irish commentator, announcing that Dorigo would be coming on to replace Mike Whitlow, asked the crowd to 'Please welcome Leeds' record signing, Tommy Dorigo.'

The Aussie thought nothing more of it, but Wilkinson turned to him in the dressing room. 'You played a great game, well done, Tommy.' His team-mates burst out laughing and Dorigo was forever known as Tommy.

Wilkinson also bolstered his midfield, paying £900,000 for Forest's England international, Steve Hodge.

Wilkinson first met Hodge while managing the England Under-21 side in 1983 and approached him about a move to Sheffield Wednesday in 1985.

The move to Leeds seemed to make perfect sense, giving Wilkinson the fifth midfielder he had always wanted – it meant he could switch things round if Plan A wasn't working.

The theory was sound, but things never worked out. Wilkinson and Hodge were at odds for the majority of the midfielder's time at Elland Road.

The problem lay in Hodge's susceptibility to injuries. He struggled to finish games, frequently being afflicted by cramp. Despite undergoing an operation on his calves to alleviate the problem, there was no improvement. Wilkinson seethed with frustration, he could not help himself; whatever investigation his medical team carried out, they just could not come up with a solution. Wilkinson, concerned he had wasted £1m, deemed Hodge a malingerer. There was no way back for him after that, regardless of his efforts.

That was no excuse for Wilkinson's constant digs in front of the other players. 'Well done, Hodgey, you nearly made it through a pre-season there … As I came in to training this morning, I saw an illusion. I actually saw Steve Hodge training … You're a museum piece, living in the past with your medals and your England caps. Why don't you just put in a transfer request now and we can get it out in public?'

Hodge had to grit his teeth at the jibes, but never once bit back. It was a tribute to his professionalism – this was hardly the way to motivate a former England international.

It's somewhat disconcerting, then, to read Wilkinson's autobiography. 'When you itemise the characteristics required in a top-quality midfielder, you realise Steve possesses the lot. The late Don Revie always maintained that the ideal midfield man should be able to pass, tackle and run and score goals. Many players have earned themselves lofty reputations by doing just two of those things. Hodgey can do the lot.'

There was no irritability in the summer of 1991 when Wilkinson took his squad to Tokyo for a pre-season friendly against Botafogo of Brazil. Leeds lost to a dubious first-half penalty. Wilkinson commented, 'It was a reasonable performance, and I think a draw would have been a fairer result. Our two central defenders and David Batty all played very well. We carried the game to them and though they looked a very good side we certainly matched them.'

Around ten one evening, a group of supporters, including the legendary Gary Edwards, wandered into the Leeds players' Tokyo hotel. They came across John McClelland and asked him where everyone was. He revealed that Wilkinson had them out jogging and that he'd been let off due to a minor injury.

'Everyone has been told to stay on English time, so for us it's only one o'clock in the afternoon.'

Wilkinson had given the bizarre direction, which meant getting up at four in the afternoon, having breakfast, going training at seven and then being awake for the rest of the night.

Leeds had better luck four days later, beating the same side 2-1 at Elland Road.

Wilkinson declared his target was simply to amass more points than the previous season. Leslie Silver recalled later, 'Our aim was to try and launch a serious bid for the championship, not this season, but next. I felt that winning a place in the UEFA Cup was an attainable target and one which we might achieve if all was to go well out on the field of play. It might be difficult to believe but Howard Wilkinson and myself never once discussed the possibility of us winning the title during the course of the season.'

Making a good start was critical, but the fixture list was not kind. Five of the first seven scheduled games were against sides from the previous season's top eight.

The season was due to start at Crystal Palace but the south Londoners threw United's plans into disarray by announcing just days before the game that it could not go ahead. Building work to comply with regulations had not been completed and the fixture had to be rescheduled.

United hastily arranged a friendly against Aldershot at Elland Road. It gave Wilkinson the chance to try out his new-look team and Leeds won at a canter, 3-1.

Gary McAllister lashed home the opener from 30 yards and Rod Wallace made it 2-0 early in the second half. Lee Chapman netted the third seven minutes from time to kill off a plucky Aldershot side who had pulled one back nine minutes earlier.

Hodge made his first appearance as a second-half sub for Gary Speed with Wilkinson commenting, 'I just said to Gary Speed, "Well done, you deserve a rest after playing in all the pre-season games."'

McClelland deputised for Mel Sterland, who was recovering fitness after a hernia operation. He retained his place as Wilkinson named the same starting line-up for Leeds' first game, in midweek at home to Nottingham Forest.

Leeds' shirts were adorned with new sponsorship, courtesy of the *Yorkshire Evening Post*, and there was also a new look to Elland Road, with the opening of the South East Corner Stand. It filled the space between the South and Lowfields Stands and provided a full corner stand for away supporters.

Silver and the board were persuaded to approve the £1m construction after United's promotion and their successful return to the First Division. It took 12 weeks to complete and provided an additional 1,395 seats.

Dorigo enhanced the threat from the left, but McClelland showed that he was no Sterland – he was solid enough in defence but lacked Sterland's ambition. He did, however, bring a different option with his long throws into the Forest area. Batty played remarkably deep, frequently found between his centre-backs, mopping up loose balls and allowing his team-mates to push on.

Further forward, Wallace brought energy and purpose, buzzing around Chapman.

McAllister's 13th-minute goal, driven low under goalkeeper Mark Crossley, gave Leeds the victory. They had numerous chances to increase their tally, but Speed missed several of them. Forest pressed hard in the second half with their neat pass-and-move football and Leeds had to thank John Lukic for several key saves.

Brian Clough admitted that Leeds were the better side and deserved to win. Wilkinson for his part was relieved to get the points, saying, 'Had we not been at our fighting best we might well have lost it. This was a good one to get out of the way.'

Wilkinson was content with the performance, but wouldn't say as much to the players, desperate for them to push on to higher things. Even man of the match Dorigo got a rollocking at half-time for drifting too far infield to cover for his centre-back when he slipped. 'Keep out wide, Tommy, that's where I need you.'

Leeds almost came a cropper at home to Sheffield Wednesday. They fell behind to a David Hirst goal in the second half and another Hirst effort came out off the inside of Lukic's post. Hodge came on as sub and equalised with three minutes remaining.

Any fears that Leeds would be victims of second-season syndrome were allayed in the following game, a 4-0 triumph at Southampton. Speed earned the plaudits for his two-goal display and Gordon Strachan completed the scoring with two penalties. The result made it clear exactly how good Leeds were.

They were helped by the dismissal of centre-back Neil Ruddock after he conceded the first penalty for flattening former team-mate Wallace, but the truth was that Leeds were a class above their physical opponents.

Chris Fairclough limped out of the game early, the victim of some brutal Southampton tackling. His injury kept him out of action until October.

This allowed Sterland to return with McClelland reverting to his preferred role in the centre of defence. When Sterland replaced Fairclough at Southampton, he was outstanding, laying on Speed's first goal and making Leeds more dangerous down the right.

Now came the big one – away to Manchester United at a sun-soaked Old Trafford.

Leeds travelled without fear and took the lead after seven minutes when Peter Schmeichel misread Speed's centre. An unmarked Chapman nodded home at the back post. It was Manchester's first concession of the season.

While 17-year-old wonder kid Ryan Giggs caused Leeds some disquiet, it looked like they would hold on for three points. However, with five minutes left, Red Devils captain Bryan Robson equalised from six yards. It was a real kick in the guts, but Wilkinson went away satisfied with a point from one of the season's most challenging fixtures.

He commented, 'You could see the equaliser coming and you felt there was little you could do about it. People tend to remember the last quarter of an hour of a game, which is when they started really turning the screw on us, but for the first 45 minutes, we looked like we were the home team. It was a typical Manchester United home surge at the end and an emotional last 25 minutes.'

McAllister: 'Very few teams would leave Old Trafford complaining about only having secured a draw, but we felt slightly annoyed with ourselves simply because we were within sight of the final whistle when United finally managed to get their goal.'

Leeds' fighting spirit was evident when defending champions Arsenal came to Elland Road. The Gunners took a two-goal lead, but Leeds forced a draw.

Arsenal might have played the better football, but Leeds' resilience was astonishing – they might even have snatched victory at the death but missed two chances.

Leeds had held their own against some of the best sides in the country and a 3-0 victory over Manchester City demonstrated that they meant business. It also produced a landmark moment.

Everyone knew that Batty didn't score goals. His only previous goal had come four years earlier, against the self-same City. It didn't stop the Elland Road crowd booming, 'Shoot' every time Batty came within 20 yards of the opposition goal.

Tony Dorigo: 'The first goal that I scored for Leeds was at Elland Road against Manchester City. The ball came out from a corner, it bounced, and I've half-volleyed it, pinged it, right into the top corner. It was a very good goal and I was delighted. A few minutes later Batty scores. Oh … my … God. It was like an earthquake, the noise. It was a sh*tty tap-in, doesn't matter, mine was forgotten. You felt the warmth for David Batty. Fantastic.'

Leeds moved up to second with a win at Chelsea, their highest position in the league since January 1976.

On 21 September Leeds faced another major test, against Liverpool at Elland Road. The Merseysiders were Leeds' bogey side – one had to go back to October 1973 for United's previous victory.

But this Leeds team was very different from previous seasons. Wilkinson had found a blend which could mix it with the country's best.

Hodge, given his first start in a five-man midfield, scored the only goal after 25 minutes. It came from a scrappy corner, smashed into the roof of the net after the ball ran loose.

Leeds had already had plenty of chances and Hodge was prominent, desperate to show Wilkinson what he was capable of. Liverpool struggled to contain Chapman, while Strachan, playing his 100th league game for Leeds, was only denied by a deflection after wriggling his way into the area.

Leeds were good value for a win that took them five points clear of Graeme Souness's team and consolidated their position in second, four points behind leaders Manchester United.

Gary McAllister: 'That victory was vital for us in more ways than one because it meant that people really did have to start taking us seriously. It made people all over the country sit up and take notice.'

Wilkinson was determined to keep the pressure off his men and did everything he could to keep the players' feet on the ground, as recalled by McAllister. 'He never once sat down and talked about us possibly becoming the champions.

That just isn't his style at all. He just kept telling us to carry on the good work and to concentrate on what we had discussed and what we had gone through out on the training ground. His approach to things … certainly helped a great deal.'

In theory, the Liverpool game marked the end of a difficult start, with games to come against some of the division's weaker sides. It didn't look that way, though, when United could only take a goalless draw from Fourth Division Scunthorpe in the Rumbelows Cup. The hamstring injury suffered by Strachan sidelined him for four games.

Imre Varadi had been nowhere near the first team for months and even when Wilkinson added him to the squad that travelled to Norwich, he was convinced that he would not even make the bench. So, on the eve of the game, he went out with his mates, a bunch of car dealers from Manchester. He got riotously drunk and was out until five the next morning.

Varadi boarded the coach for Norwich feeling decidedly the worse for wear. He got a rude awakening when Wilkinson turned to him and said, 'Gordon's out, Imre. You okay to play midfield?'

The colour drained from Varadi's face, but he couldn't let on. 'Yeah, sure, boss.'

He had never sobered up so quickly in his life and spent the first half running around like a headless chicken before being replaced by Shutt.

The game reached the break without a goal, but Leeds had good grounds for a penalty after 58 minutes. The ball struck Ian Butterworth's hand before he hoofed clear for Robert Fleck to chase into an empty Leeds half.

Batty, captain for the day in Strachan's absence, chased down Fleck. He took him out as he approached the Leeds box, but the tackle was adjudged fair. The danger seemed to have gone, but Leeds were victims of complacency when Dale Gordon intercepted a poor pass from Speed. He combined with Ruel Fox to find space in the box and hammer past Lukic.

Within three minutes, Leeds equalised when Dorigo fired a 20-yard free kick through the Norwich wall and into the top corner.

Ten minutes later, a towering header by Whyte allowed Speed to beat the offside trap, control the ball and fire low past Bryan Gunn from the edge of the area.

That should have been enough for Leeds to capture the points, but three minutes later, slack defence allowed Gordon to score his second.

Wilkinson must have seen something from Varadi because he retained him for the rescheduled match at Crystal Palace.

United's unbeaten start was ended when Mark Bright scored the only goal after the controversial award of a free kick to Palace deep into injury time.

Hodge was so incensed by the decision that he called the referee a cheat. The FA fined him for the offence.

Leeds rediscovered their form in a 4-3 victory against Sheffield United with Hodge and Sterland each scoring twice.

They got off to a flier, with Hodge opening the scoring after five minutes following a long throw by Sterland. The latter scored from a free kick to double the lead, and Leeds were cruising.

Before the game reached the break, Leeds had the chance to extend their lead when Ian Bryson fouled Tony Dorigo to concede a penalty. Suddenly, there was another case of handbags between Sterland and McAllister; Sterland, who was the regular penalty-taker, and McAllister, who had assumed the role when Sterland was out injured, had a heated argument over who should take the spot kick.

The language was florid as they bickered like two schoolchildren. Wilkinson looked on wide-eyed as Sterland, refusing to step down, especially against Sheffield United, snatched the ball from McAllister. The pressure on him was even more intense knowing that failure would earn him the bollocking of a lifetime off his manager.

Sterland didn't let it show, hammering the ball into the net. That prompted more abuse from the Blades fans. Sterland took their jibes about his weight in his stride, taunting them by rubbing his stomach as he returned to his own half.

Leeds led comfortably by 3-0 at the interval. Hodge, scoring his second goal of the game early in the second half, seemed to have killed the game at 4-0. Dave Bassett's men had other ideas. Jamie Hoyland pulled one goal back, then Tony Agana made it 4-2. Carl Bradshaw capitalised on a poor clearance by John Lukic in the 83rd minute, adding a third goal for his team.

Leeds survived an edgy final seven minutes, but it was a close call and you could see the nerves etched on Wilkinson's face.

Leeds followed up with a 3-0 trouncing of Scunthorpe in the Rumbelows Cup and then a 4-2 victory at Notts County.

The Full Members' Cup defeat at home to Forest was unimportant in the context of United's season, and Wilkinson was far more concerned with the league match at home to Oldham.

Brian Kilcline put the ball past his own keeper to decide an untidy game. The big defender had earlier headed against Lukic's crossbar as the visitors threatened to spoil Leeds' day. With Manchester United losing their unbeaten record at Sheffield Wednesday, Leeds topped the First Division for the first time since 1974.

They advanced in the Rumbelows Cup, defeating Tranmere 3-1, but then suffered a goalless draw at Wimbledon. As the season approached the international break, the dropped points allowed Manchester United to regain the leadership with victory at home to Sheffield United. They had 31 points, one more than Leeds despite playing a game fewer. It looked like a three-horse race between Leeds and the two Manchester clubs with City on 28 points. Fourth-placed Sheffield Wednesday were on 25 points with Arsenal, Aston Villa and Palace a point further back.

This was beyond the expectations of Silver and Wilkinson, though injury problems were mounting and a paper-thin squad suggested that Leeds might struggle in the run up to Christmas.

Batty was the latest casualty, missing the Tranmere and Wimbledon games with a foot infection which kept him in hospital overnight. Strangely, Wilkinson had added to his problems by selling Chris Kamara to Luton and sending Glynn Snodin, Dylan Kerr and Bobby Davison out on loan.

There was speculation about a move for a new striker, with Dean Saunders, Brian Deane and Ally McCoist all linked.

None of the gossip had any substance. Wilkinson stubbornly declared himself satisfied with the squad at his disposal, as if determined to prove the media wrong.

Only time would tell whether his faith was justified.

TV Personalities

*I know from meeting the ITV and
BBC executives that they were invariably
delighted by the entertainment level
and exciting crowd atmosphere generated
at our games.*

BY NOVEMBER 1991, Leeds United had emerged as Manchester United's only rival for the league title.

Many expected it would be a cakewalk for the Red Devils in the spring and a serene march to a first title since 1967. They had already been anointed as champions by some. Howard Wilkinson was not one of them.

He knew that three points from the home game against relegation-threatened Queens Park Rangers were critical to Leeds' push. As he accepted the Manager of the Month award, Wilkinson was relieved to be able to name a full-strength team.

Leeds dominated the first half but couldn't beat keeper Jan Stejskal. Nerves began to grip as the game approached the hour mark.

Leeds were awarded a free kick which was closer to the halfway line than the Rangers goal. Few could believe it when Mel Sterland shaped up for a shot at goal. What's he playing at? His speculative effort wasn't the most powerful, but a deflection took it past Stejskal, giving Sterland his 50th league goal.

Three minutes later, Rod Wallace settled the outcome by flicking home his first goal for Leeds from close range after Rangers failed to deal with a Strachan corner.

The evening wasn't an unqualified success – Gary Speed was carried off with a damaged ankle, much to Wilkinson's consternation.

Manchester United were held to a goalless draw by local rivals City, allowing Leeds to reclaim leadership of the division.

While popular opinion remained with Manchester, Leeds looked resilient. The home fans had sporadically booed them for wasting time in the second half with a succession of back-passes to John Lukic. Wilkinson stoutly defended the tactics – the lesson of conceding three second-half goals to Sheffield United in October would not soon be forgotten.

The following weekend brought a trip to Aston Villa. With ITV wanting to broadcast it live, the game was switched to Sunday afternoon. That allowed Manchester United to regain top spot on Saturday with victory at home to West Ham.

Villa came into the game on the back of five consecutive wins, and another victory would take them third. They were heavily backed to get something out of the game.

Wilkinson had other ideas. Forced to reshuffle in the absence of Speed, he rejected the 'obvious' solution of recalling Steve Hodge and instead assigned Chris Fairclough to man-mark Villa danger man Tony Daley. Wilkinson famously once said of the Villa wide man, 'Once Tony Daley opens his legs, you've got a problem,' and he was determined to eliminate his threat. John McClelland partnered Chris Whyte at centre-back.

The change proved a masterstroke, allowing Sterland and Tony Dorigo free rein. They gave massive performances, posing a threat every time they pushed forward down the flanks where the pitch was truest.

Despite the poor state of the playing surface, Leeds settled quickly, with David Batty, Gordon Strachan and Gary McAllister dominating and Lee Chapman a willing target up front.

With Daley's threat nullified, Villa struggled to give their fans anything to cheer. They were frequently caught in Leeds' defensive net and couldn't get near Lukic's goal.

As the home side ran out of ideas, Leeds upped their game, with Wallace having a decent chance and then Sterland firing in a long shot. Keeper Les Sealey then reacted smartly to deny Chapman from a corner.

Dorigo was getting more involved, but Leeds' momentum was frustrated by Wallace persistently allowing himself to be caught offside. They raised their game as half-time approached and were rewarded with a well-deserved goal.

Villa expected Sterland to throw the ball long and were caught out when he exchanged it short with Strachan before chipping a cross to the near post. Despite Sealey's fingertip save, Chapman's towering header appeared to be sneaking in at the back post but Wallace slid in to make sure.

Batty nearly made it two at the death but his shot from the edge of the area drifted wide.

Batty and Strachan's low centres of gravity gave them an advantage over some of their taller fellows, and Leeds were making good use of the ball. They knew it would be criminal to let Villa back in before the break, so they used up time with careful passes back to Lukic.

'Quite pleased,' commented Wilkinson at half-time, reserving his main comment for the poor state of the pitch.

Half-time media chatter was all about the likelihood of Leeds closing the game out with blanket defence, but such predictions were quickly given the lie. Within a minute, Sterland plunged in to head home from a Strachan corner.

Leeds made it three from another corner after ten minutes. McAllister and Strachan combined well, with the latter finding the byline before poking the ball across the face of goal for an unmarked Chapman to flick home in front of the Leeds fans.

Leeds had their tails up now, calm and assured and giving Villa no room. It was the epitome of professionalism.

Villa manager Ron Atkinson brought on Gordon Cowans for Mark Blake. There was an almost instant reward – Lukic parried Dalian Atkinson's shot, but the ball ballooned up for Dwight Yorke to touch home.

The goal should have sparked a fierce Villa surge, and certainly the crowd was up for it. But Leeds looked a class apart, solid in defence and assured in midfield, always ready to hit Villa on the break.

Man of the match Dorigo fired in a long-range effort that tested Sealey, and Strachan slipped the ball narrowly wide with the keeper beaten as Leeds showed they had something to spare. The only surprise when Leeds registered their fourth goal was that it took until the final minute. Strachan brought the ball out of defence, fed the overlapping Sterland and the perfect cross came in for Chapman to bury with his head.

Wilkinson described it as one of the best performances of his career, adding, 'We had to work hard initially because Villa were on full song and obviously very confident. We had to deal with that first and we did that very well. We gradually made room, time and space to start to play in difficult conditions, because it is not a good pitch.'

Asked about the chances of the title, he added, 'We've been there now two weeks, which should be an encouragement, but every game will be as hard.'

Years later he said, 'That was a fantastic game for the players because it brought everything that we were trying to do together. It all happened in one game. You do get games where it all comes together and that was one of them.

'It must be the same in musical theatre or whatever, wherever you've got dynamic flow and movement, etc. To actually practise, rehearse and then on the night pull off the best performance which has got everything in it that you've practised but you'd only been able to recreate a bit there and a bit there, to bring it all together, it's extra satisfying.'

Certainly, the television audience lapped it up, seeing Leeds at their best: difficult to beat, free-flowing and dangerous going forward.

Prior to the broadcast, most people believed the popular clichés about Wilkinson's football: robots, willing triers, long-ball merchants, dour, defensive football, kick and rush, functional. Seeing them live put an end to that once and for all. Some of Leeds' football was stunning – the elegance of Dorigo, the tiptoeing and turns of Strachan, the passing of McAllister, the drive of Sterland, the economy of Batty, the cutting edge of Chapman – this was a team with direction and purpose. Drilled they may have been, but no one could call them one-dimensional. As they carved open one of the best teams in the country, their effervescence was palpable.

It wasn't beautiful, or even particularly pretty, but it was uplifting and invigorating. Leeds had needed to win the ugly football contest first to earn the right to play their game.

Certainly, they looked like they could last the pace and a third four-goal haul on opposition territory could not be dismissed as flukey – Leeds were the real thing.

For those who relied on facts rather than headlines, Leeds were actually doing better than Manchester United. Other than a 2-0 opening-day win against Notts County, a 3-0 defeat of Norwich and a 5-0 trouncing of Luton (all at Old

Trafford), the Red Devils had to scratch around for single-goal victories.

They had the big names – Robson, Ince, Bruce, Pallister, Hughes, Kanchelskis, Sharpe, Schmeichel, Irwin and Webb – but were trading more on their reputations than their performances. The press, though, were bedazzled by the surface sheen. They spouted the myth of 'the country's premier attacking side' in the 'best tradition' of the 'Theatre of Dreams'. It suited Alex Ferguson, and the press continued to propagate the 'inevitability' of his team's coronation.

Wilkinson saw an opportunity to be exploited, readily talking about how Manchester United were 'the best team in the country according to all the experts' and instructing the players to repeat the same mantra in public: 'It's Man U's title, it's a competition for second.'

In private, he told his players, 'We can do this!' He urged his men to keep going. 'Average two points a game and any other team will struggle to finish ahead of you.'

'That reverse psychology was there,' recalls Gary McAllister. 'He kept us concentrated.'

Leeds kept the run going with the defeat of Everton, a 4-1 triumph away to the same side in the Rumbelows Cup and then victory at Luton. Wallace was on a roll now, scoring in five successive games.

Manchester United kept pace, trailing by a point with a game in hand, but third-placed Sheffield Wednesday were ten points in Leeds' wake as the title race narrowed to two horses.

Suddenly, there was a stutter in Leeds' gait as they suffered a succession of drawn games.

Wilkinson warned that Tottenham might not roll over at Elland Road and was proven right when they had the best of a 1-1 draw. He said after the game, 'Good players will always be turned on by being in so-called intimidating situations. If you are playing against a good side and people are making a lot of noise that is not, in my opinion, intimidating to good players.'

Christmas week saw Leeds drop a further four points, held to a goalless draw at Forest and then sharing six goals at home to Southampton on Boxing Day. The stalemate against Brian Clough's men wasn't of great concern but Wilkinson was annoyed by the failure to defeat the Saints. It was especially galling with Leeds 2-0 ahead and cruising after half an hour thanks to a two-goal contribution by Hodge.

Even when Iain Dowie pulled a goal back five minutes into the second half, there looked to be little danger and when Gary Speed restored the two-goal advantage after 73 minutes, Leeds appeared to be home and dry.

Uncharacteristic defensive slackness saw United collapse over the final 11 minutes as the Saints staged a fightback. Twenty-one-year-old Alan Shearer made it 3-2 and then Dowie notched his second goal with five minutes remaining.

Shearer's would be a name to haunt Wilkinson over the years to come; his goal that day was his first in four games for the Saints against Leeds, but it began an astonishing run. For Blackburn and Newcastle, his return was a remarkable 20 in as many appearances.

Gary McAllister: 'The Southampton game was one that really stuck in our throats for weeks afterwards. Normally, we can forget poor performances very quickly at this club but that really annoyed all the players because we threw the game away. After that sort of thing has happened to a team they just can't wait to get out on to the pitch and put things right.'

Wilkinson was galled but continued to keep the players level – they were not world-beaters after defeating Southampton 4-0 and they were not a poor side after the 3-3 draw. 'These things happen. It's the manager's responsibility to manage expectations and one of the ways is to look at it in a longer-term way. It just takes away some of the up and down nature which is sometimes generated by results. Even the public now looks at it a little bit more philosophically when they see the amount of possession the team had and the amount of strikes a team had and they've come off and lost 1-0. Even the public now see that that 1-0 was not as bad a result as what it seems – what the stats are saying is it was a game we could have and should have won but unfortunately in football luck plays a far greater part than many people are prepared to accept.'

Despite Wilkinson's soothing words, Leeds appeared to have lost their way. They retained second place and a seven-point advantage over Sheffield Wednesday but now Manchester United were two points ahead with two games in hand. It was an emphatic lead, earned on the back of six successive victories. The Red Devils had rediscovered their scoring boots with four against Coventry, three against Palace and Chelsea and six at Oldham – they looked ominously good.

And who should be up next for Leeds but Manchester United, at Elland Road on 29 December?

The league clash was the first of a classic triple-header – over the course of the following three weeks, the two clubs would also meet in the Rumbelows and FA Cups.

Ferguson queried whether there was more than Fate involved. 'My suspicions were "what part has television got in this?" It's tremendous for television, incredible.' Wilkinson declared himself equally amazed.

Ferguson fully appreciated what a challenge it would be at Elland Road. Animosity festered between the clubs over the decades and the mood had been embraced by Wilkinson's combative squad. The atmosphere was hostile.

As the players prepared for kick-off, Ferguson told them, 'Get in there, get a result and get out as quickly as we can because we are not welcome here.'

Wilkinson's cause was not helped by doubts over Strachan's fitness, chronic sciatica threatening his availability. The manager greatly valued his presence, agreeing with ITV's Elton Welsby when he said beforehand, 'Leeds are a different proposition when he's orchestrating the play.'

Strachan had been missed against Southampton, and Wilkinson, reasoning that the gamble was worthwhile, recalled his totem.

It was a wise choice and Strachan proved his worth in the early exchanges as Leeds got a grip on the game. Manchester, however, were well schooled by Ferguson in how to win and grew into the game as they negated Leeds' stronger points.

Big-money centre-back Gary Pallister seemed to have Lee Chapman in his pocket, as recognised by Jack Charlton in the ITV studio. 'Pallister hasn't lost the ball yet against Lee Chapman. If nothing happens with Lee Chapman, nothing happens. Pallister has won it hands down up to now.'

Wise old bird Charlton had put his finger on it – Chapman was the focal point of Wilkinson's game, the strategy all about getting the ball to him as quickly and directly as possible. With him neutered, Leeds were dragged into a dour midfield battle. For all Leeds' vaunted quality in the middle of the park, Manchester could match them with experienced internationals in Brian McClair, Neil Webb and Paul Ince. Andrei Kanchelskis was a constant threat wide on the right with his pace and close control and teenage wonder boy Ryan Giggs starred on the other flank.

The presence of two such tricky wingers nullified the attacking threat of Sterland and Dorigo and Leeds played into Manchester's hands. The Leeds crowd was left to bay empty hatred for their opponents. Mark Hughes bore the brunt of their vitriol, fiercely barracked every time he got the ball, jeered mercilessly whenever he tried to buy a foul.

At the start of the second half, the Welsh war horse held off Batty and Whyte deep on Leeds' right flank before back-heeling Giggs into space. Sterland cut off the cross at the expense of a corner.

The flag kick beat Pallister and Fairclough as they competed on the edge of the area and fell to Webb, lurking in the D. He steadied himself as it bounced up and half-volleyed consummately to beat Lukic's dive.

As Leeds sought to rally, Strachan pulled up sharply as he was chased down by Giggs – it looked as if his hamstring had let him down. The Leeds crowd feared the worst but Strachan saw out the game, leading his men in their assault as Manchester began to protect their lead, relying almost exclusively on the breakaway. The speed of their wingers was a worry and Leeds could never wholly commit to kitchen-sink attack.

The visitors were already doing whatever they could to waste time, dwelling as long as they dared over every free kick and throw-in. It provoked jeering from the terraces, with Bruce and Schmeichel the main targets, while referee Bob Nixon's tolerance of some ferocious tackling increased the likelihood of tempers boiling over.

Wilkinson fretted anxiously in the dugout, his frustration increasing with every missed opportunity. Leeds' passing into and around the Manchester penalty area began to create some threat and on the opposing bench Ferguson was intense, wide-eyed and seething at every Leeds foul, imagined or actual.

Chapman had the ball in the net just after the hour, but the referee had already given a foul for a high kick on Batty. The official had allowed play to proceed for far worse.

McAllister was played clean in on goal but could only get a back-heeled flick at the ball, which fell nicely into Schmeichel's welcoming hands.

Batty, already booked and always likely to get a second yellow card, made way for Steve Hodge as the Leeds storm grew, but they were playing on the edge, rushing things a little too much, their passes fractionally short.

Suddenly, a breakthrough with ten minutes left. Pallister went diving in as McAllister chased Wallace's flicked pass into the area and Leeds were awarded the penalty.

Patently aware he was struggling, Strachan allowed Sterland to take it. The full-back calmly sent Schmeichel one way as he stroked the ball inside the opposite post.

The action was all in the red half now but the defence soaked up everything and the game ended honours even.

'It was vital we didn't lose,' admitted Wilkinson. 'We more than earned that draw against the team who virtually everyone who's supposed to know about these things are saying is the best team in the English league.'

He was absolutely right, of course – three points would have been perfect, but a draw kept things in the melting pot.

The match had told us much we already knew – Manchester had the class, the composure and the intelligence, but Leeds had the heart, the spirit and the resilience. It was a case of unstoppable force meets immovable object. There was little to choose between the two sides as 1991 ended, though the bookmakers thought Ferguson's team would have the final say, as the odds of 9/2 on testified.

New Year's Day looked like it would improve their chances – Leeds were away to West Ham, while Manchester United welcomed Queens Park Rangers to Old Trafford, a home banker if ever there was one.

How Ferguson, who had just celebrated his 50th birthday, must have wished that logic had held good, but not a bit of it. In another match televised live by ITV, the Londoners gave Fergie a day to forget.

There were just three minutes on the clock when Simon Barker and Roy Wegerle created an opportunity for Andy Sinton to fire into the bottom corner.

Almost immediately, Rangers repeated the feat when the unsung Dennis Bailey latched on to a through ball and shot. Schmeichel got to it but could do no more than take the pace off, watching in horror as it rolled on into the net.

The cameras cut to Ferguson's haunted face as he wondered what he had done to deserve this.

Ian Holloway and Bailey went close as Rangers' whirlwind start continued but United's luck held.

Things calmed down after that and there were no more goals in the first half, but then Bailey added his second, running through a gaping United defence to chip Schmeichel.

McClair pulled one back for United in the final ten minutes but then Bailey completed a startling hat-trick, netting the rebound after Sinton's shot hit the woodwork.

They might even have had a fifth when Bailey left Bruce on the seat of his pants before laying on an opportunity for Wegerle, but the ball went soaring into the crowd behind the goal.

'A horrendous performance,' Ferguson said. 'That was just unbelievable and we got what we deserved. It was a lack of determination in clearing the ball and defending properly. We hadn't even got started when QPR were 2-0 up.'

Ferguson attributed the result to the 'cabbage patch' of a pitch. At the end, the triumphant Bailey entered the United dressing room looking for Manchester players to sign the match ball. Steve Bruce angrily hurled it through the door.

Leeds took full advantage, winning 3-1 at West Ham, thanks to a Chapman brace. It was their first victory in almost a month.

Wilkinson's face showed no flicker of emotion, but inside he was glowing with satisfaction as Leeds reclaimed the leadership. More importantly, he was reminded of Manchester's fallibility, of how they could crumble under pressure. He filed his notes away for a rainy day.

The country also marked the results – this would not be the formality that they had expected.

The two Uniteds were scheduled to meet in the FA Cup a few days later but two hours before kick-off a downpour saw the game postponed. They met again almost immediately, in the last eight of the Rumbelows Cup.

Leeds were well up for the test and oozed confidence. Batty, for whom it was the last appearance before a two-game suspension, commented, 'I fancy us to beat Manchester United in both the FA Cup and the Rumbelows Cup because we can now consider ourselves the best team in the country. The encouraging thing is that we've been gathering points when we have not played well. We are due a convincing performance. I wonder what we are capable of when we really click. There won't be a replay.'

Leeds pushed Manchester back at the start, but were almost caught out by a quick attack. After clearing away a dangerous ball across the area, Whyte furiously berated his team-mates.

Leeds bounced back to take the lead. Lukic's long kick downfield caused havoc with Batty and Rod Wallace combining to set up Gary Speed on the left. There was no hesitation as he calmly smashed the ball past Schmeichel, but the partisan home crowd was anything but calm as they celebrated.

Unfortunately, that was as good as it got for Leeds. The visitors forced their way back in, Clayton Blackmore curling a long-range free kick into the top corner.

That set the stage for Ryan Giggs to show that he had what it takes. He had performed reasonably at Elland Road in the league, but now he was unplayable. He was a constant menace with his direct running and at the start of the second half, he set up Kanchelskis to fire Manchester ahead.

He added a third himself four minutes from the end to wrap up the game.

A few days later, Manchester scraped home by a single goal at home to Everton to regain top spot, throwing the ball back into Wilkinson's court.

Away to his former club Sheffield Wednesday the following day, the nation waited to see the Leeds response.

Wednesday were in good form, undefeated since the end of November and upwardly mobile. They were fifth but only a point behind third-placed Liverpool.

Again, the ITV cameras caught Leeds on song. They wasted no time settling down and had the freedom of Hillsborough from the moment Chapman opened the scoring in the ninth minute.

Tony Dorigo had already threatened, cutting in from the left to unleash a powerful right-footed strike from outside the area. Keeper Chris Woods did well to turn it over for a corner but Leeds were not to be denied. Fairclough nodded McAllister's flag kick down for Chapman to sweep home from deep inside the six-yard box.

Wednesday knew as well as anyone what was coming, what Leeds intended, but they could do nothing to prevent the execution. The men in bright yellow could see they were there for the taking.

Hodge was having a wonderful game in midfield as deputy for Batty, showing what he could bring to United's play. Further forward, Dorigo and Wallace were wreaking havoc from the left with some gorgeous crosses and Chapman went close several times, one shot crashing against Woods' bar.

Dorigo struck next as the game reached 30 minutes. Entrusted with a free kick from 30 yards, the Aussie made no secret of his plan as he launched into a full-blooded drive. Woods could not get near it as it flashed into the top corner. It was a stunning strike, caught so clean and sweet that the goalkeeper never had a prayer.

Leeds' equanimity was rudely interrupted shortly afterwards as Wednesday briefly threatened to get back into the game. Full-back Roland Nilsson poked the ball through the Leeds penalty area. It looked innocuous enough but caught Whyte in two minds, unsure whether to leave it to Lukic or clear his lines. He did neither and the ball would never have reached the goalkeeper. As Whyte dallied, Wednesday striker Gordon Watson slipped past him. Whyte got the faintest of touches to nudge the ball wide but Watson took it into his head to indulge in the most shameless piece of cheating. He was beyond Whyte when he decided to throw himself into a dive. It was no half-hearted effort, a kicking out of his legs under him as if searching for a fellow pair to play footsie with. It was a bizarre act of circus-like proportions and he rolled over and over in mock agony.

The furious Leeds defenders were ready to give Watson the roasting of his life for his gamesmanship but stood open-mouthed as referee Philip Don bought the dive, pointing to the penalty spot.

'It was a stonewall penalty' protested Watson for ever afterwards, but everyone knew the truth.

When the dust settled, John Sheridan stepped up to take the spot kick. Lukic pushed the first effort on to the post but Sheridan followed in to poke home the rebound as Leeds continued to protest.

If the Wednesday fans thought it would spark a fightback, their hopes were killed off within minutes when Chapman rose to nod home a lovely cross from Speed.

Into the second half and Chapman completed his hat-trick, nodding in from practically on the goal line after Speed headed a corner on to the Wednesday bar.

Wilkinson leaned smugly on the glass window surrounding the Leeds dugout, well satisfied with life.

After 70 minutes substitute Mike Whitlow rose to nod home Wallace's steepling cross to make it five.

There was still time for a sixth as neat Leeds combination work left Wallace in the clear just inside the Wednesday area and he clipped the ball over Woods.

The victory was breathtaking and Leeds coolly glided back into top spot. Despite the pleasure of the performance, there was a downside for Wilkinson, who was sent off for his reaction to Watson's antics. The linesman reported to the referee that he had raced towards him and given him a load of abuse.

Wilkinson was adamant that he had done nothing of the sort; rather he had been rebuking his players for their lax defending.

The next morning, media friend David Walker rang Wilkinson.

'I hope you're going to appeal?'

'How can I? It's my word against his.'

'It was on television, it was on ITV. We'll get the video.'

Football reporter Gary Newbon recalls, 'I was ITV's touchline reporter, standing next to Wilkinson, who was in the dugout. What he was actually doing at that moment was shouting at Tony Dorigo.

'The said linesman – neither Wilkinson nor I can recall his name – was not in our vision.

'Two or three days after the game, Wilkinson rang me to explain that he had been charged by the FA and would I please find any useful video evidence and would I appear for him at the hearing.

'Luckily, I found an untransmitted piece of video from our live match coverage that proved Wilkinson was in his area, that I was next to him and that the linesman was a long way from the incident at the other end of the pitch!'

Wilkinson persuaded the FA to review the video evidence. He wheeled a massive television and video player into a Lancaster Gate meeting room and insisted that the disciplinary panel watch the tape.

'The video clearly showed that both at the time the penalty was awarded and thereafter at no point did I run down the touchline 20 yards and say to him what he said I'd said.'

Newbon: 'The FA Commission was chaired by Geoffrey Thompson, who was completely fair in every way. ITV's video clip proved Howard's innocence and the charge was soon dismissed.

'To my knowledge, the linesman involved did not have top duties again.'

The charges were dropped, much to Wilkinson's satisfaction, and he was left to reflect on an excellent afternoon's work as Leeds regained leadership of the division with the kind of performance that dreams are made of.

No one would have believed Wilkinson if he had continued to play down Leeds' chances of the league championship.

For weeks he had told his players, 'Let's see where we are after Christmas.' Now he just told them, 'We're nearly there. Just kick on for home.'

Asked later when he started believing that Leeds could win the title, Wilkinson admitted, 'Possibly three months before the end of the season just because of where we'd been and who we'd beaten, as it were. You've got to take it while it's there.'

Hillsborough took his breath away, the performance as good as his Leeds had ever given. They had destroyed one of the country's finest sides and confidence was soaring.

Alex Ferguson could only look on from the Theatre of Dreams and wonder what the next three months would bring.

A Touch of Chic

If you hire people who are smarter than you,
maybe you are showing that you are a little
bit smarter than them.

15 JANUARY 1992.

'As the ball approached me, I felt certain I was about to score the equalising goal. Such was my concentration, I could only focus on the ball and was totally unaware of Pallister as he backed into me and knocked me off balance, just before I made contact ... In an attempt to break the fall, my left arm had taken my full weight of nearly 14 stone. As I picked myself up, I felt a searing pain above my wrist. I looked down and saw my lower arm grotesquely out of shape, with a huge lump protruding from its upper surface. I knew instantly it was broken.'

As Lee Chapman suffered the agony of a second serious injury in 12 months, Leeds United's entire season was in the balance.

Alan Sutton raced over to tend to Chapman. He could see at once that he was in trouble, but out of habit he turned to the customary magic sponge. 'He were squealing like a pig and I was just trying to do something ... sometimes cold water works.'

Leeds were playing their greatest rivals, Manchester United, at Old Trafford in the delayed FA Cup third-round tie.

Leeds hadn't beaten United since 1981 but had high hopes they could put an end to that run.

Leeds made all the early running with Mel Sterland and Tony Dorigo on almost constant attack. Chapman was getting the better of Gary Pallister and it gave the Whites an advantage.

'We were never in the race,' admitted Alex Ferguson, though Mark Hughes gave his team the lead before half-time against the run of play. Gordon Strachan, missing through injury once again, told the BBC during the interval it was 'an absolute travesty'.

With Leeds looking like they must equalise, Chapman was laid low by a crashing challenge – Pallister barged into him with no intention of playing the ball and it should have been a penalty, but referee Ray Lewis didn't even consider it.

Howard Wilkinson, Mick Hennigan and Sutton were too concerned about Chapman to protest, and Leeds' chances of an equaliser vanished with Chapman into the night sky. He would be out of commission for several weeks while his double fracture mended.

In retrospect, the old adage about 'being able to concentrate on the league' could not have been more accurate or more telling. Manchester United put Leeds out of both Rumbelows and FA Cups in the space of a week but landed themselves with the complications of fixture congestion. They already had two more league games to play than Leeds and there would be a further five to come in knock-out football.

Wilkinson stored that away in his locker, fully appreciating the pressure it would bring for Ferguson and his players.

The Leeds manager had more pressing issues to concern him – how to cope with the absence of his talisman.

There was newspaper conjecture about Tony Cascarino, Brian Deane and Steve Bull, while Carl Shutt, Bobby Davison and Imre Varadi had their own claims. Wilkinson, however, decided to test out Gary Speed's versatility, asking him to lead the line against Crystal Palace.

Wilkinson, able to welcome back Batty and Strachan, was confident of getting something out of the game and had no doubts about gambling on Speed up top. 'The great thing about Gary Speed was his ability in both boxes. He scored goals and he stopped goals. He was as good a centre-half as he was a centre-forward, the number of goals he got at the back post coming in.'

Wilkinson sought to gee up the fans before the game, saying, 'In my time at Leeds there has probably never been a more important time for the contribution supporters can make. We need the fans' support, not just at the start or if we happen to be ahead, but throughout the game.'

Leeds made a good start, but Palace stunned everyone after 17 minutes when Geoff Thomas scored from the edge of the area. The Londoners gave Leeds a thorough test, Mark Bright almost grabbing a second.

Steve Hodge had two chances to equalise within five seconds but was denied by Palace keeper Nigel Martyn, a big-money buy from Bristol Rovers.

After 30 minutes, Speed laid on Leeds' equaliser, flicking on a corner. Chris Fairclough thumped home from close in.

Speed and Rod Wallace both found the woodwork in the second half, but Leeds had to settle for a point which left them on top of the table with Manchester lucky to draw at Notts County.

Leeds had the luxury of a week off after being eliminated from the FA Cup. Hennigan took the squad away on a break to La Manga while Wilkinson stayed at home to consider his options.

Released from the pressure cooker, Batty and Speed were involved in an incident that resulted in their rental car being wrapped around a lamp post. Hennigan gave them the bollocking of their lives but kept the details under wraps and Wilkinson remained blissfully ignorant.

The break stiffened Wilkinson's resolve and he persisted with Speed up front when Leeds met Notts County at Elland Road. Manchester United regained top spot by beating Aston Villa in one of their games in hand, but Wilkinson wasn't bothered about what his rivals were doing.

Sterland nodded Leeds ahead early on against County to settle their nerves, and then the second half saw the most surprising of interventions. Batty abruptly cast all caution to the wind. He raced out of defence to beat a Notts man to a loose ball and set off on a dash forward which took him to the edge of the opposition area. Batty ignored Wallace and Strachan in the centre and smashed the ball into the top corner to spark amazing celebrations as he ran to greet the adoring Kop.

Wallace completed a comfortable victory by heading in from close range after a Strachan free kick caused confusion in the County area.

Leeds' unbeaten league run now stood at 16 games, the best since Wilkinson's arrival. They regained top spot after Manchester United drew with Arsenal thanks to their superior goal difference.

The day brought some stories that Wilkinson was interested in an international striker plying his trade in France, Kalman Kovacs. The rumour-mongers had everything right but the name.

Eric Cantona possessed God-given abilities, but he was a maverick who had fallen foul of the French football authorities.

While playing for his fifth club, Nimes Olympique, against St Etienne on 7 December, Cantona took exception to a decision and hurled the ball at the referee. Cantona disdainfully strutted from the pitch rather than waiting for the inevitable red card.

The disciplinary panel suspended him for four matches, the sanction influenced by his reputation. The chairman told him, 'You can't be judged like any other player. Behind you there is a trail of the smell of sulphur. You can expect anything from an individualist like you.'

Cantona could not contain himself, approaching each member of the panel and calling them an idiot in turn. When his ban was extended to two months, Cantona immediately announced his retirement.

He began to regret the decision as the weeks passed. One of his greatest advocates, national team manager Michel Platini, suggested a fresh start in England. Cantona took Platini's counsel; assistant manager Gérard Houllier acted as an intermediary and worked with agent Dennis Roach to find a club.

Cantona began negotiating an exit from Nimes. On 16 December, the club agreed to cancel his contract, a move which for once lived up to the clichéd 'by mutual consent'.

Platini told Liverpool manager Graeme Souness, 'I've got a player for you, he's a real problem in France but he's really talented and he'd be perfect for your club.'

'Look, Michel, I'm fighting fires here at the moment. I'm trying to get some people out of the door that are resisting, I'm fighting a dressing room here. The last thing I need is another controversial figure.'

Cantona had discussions with Sheffield Wednesday, looking to find cover for the injured David Hirst.

Wednesday fans waited with bated breath as the Frenchman considered a new start in Sheffield.

Wednesday manager Trevor Francis agreed to a week's trial. The relevant week fell in the midst of a bleak English winter, with frost rendering pitches unplayable. Francis selected Cantona for an indoor six-a-side game against American tourists Baltimore Blast, but outdoor training was impossible.

Francis was reluctant to commit to a deal without seeing Cantona on grass. He named him in his provisional side to face Luton and offered to extend the loan arrangement, but Cantona hurled his toys out of the pram and walked out.

Francis claimed that Wednesday only allowed Cantona to train with them as a favour to Roach and Platini to allow the forward to regain his fitness.

'There was never, ever any suggestion of us signing Eric Cantona,' said Francis. 'The kind of contract he would have wanted would have killed my whole budget as we were a team that had just come out of the Second Division.'

Cue the entrance of Howard Wilkinson and the beginning of an extraordinary episode in English football.

It's difficult to imagine a more implausible Wilkinson signing, but the Leeds manager was desperate.

'I'd seen him play before in a France Under-21 game at Highbury and I'd spoken with Gérard Houllier about him,' recalled Wilkinson. 'I'd heard that Eric had burnt his bridges over in France. It was a gamble but, as it turned out over the short term, the gamble paid off.'

Wilkinson did his due diligence on Cantona by calling people whose judgement he trusted – Platini, Houllier and Glenn Hoddle, who had just finished playing for Monaco. 'They gave me a brief potted history, that he'd had ten clubs, I think, and had had a difference of opinion with somebody. All said the same thing – brilliant, absolutely unbelievable player but, shall we say, he has his moments when he can be difficult, hence the number of clubs he's had. Anyway, I got him over on loan, with an agreement to buy him in April if it worked out.'

The short-term arrangement would cost £100,000 with an option to make the transfer permanent for £900,000.

Wilkinson invited Cantona to watch Leeds play Notts County. A contract had not yet been signed, but Cantona confidently asserted, 'We knew quite well that a mutual adventure would soon be bringing us together. There would be no question of a trial period.'

He revealed that Wilkinson was convinced of his worth, assuring him that he could quickly became a star, not only at Leeds, but also for British football. He was cautious, however, not to rush Cantona too quickly into the fray. Scepticism still prevailed towards foreign players and their perceived ability to adapt to the physicality of the English game. Assured by Platini and Houllier that he was 'made to get on with British football', Cantona, for his part, harboured not one iota of self-doubt.

Cantona stood out from the crowd in both looks and behaviour. He had a monobrow and pronounced Gallic features, his gait always ramrod straight, like a soldier, with his collar turned up in an insolent gesture of defiance. He strutted across the football field like an aloof colossus, different from the rest, above lesser men.

As Andy Peterson of podcast *The Square Ball* observed, 'He was very much an unknown quantity. He just stood there and glowered and was brilliant and then stood there and glowered and was rubbish.'

'He scored a goal in training that none of us could believe,' recalls Tony Dorigo. 'The goals were on the 18-yard box and the ball was thrown to him on halfway, on an angle running away from goal. It was miles out. Before it landed, he volleyed it back across the other way and into the top corner. The keeper didn't move.'

Football in the community officer Ces Podd remembers Cantona's arrival. 'The lads all took to him straight away. You knew that because they hung his boots – he had these big boots that came halfway up his thigh – you know, you just don't wear them things at Elland Road and all that – I went to the changing rooms and somebody had hung them up, you know, on the ceiling. I don't know how they got up there and I can remember Cantona. "Why, why have they done this?" And the boys are saying because they like you, welcome to Leeds United.'

There was an arrogance about the newcomer. One Saturday evening, he went to The Majestyk nightclub in the city centre with the rest of the squad. Cantona was told that if the players wanted to talk to girls, they had to go down on the dance floor or to the bar and make an effort. He haughtily informed them, 'This isn't how it works. The girls should come to me.'

A mickey-taking reporter questioned Wilkinson in French about why he had signed Cantona. He was dumbfounded when Wilkinson coolly responded, 'Parce qu'il est un bon jouer. Nous avons besoin d'un bon jouer au football.'

'You weren't supposed to be able to answer that. You can obviously speak quite well towards him, then?'

'I can understand him better than I can understand Gordon Strachan and Gary McAllister.'

Wilkinson said later, 'He attracted more media coverage than any player I've ever signed, including Gordon Strachan. Journalists arrived from all over Europe to meet him and he was not just contributing to sports articles, either. He gave interviews on art, philosophy and politics. A natural room-mate for David Batty, I thought immediately.'

The signing brought both benefits and risks: Wilkinson had found a genius, a bag of tricks capable of bringing the completely unexpected to the party, amazing goals, incisive passing and wonderful feet. It was unclear, however, how he could be integrated into the team – certainly not a direct substitute for Chapman, he was an individualist of unpredictable mood, a loner; his inclusion would bring disruption, someone would be displaced with an inevitable impact on both spirit and formation.

Even at an early stage, one could see that there might be trouble to come between Cantona and Wilkinson.

Chris Kamara, in his autobiography, recounts a story which demonstrates the tense dynamic between the two men. In 1992, while pursuing his A licence coaching badge, Kamara requested Wilkinson's assistance with a training session. Cantona and a number of other players lined up to participate.

Kamara describes an incident from the session. The ball was delivered neatly to Cantona. He halted his run to wrong-foot his marker, and suddenly sent the ball flying goalwards. His shot arced through the air and dipped just under the crossbar, leaving Lukic stranded. The other players could only stand back and watch in awe. It was a glimpse of the genius that Cantona would later take to Manchester United.

Applause filled the air. All but one joined in the ovation. Wilkinson casually sauntered over from the touchline, his finger wagging in disapproval.

'Whoa, whoa, whoa,' he bellowed. 'Eric, you had better options there.'

Chiding Cantona for not passing the ball, Wilkinson suggested that he should have brought Strachan and McAllister into the move. He dismissed Cantona's artistry as something that would have been impossible to pull off during a real match.

Cantona froze, his hands on his hips, his burning eyes locked on Wilkinson. It wasn't clear whether he failed to comprehend Wilkinson's words, or he was just shocked at the audacity of this peculiar Englishman.

Cantona was named in the party that travelled to Oldham. He attracted dozens of French journalists to Boundary Park.

Roy Butterworth, an Oldham matchday press officer, recalled, 'He was sub that day. We had 66 in the press box. Twelve journalists arrived from France and the chairman, Ian

Stott, said, "Tell them they can come next week, we're at home to Queens Park Rangers." He gave the Parisian newspapers my office number and my phone was red-hot. I said, "You can come but you arrive at two o'clock and you may have to stand at the back of the press box because it's full." We only had 45 seats and one of them was mine.

'They arrived at 10am. I was nearly ready but I was still at home. I threw my clothes in the car and was here for about 20 past.

'The club made them their breakfast, bacon and sausage sandwiches. We said, "At 2pm you've got to come to the press box." Then at 2.40 – in the days before they had proper warm-ups – the chairman appeared in the directors' box. The journalists should have been on my right, they were in the bloody centre circle. I jumped down the steps, out on to the pitch and shouted, "Non!"'

According to Strachan, the focus on Cantona helped the rest of the squad. 'He took a lot of pressure off us when he turned up. There was something else to talk about, you know, for other people. The way he went about his job, he was different. It was fun for us with this new fella who didn't say much.'

The other players could fade into the background, free of the usual speculation as to whether they could maintain the title chase.

It was a bitterly cold afternoon in the humble surroundings of Boundary Park, the icy air making breathing a laborious task. The playing surface was still bedding down after the plastic pitch was replaced by turf.

Leeds were soon a goal down. Hodge was made scapegoat for a sluggish first half, dragged off to let Cantona make his debut. There were a couple of flashes of brilliance but for the most part he was a lost soul, having to compete for the high balls that were meat and drink for Chapman. Strachan and

McAllister did their best to give Cantona something to feed on, but Oldham's prosaic football rendered him a passenger. As the game entered its final three minutes, Oldham broke away from prolonged United pressure to double their lead. A disconsolate Wilkinson looked lonely and weary on the touchline.

Elsewhere, Manchester United had to settle for a point at home to Sheffield Wednesday. It took them clear and they headed into an FA Cup replay against Southampton in good heart. It did them little good – the game was still level after extra time and the Saints went through on penalties.

Ferguson could have done without the extra 30 minutes, but it had little impact with both Uniteds enjoying a day off when the fifth-round ties were played.

Wilkinson filled the void with a friendly at home to Gothenburg and he used the game to give Cantona a start, up front alongside Wallace.

Mike Casey reported for the *Yorkshire Evening Post*. 'Showing an almost reckless unconcern for his safety and an insatiable hunger to be in the thick of the action, he is set to become a favourite with the Koppites. They cheered his every move. With his shirt outside his shorts – I wonder which referee will have the nerve to try to explain that it's against the rules – Cantona roams menacingly. He had the look of a man who could become Public Enemy Number One to First Division defenders. He produced enough clever touches, a few goalworthy efforts and a hunger for the action.'

Cantona came close to a goal twice in the five minutes before the interval as he showcased his potential.

Wilkinson was not yet convinced and sought insurance, bringing in former Sheffield United striker Tony Agana on loan from Notts County. It was a far more typical signing for the manager.

Nonetheless, Wilkinson saw enough to give Cantona his debut, away to Everton on 23 February, but it was Carl Shutt, on as substitute for Wallace, who did the business, scoring Leeds' goal in a 1-1 draw.

It was a decent point, but their lack of victories was eating away at Leeds' confidence. They had won just three of the previous dozen games. Manchester United beat Crystal Palace and were now three points clear with a game in hand. Everything pointed to them securing their first championship in 25 years.

Both teams faced sides from the bottom six on the last day of February – Leeds hosted Luton, while Manchester were at Coventry. Luton had gone 20 away games without a victory while Coventry had won only three times in 16 matches, losing the reverse fixture 4-0. Neither United managed the easy victory that seemed to be on the cards.

While Manchester finished goalless, Leeds scraped a win but it was a near thing.

Chris Kamara, returning to Elland Road for the first time since joining Luton, was greeted enthusiastically by the crowd, although they reserved their best cheers for Chapman, sporting a cast on his damaged wrist. Cantona and Agana warmed the bench.

Leeds pressed Luton back in the first half, and even the loss of Dorigo after 28 minutes with a nasty knee injury did not derail them as Wilkinson summoned Cantona from the bench.

Despite their dominance, Leeds couldn't get the goal they deserved and Luton were always a threat on the break. Mick Harford put in a real shift up front, though he fluffed two chances.

Near the end of the half, Fairclough headed a Strachan corner against the bar. It was a golden opportunity spurned and the crowd were fidgeting as the half-time whistle sounded.

Leeds' anxieties were evident after the interval, with Luton on the front foot. James robbed Wallace, played a one-two with Hughes, and delivered a perfect right-wing cross. Harford escaped his markers to meet it but headed over.

The striker set up Preece and his beautiful chip was destined for the top corner until Lukic made a flying save.

Leeds were stung into a response. Cantona got through on his own but clipped his shot over; then James missed a tackle on Wallace, who whipped in a 20-yarder which crashed against the underside of the bar and into the hands of keeper Sutton.

Leeds' pressure told just before the hour after Strachan put McAllister through. Sutton brought him down and it should have been a penalty, but Leeds spared referee Allan Floyd the decision. Cantona smashed the loose ball into the empty net for his first Leeds goal.

He celebrated joyously, milking the applause of the home support. 'As soon as I came on, I knew I felt good and that I was going to score my first goal,' he said. 'At that exact moment when the ball went into the net, thousands of supporters behind the goal seemed to plunge towards the turf. In scoring this goal at the Kop end I became seduced. I had met, it seemed, my new family.'

As Luton rallied, Hughes and Harford both headed wide, while Stein, on for the final quarter of an hour, headed straight at Lukic and then shot inches wide.

Leeds weathered the rally and secured the points with five minutes left.

Sutton sprinted out of his area to head clear from McAllister's high ball over the defence but he managed only to return it to McAllister, who lobbed it back into the area.

Sutton had recovered his ground, but Dreyer botched his clearance and Chapman volleyed into the corner.

Asked about Cantona, Wilkinson told the press, 'Jewels like that are hard to find.' He admitted that Leeds did not dominate the game as he would have liked, picking Kamara's performance out as a key factor.

Wilkinson had long since abandoned any ambitions of playing free-flowing football. All that counted now was results – ugly wins were far more valuable than pretty-pretty play.

Leeds struggled again a few days later at Elland Road, held to a goalless draw by Aston Villa. The game could have gone either way.

Agana, preferred to Cantona, had the chance to score within the first four minutes but slipped the ball wide. At the other end, Dalian Atkinson saw a goal ruled out for muscling Fairclough off the ball as he broke into the area.

Leeds had the benefit of a dubious late penalty, but goalkeeper Nigel Spink smothered Strachan's effort. They remained a point behind Manchester United, who drew the first leg of their Rumbelows Cup semi-final against Middlesbrough.

With the second leg the following Wednesday at Old Trafford, the Red Devils had the weekend off, giving Leeds the chance to recover top spot as they faced Tottenham at White Hart Lane.

The pitch was so heavily sanded that it resembled a beach but Leeds played the conditions far better than the home side. Eight minutes before half-time they took a deserved lead.

Spurs goalkeeper Erik Thorstvedt punted the ball downfield. It was gathered by Strachan, who slipped it short to Batty. He played Wallace through between the two centre-backs and the forward clipped a shot past the keeper.

Paul Allen equalised for Spurs three minutes into the second half after some nice one-touch football but Leeds responded strongly, netting twice within the space of a couple of minutes. After 76 minutes Jon Newsome headed home at the back post from a Strachan corner and then Strachan broke forward to feed Cantona, who had come on for Dorigo. He cut back inside and squared the ball for McAllister to race on to and slide under the advancing Thorstvedt.

The result opened a two-point lead on Manchester United, though Leeds had played two games more.

The game marked the end of Sterland's season. He sustained an ankle injury against Notts County but continued to play, eased through games by painkilling injections. He had to admit defeat after coming off against Spurs and was admitted to hospital for an operation. There was an abortive comeback the following December, but Sterland would only appear five more times for Leeds.

In his absence, Wilkinson turned to Jon Newsome. The 21-year-old let no one down, but he was no Sterland and a major source of Leeds' attacking threat was gone.

With Manchester United seeing off Middlesbrough on 11 March to book their Rumbelows Cup Final place, Leeds had the chance to turn the screw in the league. It was not to be – they caught QPR in the same mood as when they swept Ferguson's team away on New Year's Day. In fairness, it might have been expected as Rangers had beaten Manchester City 4-0 a few days earlier.

There were few signs of the calamity to come in the early minutes as Leeds settled into a decent rhythm with Batty and McAllister taking control of midfield. After 11 minutes, their dominance was rewarded when Speed headed home from Newsome's cross.

It was classic Leeds, but they were swept aside by a QPR side in full flow.

Leeds had to thank an alert Lukic for thwarting Andy Impey from close range as Rangers swarmed forward.

The reprieve was brief – Les Ferdinand reacted faster than the Leeds defence at a corner and scored from six yards.

The game was still level at the hour mark, but Leeds were opened up twice inside a minute.

Ray Wilkins played Bradley Allen through after QPR broke from deep within their own half. He moved wide to his right to round a panicky Lukic and a lumbering Whyte, and into an impossible angle before slickly cutting the ball back into goal.

Rangers were instantly back to pressurise Whyte, whose poor clearance allowed them to pour forward. The first couple of chances were squandered before Andy Sinton fired in from wide left. It was a goal entirely of Leeds' own making.

Wilkinson sent Cantona on for McAllister but it was far too late and the game was dead and buried with seven minutes remaining.

As Sinton reached the area and steadied himself to beat Lukic, Whyte reached out from behind to drag him down. He was shown the red card before Clive Wilson buried the penalty to end the agony. Leeds looked dead on their feet, fearing that their title chances were gone.

Wilkinson was strangely phlegmatic after the game. 'It's important that we bounce back and I believe that we shall. A lot of people at this club including myself have a lot of experience in football and we're not upset by setbacks. People like Lukic, Strachan, Sterland, Chapman and McAllister have seen it all and done it all. They know what's needed at times like these. Their experience and leadership will be a boon to their team-mates. It's a big prize they're playing for, the title, and they will give it their all.'

Wilkinson needed a reaction, and he got one when Leeds came up against Wimbledon. He went with an attacking line-up, starting Cantona alongside Wallace and Chapman but sporting the No 3 shirt. It paid off, as each of the three scored. With Dorigo and Whitlow both injured, Speed filled in at left-back.

Leeds made their intentions clear well before Chapman opened the scoring after 23 minutes. They subsequently missed two further opportunities but made it 2-0 within four minutes of the first goal. Wallace charged down Warren Barton's clearance, took it wide and chipped the ball to the six-yard line. Chapman had the freedom of Elland Road to nod home.

Four more minutes and Strachan's lofted cross came in from the right. Three defenders crowded Chapman, but the ball bypassed them all and Wallace finished easily.

Paul Miller pulled one back early in the second half, but the Dons never threatened to get anywhere near Leeds.

With 16 minutes left, John Scales misjudged his backpass and Cantona was on it in a flash. He ran on to coolly add the fourth to prompt cries of 'Ooh aah Cantona' from the Kop.

Chapman scored his third goal in the 80th minute. Carl Shutt's cross from the byline was perfect, but Chapman mistimed his header. It dropped at his toes before trickling apologetically into the net.

Little did he care as he snaffled his second hat-trick of the season, substantially improving Leeds' goal difference.

Manchester United ruined what might have been a perfect day. Despite surrendering the first goal against Sheffield United, they won 2-1 thanks to a Clayton Blackmore winner eight minutes from time.

Fergie's men had three games in hand, two of which they would play during the next seven days. With Leeds' game at Arsenal not taking place until the Sunday, Manchester might have been four points clear by then.

He might not have shown it, but Wilkinson feared the worst. He could only hope for the best, and he almost got it – the Red Devils lost 1-0 at Nottingham Forest on Wednesday night to a last-minute Nigel Clough goal, and were then held to a goalless draw at Old Trafford by the same Wimbledon side that had capitulated so meekly at Elland Road.

With Leeds still top, Wilkinson was reminded of the fault line running through his rivals.

Leeds' game at Highbury provided an opportunity to extend their lead but defending champions Arsenal had found their form with a seven-game unbeaten run.

Leeds welcomed Dorigo back, with Cantona donning the No 2 shirt that he took for the next three games. The Aussie played on the right with Speed continuing at left-back.

It was a tight game but Leeds contrived somehow to take the lead after 73 minutes, Chapman flicking a Wallace cross almost through David Seaman. It was typical Chapman – he had the happy knack of finding space in the right area. He might not have been the most elegant of footballers but he was deadly within the six-yard box.

Could Leeds gain an unexpected win? Regrettably not. With nine minutes remaining and Leeds soaking up pressure, Paul Merson intervened. He deftly flicked the ball over the United defence, sprinted on to it himself and nonchalantly beat Lukic to level the scores.

It was a point gained at a difficult venue, but given the circumstances, it felt like two dropped.

The following weekend seemed to offer another opportunity for Leeds – Manchester United were away to QPR, while Leeds hosted bottom club West Ham.

Both games ended scoreless, and Leeds were fortunate. They looked shaky at times with Whyte suspended, and the Hammers should have made them pay.

Leeds had their chances, with Chapman missing the easiest of the lot. Cantona teed it up with a delightful pass into Chapman's scoring zone. Cantona, appearing to have established himself in Wilkinson's side, was playing decent stuff and put the ball in the net himself shortly afterwards, but he was adjudged offside.

Ferguson crowed over the evening's outcome, claiming that Leeds were feeling the nerves that came with never having won a trophy.

Three days later, Manchester won 3-1 at Norwich to go top. As the season moved into April, they appeared to have broken the back of Leeds' challenge.

'The players are doing everything asked of them,' was all Wilkinson would say, refusing to be drawn into Ferguson's mind games.

Toughing It Out

Not all of those players would have been
seen as the best in the world, but they
were committed to excellence.

AS THE season entered its final furlong, the destination of the championship appeared to have been settled. Leeds United, with six games remaining, trailed Manchester United by a point and had played an extra game.

The victory Alex Ferguson's side inflicted on Norwich City on 31 March ended a three-game winless run and appeared to have soothed their nerves.

Getting something from a trip to Maine Road four days later was essential for Leeds. With Manchester City reaping a single point from four games, Howard Wilkinson had every reason for optimism.

City's dismal form saw them slip from third to sixth, and the knowledge that every point gained by Leeds would damage their Manchester rivals suggested the Sky Blues might not put up a serious fight.

So much for the theory: City won 4-0.

While the score flattered them, it was the first time under Wilkinson that Leeds had lost by such a margin – the game appeared to be up.

When asked whether the result had ended the chase, the most positive answer Wilkinson could offer was 'I don't know', before conceding, 'What I do know is that we have now left ourselves with a great deal to do.'

Away from the prying eyes of the media, Wilkinson maintained extraordinary composure, never betraying an ounce of doubt or emotion. 'Listen, this can happen, you know, this can happen,' he would tell the players, redirecting their attention to what they did rather than worrying about what was going on around them.

'We just need to beat what's in front of us. What happens elsewhere, we'll see what happens at the end of the season.'

'It was, I think, his calmness in front of the TV cameras as well,' added McAllister. 'Players say they don't watch it, they don't watch their manager speak. They do. They can see how he's reacting to the whole situation. It was incredibly calm, you know, "We can win this, but we've got to play, and we've got to stay focused." And it was his manner around the place as well. Everybody was calm but there was a belief, you know, there was a belief that things weren't going that well across at Manchester United.'

Wilkinson was matter-of-fact in his approach.

'Inevitably, I faced calls to make wholesale changes to the team, to punish the players who had not been up to scratch against the Mancunians. I decided the right approach to the run-in was to go back to our most experienced, proven team. Instead of chopping and changing I chose to back the players who had performed so creditably for the previous six months and leave them to win or lose the title. In my wisdom I felt it was better to return to the pattern and team play we had developed through an informative pre-season period rather than to clutch at straws and pray for one-off football miracles.

'There was a real air of doom and gloom after that defeat and I remember going home and then spending all Sunday thinking about what I would say to the players, just going back over the games and going back over the records. That group of players, over the last two seasons, had done well. I'll take the uncertainty out of the next games.'

Wilkinson went in on the Monday and told the squad, 'Here's my plan for the next five games. We can win four; we've got to draw the other one, at Liverpool. On the penultimate game of the season we play Sheffield United in the morning, and Manchester United have to go to Liverpool in the afternoon. If we do what I say, we may just put pressure on them to get a result from that game and I don't think they will. So, I'll pick the same team every week, unless we get injuries, but against Liverpool I'll make one change.'

He didn't tell them what his tweak would be, but one man had an inkling.

The following morning, Gordon Strachan went to see Wilkinson. 'I've come to save you the embarrassment and tell you to leave me out when we play Liverpool. Don't give me any bullsh*t about you wanting to keep me fresh for the home game. We need one point there as you say, and you're right, I'm not the best person to get one.'

Wilkinson breathed a sigh of relief but the exchange between the two men was typical of their relationship: trust, respect, honesty. Individuals' wants were subordinate to the needs of the club as a whole. It was a mature approach, devoid of ego or tantrums, and it set the tone.

David Batty maintains that no such conversation ever took place; certainly, he wasn't paying attention if it did happen, as per usual.

Wilkinson's decision meant that Eric Cantona would be consigned to the bench. Given the affection the Leeds fans had for the Frenchman, it was a huge risk.

'I knew the crowd wanted to see him in action,' recalled Wilkinson, 'but I recognised Eric would have to be deployed in a sensible, tactical manner to help him adapt to life in England.

'I spoke to him privately in my best French to make sure he understood. I realised he might not like the news but it had to be done. I subsequently learned that he was somewhat shocked and disappointed but he never failed to give of his best when he was called on.'

Over at Old Trafford, Ferguson prepared his men for the Rumbelows Cup Final against Nottingham Forest, certain that they had enough in the tank to see off Leeds' faltering challenge.

The two points the Red Devils relinquished against Manchester City in midweek appeared inconsequential in the context of their position – they had a two-point lead on the Whites and the cushion of a game in hand. The four goals City put past John Lukic had wiped out Leeds' goal difference advantage.

Leeds had the opportunity to build some pressure over the weekend. The day before Fergie's men met Forest at Wembley, the Whites faced Chelsea at Elland Road.

Most people were surprised to see Cantona on the bench in a game that Leeds simply had to win, and the early signs were not encouraging. Neil Midgeley's whistle-happy refereeing prevented Leeds from building any rhythm in a goalless first half.

However, they nudged themselves into the lead ten minutes after the restart when Strachan forced his way into the Chelsea area. He found Rod Wallace, who coolly switched feet to create space before slipping the ball past goalkeeper Dave Beasant.

Failure to capitalise on that advantage set nerves jangling around Elland Road – you could almost smell the fear that Chelsea could yet claw a way back into things.

Leeds were edging their way to victory and eager to run the clock down. Wilkinson had already brought Jon Newsome on for Steve Hodge to stiffen things up and he used his second sub with five minutes remaining. Cantona took Wallace's place – he had an extraordinary impact.

Leeds added a critical second goal after only a minute. When McAllister sent a ball from the left across the area, Cantona calmly set up Chapman, whose first shot through the legs of Andy Myers found the post. When it came back out, Chapman used his knee to poke it over the line.

You could sense the relief in the stadium and the mood improved further as Cantona showcased his wares.

He took a throw from Strachan in his stride and closed in on goal, his mind racing. Chelsea defender Paul Elliott was shadowing him, but Cantona flicked it over Elliott to wrong-foot him. As the Chelsea man turned, Cantona flicked the ball back to the right, cushioned it and arrowed a sumptuous shot into the net. One of the greatest goals ever seen at Elland Road, it was a breathtaking piece of artistry, delighting all who witnessed it.

Cantona hurdled the barrier behind the goal to milk the moment with his adoring fans in the Kop.

Leslie Silver, sitting next to Wilkinson, turned to him and whispered, 'That's just cost me a million quid.'

Neither man had been certain that the loan from Nimes would result in a permanent move, but they were left with few options after such a show of extravagance. They would have been lynched by the Kop.

'He scores a wonder goal and it's the day before we've got to ring up and tell the club whether we're going to take him or not,' recalled Wilkinson, 'and the chairman whacks me in the ribs with his elbow and says, "That's just cost me."

'We had an understanding that if we wanted him after a certain date we had to pay. We expected him to go back but we never had a choice after that.'

The result was a boost, even if the performance was nervy, as Leeds moved a point clear.

The following day, Manchester won the Rumbelows Cup thanks to an early goal from Brian McClair against Forest. Four days later, a second-half strike from Andrei Kanchelskis was enough to secure three points against Southampton. They had five games left to Leeds' four and a two-point lead. Surely, the Yorkshiremen's opportunity had gone?

Hodge duly took Strachan's place on Easter Saturday, when Leeds battled manfully to earn a goalless draw at Liverpool, just as Wilkinson had predicted. John Lukic showed what a fine keeper he remained, denying Liverpool at every turn.

Manchester United fans were upbeat on the three-hour trip to relegation-threatened Luton, gloating over the headline in the *United We Stand* fanzine: 'Champions At Last – Prediction: Luton 1 Champions Elect 3'.

They took the lead midway through the first half, but Luton bounced back after 50 minutes, with Mick Harford scoring from the rebound after his first header hit the bar.

Imre Varadi and Chris Kamara were both in the Luton side against Manchester, and a note of appreciation went winging its way south.

The draw was disappointing yet seemed to be of little consequence – popular opinion had it that the Red Deveils would still cruise to the title. Indeed, the *Sunday Times* proclaimed as much: a condescending report of 'the gallant Yorkshiremen's failure' to win at Anfield deemed it the death knell for Leeds.

Alex Ferguson's mood was dark, as he recalled in later years. 'There was no rhythm in our play. We moved into a lead we didn't deserve but still couldn't win the match. Luton played to avoid relegation and, looking back, it was an ominous result for us.'

His players fluffed their lines in the Easter Monday lunchtime match at home to Nottingham Forest.

Manchester's Rumbelows victory over Brian Clough's side filled everybody with confidence, but the Red Devils had injury concerns and there were anxieties in their camp. Bryan Robson was a long-time absentee, and now Paul Ince and Paul Parker were added to the list of those missing in action.

After 33 minutes, Ian Woan's speculative shot from outside the area somehow bobbled under Peter Schmeichel's body to give Forest the lead, but McClair almost immediately levelled. An expectant Old Trafford bounced with anticipation.

The second goal would not come. As the final ten minutes beckoned, the game was drifting towards a draw. Then Forest launched a swift attack, and when a dummy left Scot Gemmill free on the edge of the area, the young midfielder buried the chance.

You could sense Ferguson's shoulders drooping as attention switched to Elland Road to see if Leeds could capitalise in the teatime fixture against Coventry.

From the off, nerves were jangling, the tantalising nearness of the prize militating against an easy game. Chances were few in the first half, the players' anxiety echoing that of the fans.

Then there was a breakthrough – Strachan's long free kick into the area was nodded goalwards by Chris Whyte. Brian Borrows' miskick saw the ball spin up at the back post and Chris Fairclough jack-knifed into a header that looped over goalkeeper Steve Ogrizovic.

Leeds couldn't build on their lead until the closing ten minutes. Whyte carried the ball out of defence and fed Cantona, who set up a chance for Speed. He couldn't take it but Cantona followed in. His goalbound shot was blocked by Lloyd McGrath on the line.

The ball struck McGrath's legs, but the linesman advised the referee that he had used his hands. The penalty was awarded and McGrath was dismissed.

'Eric should have spared the Coventry player that indignity by converting the glorious goalscoring opportunity with the panache we had grown to expect of him,' scolded Wilkinson.

McAllister ignored the mayhem and stroked the spot kick home.

Leeds wisely declined to look the gift horse in the mouth and ran the clock down as the ecstatic fans chanted, 'Fergie, Fergie, what's the score?' The three points left them top.

The victory guaranteed at least a UEFA Cup spot and, as Wilkinson remarked, 'That was our first target at the start of the season and I'm delighted that we have achieved it. As far as the title race is concerned, I'm just glad we've kept it alive. The longer it goes on, the better it will be for us.'

While Manchester still had a game in hand, you could hear the bottle going across the Pennines.

A trip to bottom club West Ham two days later was just what the doctor ordered for the Red Devils. The Hammers had won seven of their 39 games and were struggling for goals, nine points from safety.

Yet, Ferguson could feel the tension mounting, and he had concerns with some elements of his squad. One such was Neil Webb. The midfielder was huffy when taken off against Forest, and Ferguson, a man who brooked no half-heartedness, had suspicions about Webb's commitment. He dropped him from the side and brought Mike Phelan and Clayton Blackmore into midfield. Seeking to consolidate in the middle of the pitch, he also rested Kanchelskis.

Theirs was a tepid display, marked by hesitancy, while a carefree West Ham gave their performance of the season. Fergie described it as 'obscene' and 'almost criminal' as he wondered why they hadn't shown as much fight throughout the campaign. He also bemoaned the Lee Sharpe 'goal' that was chalked off for offside.

Schmeichel made first-half saves from Mike Small and Kevin Keen to keep it scoreless, while Ferguson's men could not muster a single shot on goal in the first half.

The Hammers continued to boss affairs after the break and Stuart Slater hit a post. After 66 minutes, their ambition was rewarded when Gary Pallister poked away a cross towards West Ham defender Kenny Brown. In the finest moment of his career, Brown volleyed the ball past Schmeichel and into the corner.

Pallister exemplified his team's dismay, sinking to his knees at the gravity of what was happening.

The Manchester United manager had other issues to contend with. The unrestrained antics of some of his younger players was a growing concern.

The evening following the defeat at West Ham, Ferguson was scheduled to make an appearance at an English Schools Football Association function in Morecambe. He could have done without the distraction but felt obliged to uphold his commitment. An innocuous chat took a turn for the worse when a member of the Association told him that he had seen Lee Sharpe and Ryan Giggs in Blackpool on the Monday night.

Ferguson initially dismissed the notion, adamant that his players were at home resting for Wednesday's game at West Ham. But his colleague was insistent, saying he had seen Sharpe in his Range Rover.

Battling the rising fury within him, Ferguson hastily made his excuses and left. He headed straight over to Sharpe's house to confront him.

Ferguson walked in on a riotous party and was not amused when he came across Giggs and three young apprentices. He went crazy and threw everyone out. When Sharpe emerged after a horizontal jogging session, Ferguson tore a strip off him and Giggs.

Ferguson didn't hold back. He was furious, particularly with Sharpe, accusing him of leading Giggs astray. There had been other signs of waywardness in Sharpe's off-field behaviour. Ferguson blamed himself for allowing him to have his own house when he was far too young. It was a bitter pill to swallow, seeing Sharpe's promising career coming off the rails. His downfall was one of the darkest chapters of Ferguson's time at Old Trafford.

Word of Sharpe and Giggs' escapades soon reached the rest of the squad. There were dark rumblings and accusations that they had betrayed their team-mates. Despite their tender age, Ferguson was convinced that they fully appreciated the depth of their irresponsibility.

The first Super Sunday, 26 April, promised to be the most dramatic of days – Leeds were away to Sheffield United at lunchtime and immediately afterwards Manchester United faced Liverpool at Anfield.

Five thousand Leeds fans made the trip to Bramall Lane that windswept afternoon, confident that they could succeed.

Yet Sheffield United promised to be difficult opponents. They were unbeaten in eight matches and had the best record in the division since the start of the year.

Wilkinson gave an emotive speech to the players before the game. 'Do it for your mums, your dads, your wives, your girlfriends, your kids and yourselves. You've given the fans all they could ask for in the first 40 games, now go and do it for yourselves.'

ITV beamed the game live to the nation, and one of their staff members situated in the players' tunnel before the game was a Leeds supporter. The home stewards shamelessly baited the Leeds team as the players lined up ready to go out. 'You'll get nowt today, you bastards.'

The ITV man had to remain neutral and could say nothing. Then the countdown came – '5 ... 4 ... 3 ... 2 ... 1 ... Out you go, ref.'

As soon as the official had gone, the ITV man was off. 'Right, you bastards, we're gonna kick seven bells of sh*t out of you today,' he began, before turning to the Leeds team. 'Get into this f***ing lot.' That was it, the Leeds players were at it, 'Right, you lot can f*** off!'

Wilkinson had drilled it into his men: 'Trust your swing.' Yet it was tough to stick to the script on such an emotional afternoon. The high wind spoiled any chance of a decent game of football. Crisp bags and other items of rubbish were swept across the pitch, caught up in the gusts of wind that were everywhere.

Leeds' start was edgy as the Blades took an early grip, forcing Whyte into a goal-line clearance to deny John Pemberton. After 28 minutes, Alan Cork scored the goal their persistence deserved. He reacted quickest to poke home a ball that ran loose after a corner caused panic in the Leeds box.

As Wilko's troops struggled to create any memorable moments in the first half, the alarm bells trilled their angry warning.

Suddenly, on the verge of the half-time whistle, they got the break they needed.

Leeds were awarded a free kick for an untidy challenge on Chapman. Ever alert, Strachan slipped a quick ball through for Wallace and chaos ensued in the Blades' defence.

Keeper Mel Rees rushed out to deny Wallace and sparked the most bizarre of equalisers.

The ball cannoned around in a frenetic pinball as Brian Gayle's rushed clearance crashed off the legs of Speed and across goal before heading goalwards off Wallace's knees. It looped into the net despite a desperate attempt to punch it away from a diving Pemberton.

No one knew quite what had happened as the Blades' post-mortem began. Leeds cared not one jot as they gleefully mobbed each other.

Rees' challenge on Wallace left the keeper struggling with a leg injury. Substitute keepers weren't permitted at the time so Rees had to soldier on. He had enough about him at the start of the second half to touch an effort from Speed on to his post, but he could do nothing when Leeds took the lead after 65 minutes.

Pemberton fouled Batty wide on the left to concede a free kick. It gave Leeds the opportunity to push all their big defenders forward.

McAllister lofted the ball towards the back post. An over-reaching Rees could only get fingertips to it and the ball continued its arc out wide of the goal. Newsome was already plunging into a dive that took him nose-down into the turf beyond the post and he somehow managed to nod the ball back into the empty net.

Weeks earlier, when Newsome scored his debut goal against Tottenham, he had no idea what to do or how to celebrate. He promised himself that if he ever scored again, he would make sure he had a big smile for the cameras. His grin was as wide as the River Aire as he was mobbed by overjoyed team-mates.

Leeds appeared to have struck a decisive blow, but back came Sheffield to equalise within two minutes.

Nervy Leeds defending resulted in a corner, and they struggled to cope with John Gannon's flag kick. It ran out wide for Pemberton to cut back so sharply that Chapman was caught unawares as the ball cannoned into the net off his knee.

Shaking off the disappointment, Leeds forced themselves on to the offensive and Batty was unlucky when his shot was diverted wide for a corner.

The decisive moment came with 13 minutes remaining.

Wilkinson had brought Cantona on for a tiring McAllister and he was inevitably involved, heading a Speed clearance on into a yawning Sheffield half and chasing it down. Wallace, his socks round his ankles, closed in from the right as David Barnes' hacked interception sailed deep into the danger zone.

Despite Cantona and Wallace's attentions, Brian Gayle seemed to have everything under control, but he was distracted as Rees began to stumble forward. The ball reared up and caught Gayle on the knee, looping into the air. He attempted to nod it back to his keeper, but Rees was further out than Gayle realised and the burly defender almost took it out of his hands, his header looping over him and on towards goal. A sick grin contorted his face as he realised what he had done.

It was one of the season's most bizarre moments. All Cantona and Wallace had to do was raise their hands in celebration as the ball bounced apologetically into the Sheffield net.

Everyone of a Leeds persuasion was on their feet as the shackles came off. Cantona tried one of his party pieces, dancing through the Blades defence only for his shot from range to sail wide.

The bright sun had given way to drizzle as Sheffield tried to spoil Leeds' moment of triumph. Deane watched an effort slip past the post, but that was it: the referee's whistle sounded to end the match. Leeds had done their part of the job. They could only wait to see how Manchester United responded.

Manchester's rivalry with Liverpool was as bitter as that with Leeds. If the game had been at Elland Road, the crowd could not have been more hostile. 'Have you ever seen United win the league?' the Kop cheerfully jeered, reminding everyone that it was 25 years and counting since Manchester had won the championship. If Liverpool could not win the title themselves, extending Old Trafford's drought was the next best thing.

Recognising the desperation of the position, Ferguson felt obliged to recall Ince and Robson to revive his wavering midfield.

Robson restored some spirit, but it was Liverpool's Jan Molby who bossed the game. His team took the lead after 12 minutes with the first meaningful attack. John Barnes deftly fed Ian Rush's perfectly timed run and Rush slotted the ball inside the post as Schmeichel came off his line. It was his first goal against United in 24 appearances.

Midway through the first half, Robson dispossessed Molby with a fierce lunge and Ince's 25-yard drive beat Hooper only to strike the inside of the post before reaching safety. Mark Hughes twice drove over, and United were denied again when Bruce and Kanchelskis both found the woodwork in a single attack.

But the bite of earlier months was gone and Manchester were second best to a determined Liverpool. Ferguson knew long before the end that this was not to be his day.

Rush was taken off with a knee injury just before the half-hour to save him for the FA Cup Final. The change was nullified by the loss of Gary Pallister, who severed an artery in a foot, and Liverpool continued to press at the heart of the United defence.

Schmeichel saved feet-first from Dean Saunders, who then saw a goalbound shot blocked on the line by Walters. Schmeichel denied Molby and with three minutes left, the keeper turned a shot from Houghton on to the underside of the bar only for Walters to complete the scoring from the rebound.

In that moment, United were finished, their challenge over. Leeds could celebrate as 'Always look on the bright side of life' rained down from all parts of Anfield.

Ryan Giggs: 'I walked out to the coach afterwards and was asked for my autograph by a Liverpool fan. He ripped it up in front of me and told me United would never win the league. I was 18 at the time.'

The Leeds players and management had chosen to spend the afternoon in different ways.

Wilkinson stayed at home with Bill Fotherby, Mick Hennigan and their wives enjoying a Sunday roast, studiously ignoring proceedings at Anfield.

Strachan's strategy was similar. 'I went to the Hilton Hotel for tea with my wife and my two boys were watching it on a TV in the gym,' recalls the Leeds captain. He gave them strict orders not to tell him the score until the game was over. Wilkinson had given similar instructions to his family.

'I went home and I didn't have the telly on at all,' recalled Mel Sterland. 'I just thought what will be, will be. I found out by phone. The telephone rings and the voice at the other end goes, "We're champions." I thought I was being kidded. The champagne came out, the lagers came out, and that was it for a couple of days. I don't think I was sober for a week.'

John McClelland: 'I was out walking my dog because I thought, "I can't focus." I was 36 and a bad decision, just one decision, Fergie time, or a situation where Liverpool dominated for 90 minutes then Man United get a dodgy goal in the 93rd minute – that would have emotionally haunted me. I was 36 and so close to getting a championship medal and I would have had flashbacks. So, I thought, "Just don't watch it."'

'I had maintained all along that the race for the title would go to the final week,' said Wilkinson. 'Perhaps I had prepared myself for that scenario too well. When we were crowned a week early, I found it difficult to comprehend the impact of that result at Anfield. I conducted a thankfully brief television interview via the telephone. I admit, on that occasion, words failed me.'

One player who did watch the match was Tony Dorigo, the supporters' club's player of the year. He had travelled south to meet up with England, who had a friendly match in Russia just three days before the final game of the season.

'I managed to get a phone call from Howard,' says Dorigo. 'He was slightly slurring his words. He'd been on the sauce by then. He'd spoken to Graham Taylor and, if myself and David Batty didn't want to go to Moscow, it wouldn't be held against us. Graham was more than happy for us to stay and celebrate the title win. So, I jumped in a car and headed back to Leeds.

'It's surreal because you've done it all season and your whole destiny is hanging on this moment. You've gone through all these games and it hinged on something there and then. When Man U went behind, you didn't want to get too excited either. You're trying to keep a calm façade, but inside you're going like the clappers.

'When it happened, I didn't know what to do. I'm thinking, "What do I do now? Do I ring the boys?" If you win it on the pitch, you're with the team, so it's all quite natural, but this was surreal.'

ITV had sent a film crew to Chapman's house where he was watching with Batty, McAllister and Cantona. The cameras were trained on Cantona while Chapman acted as interpreter, which meant that he yelled very slowly in a French accent as a bemused Cantona looked quizzically on.

According to Martin Goldman, a director at local electronics company Cathay Corporation, a club sponsor, the players congregated later in their favourite haunt, the Flying Pizza in Roundhay, Leeds.

'The place was buzzing. Then, at about 11.30pm, Batty said to me, "We are going back to yours, we are still celebrating."

'I said to Adriano, the owner, "I haven't got enough drink for this lot, give me 25 bottles of white and 25 bottles of red." In the end, about 250 people came back to mine. It was unbelievable.

'I had a house with a swimming pool and a football pitch. Eric Cantona jumped in the pool with all of his clothes on.

He was pissed out of his head. We were playing football in the garden at 3am. The last to leave were Batty, Cantona, Gary Speed and Gary McAllister – at 6.50am!'

Leeds had one final match to negotiate, at home to Norwich. Strachan was presented with the championship trophy before a game which was a mere formality that had to be completed.

Wilkinson admitted it was 'very, very difficult' to rouse the team one last time but emphasised that they wanted to go out with a professional performance.

They did so in straightforward fashion, winning thanks to a first-half goal from Wallace. It was a wonderful solo effort, his run starting in his own half as he weaved his way through what seemed like the whole Norwich defence before slotting the ball neatly inside the far post.

Leeds had enough chances to have won at a canter but couldn't add to their score. Nobody cared as they went on a lap of honour, showing off the trophy to their exultant fans.

Wilkinson had done what seven managers since Don Revie had failed to do in the 18 long and dark years since Leeds' last title triumph. He was deservedly crowned Manager of the Year.

'Career-wise, it's the most fantastic day of my life,' he remarked. 'It's one of those old dreams coming true.

'When I was 24, I thought I had better become a manager because as a player I was a bricklayer's labourer. When I decided all those years ago that I wanted to be a Football League manager, I said my ambition was to win the league and European Cup. Even then, when I was young and stupid, you could grant yourself those liberties. It was like going into politics and saying to yourself you want to be Prime Minister.

'That Leeds team was a classic case of the whole exceeding the sum of the parts. That group of players were very honest and very hard-working. Their attitude was exemplary all the way through and that meant they really earned the success.

'In the end, we got there with a centimetre to spare but they thoroughly deserved that success. We had some very, very good players. Star players, in fact. But the team was what mattered, not the individual. Every member of that squad was committed to the team rather than his own agenda.'

Wilkinson's obsession with the team as the important thing rather than individuals ran through his entire career. 1992 was when that ethos had its greatest reward.

Blowing It

*Eric likes to do what he likes when he likes
and then f*** off. We'd all want a bit of that.*

4 MAY 1992.

Rubbish littered every yard of City Square, the last dregs of a party to end all parties. Bank Holiday Monday was quiet and peaceful after the previous afternoon's chaos.

Then, the square was transformed into a sea of yellow, blue and white as 150,000 people flocked to watch the Leeds United team parade the league championship trophy through the streets on an open-top bus.

'It's not until you get to these sorts of days that you realise how it feels,' said Howard Wilkinson from the top deck. 'Absolutely magnificent. Memories like these can't be bought. There'll never be another day like this.'

On the Sunday, Wilkinson had been elated, at the pinnacle of his profession. 'Look, Ma, top of the world.'

'For me, the end of the season is always an enormous relief – just a deep exhalation, because I always found it very wearing. By the time the end of the season comes, you're whacked, you're whacked. And I learned very early on that you've got to give yourself time away, you've got to get away from it, you've got to go and do whatever it is you do but get yourself separated and concentrate on what a holiday should be about, which is in the case of the football manager these days doing nothing, just giving yourself time to take a few deep breaths, get some sunshine and just clear your head.'

Certainly, Wilkinson took a few deep breaths that May.

But someone as professional and committed to the cause as he could not take it easy. Getting to the top was the simple part – staying there was a greater test, to maintain that excellence. And there was the new challenge of the Premier League and the European Cup to prepare for.

David Batty lobbied for a more expansive role while Eric Cantona made it clear that he expected to be a regular starter. Wilkinson accepted that hoofing the ball forward in the general direction of Lee Chapman was a tactic that had reached its sell-by date. A more cerebral approach would be needed in Europe and Wilkinson conceded as much when he conferred the captaincy on Gary McAllister.

There was another development that demanded a response, a change of thinking.

For years, there had been calls for action to prevent the use of the pass back to the goalkeeper to waste time. Despite some dramatic moments, overuse of the tactic made Italia 90 one of the most boring football tournaments ever – it was an easy way to frustrate a side chasing the game. A rule was now introduced making it illegal for a keeper to pick up a back-pass.

For Leeds, the ball to the keeper was not about time-wasting – rather it was used to get the ball forward quickly to Chapman. Chris Fairclough and Chris Whyte habitually passed back to John Lukic so that he could punt long out of his hands. At a stroke, the option was removed from Leeds' armoury.

Wilkinson was a massive critic of the rule change, claiming it would increase negative football rather than reduce it.

'If the new rule is the authorities' idea of how to foster better football, then the experiment will prove counter-productive,' he protested, arguing that it would have made more sense to 'stamp out the one back-pass that does reek of gamesmanship, the case when a goalie throws possession to a defender whose sole intention is to dally and then roll the ball back to his keeper.

'Instead of improving the game and forcing defenders to turn with the ball, FIFA have inadvertently encouraged more long-ball football where teams gain an even greater advantage by pumping passes behind the opposition defence. The new ruling will be manna from heaven to a coach working with his long-ball side. He will encourage his players not to pass to people but to deliver the ball into the space behind the markers and in front of the goalie.

'The clever coach will have deputed a goalie blocker or marker, whose first duty when the ball is banged forward will be to cut off the last line of defence and the opportunity for the keeper to fly-kick the ball upfield.

'With the goalie effectively marked, all the under-pressure defender can do is kick the ball to safety in the stand and so, with one pass, the opposition will be camped in the attacking third of the field ready to take one of their long throws towards a pack of tall players in the penalty area.'

Accusing other managers of long-ball tactics drew accusations of hypocrisy, but Wilkinson shrugged them off.

The change prompted the manager to focus his recruitment on midfield, widely acknowledged as United's strongest department. Arsenal's David Rocastle cost a club record £2m and Blackburn's Scott Sellars a further £800,000 to bring him back to Elland Road.

Some were concerned when Wilkinson showed no interest in the Southampton pair, centre-back Neil Ruddock, sold to Tottenham for £750,000, and England Under-21 striker Alan Shearer, who joined Jack Walker's big-money revolution at Blackburn for a British record fee of £3.6m.

Wilkinson was satisfied with his options up front, while in the centre of his defence Jon Newsome and David Wetherall provided cover for Whyte and Fairclough. Newsome had covered for the injured Mel Sterland at right-back in the spring and Wilkinson thought he could do so until Sterland recovered from an ankle operation.

Some felt that Leeds should have pushed the boat out, struck while the iron was hot, but Wilkinson was painfully aware that any transfer fees would come directly from the personal pocket of Leslie Silver. He respected him too much to take advantage. The chairman had already stumped up £900,000 to make Cantona's signing permanent and a bullet payment of £500,000 was due to the Frenchman in the autumn.

With a profit of half a million pounds and the promise of increased turnover from an improved television deal, Leeds were nevertheless one of the big spenders in the summer, only outdone by Tottenham, Liverpool, Aston Villa and promoted Blackburn.

When questioned about his dealings, Wilkinson claimed that he 'just wanted a stronger squad in depth'.

Rocastle was a like-for-like replacement for Gordon Strachan, amid fears the Scot would be forced to retire by the twin ravages of age and chronic sciatica. That made sense, with Rocastle considered one of the game's finest young talents, but the money pouring into football from the new BSkyB broadcasting deal had stoked price inflation. Silver was forced to dig deep to bridge the gap before the television cash started rolling in.

Wilkinson had made a career out of shopping for players in the autumn of their careers and wringing a last hurrah out of them, but Leeds were now at a whole new level. They needed the best to compete on the highest platforms. It was a significant new challenge.

The manager hoped for some easy pre-season preparations and a chance to try out some new things during the Makita Tournament staged at Elland Road. What he actually got came close to a civil war.

Wilkinson opted for a 3-4-3 formation in the first game against Stuttgart with Gary Speed sweeping up at the back. The experiment was a failure – Speed struggled to come to terms with the role – though Leeds beat the Germans 2-1 to advance to the final.

Batty's virtuoso performance against Sampdoria in that match is fondly remembered. The midfielder recalled, 'It was a friendly, wasn't it? So you could do what you wanted. It was just funny.'

Italian midfielder Robert Mancini did not get the joke, protesting vigorously at Batty's strong-arm approach. Insisting with a smirk that the Italians had started the rough stuff and 'got what they deserved', Batty relished making the afternoon a nightmare for the visitors. After an opponent threw a righteous tantrum, he gave a knowing wink to Gary McAllister.

When the referee politely requested that Wilkinson should withdraw Batty before he got sent off, the manager rejected the plea out of hand. 'He felt he had been upsetting one or two people and that the game would be easier to control without him around. It is my view that is exactly what Batty is paid for.'

It was hardly a good rehearsal for what might come when the real action started – Batty would have been quickly removed if he had tried such antics in formal competition – but the home fans loved his brazen aggression.

Cantona enjoyed a brief cameo as substitute but came stage centre the following weekend when Leeds faced Liverpool in the Charity Shield game at Wembley.

On a sun-soaked afternoon, a hat-trick from the Frenchman secured a 4-3 victory. Strachan came on for the final six minutes, his only contribution a cack-handed own goal that saw the ball pinball between his ankles before trickling lamely over the line.

Cantona had excelled. When he was on his game like this, he was undroppable. With Strachan still finding his fitness and Rocastle struggling to get accustomed to Wilkinson's demands, Wilkinson opted for a 4-3-3 formation that gave Cantona the freedom to do as he would.

Two goals from Chapman were enough for a comfortable start to Leeds' title defence with victory against Wimbledon and Speed's goal six minutes from time earned a point at Aston Villa.

Job done, thought Wilkinson, as Leeds settled into the form of the previous season, but then came a rude awakening.

They found themselves 2-0 down after ten minutes away to promoted Middlesbrough. Former Leeds starlet Tommy Wright featured strongly, setting up two goals for Paul Wilkinson and then making it 3-0 early in the second half. Another former Leeds man, John Hendrie, made it four just before the hour.

With 20 minutes remaining, Cantona pulled one back but it was too late. Leeds were humbled, their midfield in disarray and their defence pierced too easily.

The goal didn't save Cantona from the edge of Wilkinson's tongue – the manager chastised him for lack of effort and Steve Hodge claimed that the game 'signalled the beginning of his getting a reputation for not playing well away from home'.

Wilkinson consoled himself with the thought that there were often shocks in the early weeks of the season. 'You do get one of these displays now and again. If I knew why it was they occurred, I would do something about it.'

There were shocks for the other expected front-runners – Manchester United and Arsenal both lost their first two games – and Wilkinson exuded calm, sticking with the selection that had started at Middlesbrough for the game against Spurs.

Tottenham keeper Erik Thortsvedt had a nightmare, having a panic attack whenever the ball came near him. John Lukic hadn't found the new law easy to come to terms with, but Thorstvedt was something else, a shaking wreck by the end of the game.

Leeds took full advantage, surging to a five-goal triumph. Cantona's hat-trick was the Premier League's first as Leeds found themselves in the top three.

The Frenchman signalled that it would be his night early on, attempting a spectacular bicycle kick, and was then involved in Rod Wallace's opening goal. Seven minutes later, Cantona added a second. He ecstatically celebrated in a way that was entirely alien to his normal aloof manner, almost like a little boy in the playground.

Five minutes more and McAllister and Batty combined to steal the ball and set Cantona up with a perfect cross. He coolly despatched it before some more high-stepping in front of the Kop. He completed his hat-trick a minute into the second half, volleying home after a miscued header by Chapman. The Frenchman then set Chapman up for a fifth goal to round off a wonderful afternoon.

Leeds had flattered to deceive – it was a month before their next league victory as they slipped into mid-table.

Of greater concern was the way the team fluffed their lines on the return to European competition.

Leeds' first opponents were VfB Stuttgart, whom they had beaten in the Makita Tournament. They were expected to be stiff opposition on their own soil in the first leg.

Wilkinson gave Rocastle his first start. He wore the No 2 shirt but played in midfield alongside Strachan, McAllister and Speed. Batty acted as makeshift right-back.

Leeds played well in the first half, which ended goalless despite Cantona twice going close, one chip saved by the keeper and a header rapping the woodwork.

At half-time, Wilkinson replaced Rocastle with Hodge, and that's when things fell apart. Just after the hour mark, striker Fritz Walter scored twice for the Germans.

It was bad but still salvageable at Elland Road, and Leeds were trying to see out time when they conceded a killer third with eight minutes left. Andreas Buck capitalised on Batty's inexperience in defence, cutting inside and firing past Lukic.

Wilkinson was distraught. 'It was an absolutely crazy result. We were comfortable for 60 minutes.'

He told his players, 'I'm not sure if I should have changed it but one thing's for sure. When we get back to our place we lose to this lot over our dead bodies!'

Leeds had few genuine prospects of pulling off a miracle in the second leg. They would have become the first British team in European Cup history to overturn a three-goal deficit.

The atmosphere was initially as tepid as United's hopes, dampened by UEFA's demand of a capacity reduction of 6,000 for security reasons – only 20,457 turned out to watch the wake.

But the few that attended saw Leeds launch a comeback that evoked memories of famous European nights in the 60s and 70s.

The manager did his pre-match work well – Leeds were primed to go for their opponents' throats and they drew first blood after 18 minutes. Strachan pumped the ball to the edge of the area and Cantona cushioned his header perfectly for Speed to volley home.

The players poured forward in waves, as if believing anything was possible, but Leeds' kitchen-sink assault left a chink at the back and Buck scored after 34 minutes. That away goal meant that United needed another four to go through.

They seemed not to care – within four minutes, they regained the lead on the night when McAllister stroked home a penalty after Chapman was bundled to the turf.

Cantona netted Leeds' third as the second half reached its mid-point, clipping the ball over the keeper after reacting first when the ball ran loose. As the clock ran down, hopes began to ebb, but with ten minutes left, Chapman headed in from Strachan's corner and faith was restored.

One more goal would be enough. Leeds came again, camping in the Stuttgart half. The Germans, paralysed by anxiety, fell on to deep defence, bringing on reinforcements to stem the tide. Somehow, they held out and the result at 90 minutes meant they were through on the away goals rule.

It was a gallant attempt, as Strachan observed. 'You can talk all you like about Italian and Spanish football, but there is no better spectacle than a British team, going at it as we did against Stuttgart.'

There was an unexpected reprieve.

Club secretary Nigel Pleasants raised an objection 'after hearing a rumour that Stuttgart had fielded an ineligible player. I actually found out from a reporter who said he had received a phone call from somebody in Cologne, Stuttgart's biggest rivals, who told him they had played four foreigners that night. After more digging, it was found to be true.'

Jovo Simanic, a Belgrade-born defender, replaced striker Maurizio Gaudino in the 82nd minute, just seconds after the Germans introduced Swiss international Adrian Knup. With Serbian Slobodan Dubajic and Eyjolfur Sverrisson of Iceland both playing throughout, Stuttgart finished the game with four 'non-nationals' on the pitch, one more than allowed.

Pleasants checked the nationalities of the German squad and faxed UEFA 'for clarification'.

Stuttgart general manager Dieter Hoeness pleaded that putting on Simanic had been an oversight. Yeah? So what?

There was some speculation that UEFA would disqualify Stuttgart, but they opted to declare the result 3-0 to Leeds, the default score in such circumstances.

Leeds were elated by the ruling, though Bill Fotherby blustered, 'Rules are rules, and we think Leeds should go straight into the next round.'

Wilkinson agreed, declaring, 'If we'd done what Stuttgart have, I would expect to concede the tie. If this was the FA Cup and you had an ineligible player on your team sheet, you'd be thrown out.'

Stuttgart president Gerhard Mayer-Vorfelder pleaded for a 'merciful ruling' and got his wish with the tie deemed even and the clubs ordered to replay at a neutral venue.

Pleasants said, 'They should have been kicked out because they had broken the rules but we learnt that German television had put about £2m into the competition and Stuttgart were their last team in it. They ended up deciding on a third game. We asked for it to be played at Leeds because that's where the offence took place but, on the Monday, we got a fax from UEFA saying we needed to be in Barcelona on Friday night, giving us four days to sort everything out. It was crazy.'

The game was staged in Barca's 100,000-capacity Camp Nou. With fewer than 10,000 in attendance, the stadium resembled a graveyard, with local schoolchildren given free tickets to make up the numbers.

Leeds were rewarded for their good start when Strachan rifled in a long-range drive after 33 minutes.

United's lead lasted seven minutes, midfielder Andre Golke diving to head home at the back post. Lukic should have done better than to let the ball squirm through his hands.

The game remained level as it entered its latter stages. With 14 minutes to go, Carl Shutt was thrown on by Wilkinson to replace Cantona, who had been a passive bystander. Shutt said to Rocastle before he took the field, 'I'm going to f***ing score here, Rocky.'

His initial task was to help defend a corner, but when Dorigo cleared the ball long, the striker made ground against a sparse German defence. He appeared to have surrendered possession, but the ball fell loose and Shutt was on it again.

Strachan, storming forward into acres of space, screamed for the ball, but Shutt ignored him, eyes only for goal. He appeared to have taken it too wide, but his shot went through the keeper's legs, stunning everyone, including himself.

It was the pinnacle of Shutt's career, 'a great night', as he recalled. 'There weren't many fans but they made a lot of noise and it was great to reward them.'

Wilkinson let the players enjoy the night out in Barcelona after the game, but they couldn't get in anywhere until Barca striker Steve Archibald turned up to ease the way.

Back from the brink, Leeds' reward was a 'Battle of Britain' tie against Glasgow Rangers.

Cautious about potential disorder, the police directed that away fans were excluded from both legs. Leeds laughed the imposition off, although there was a moment of apprehension as they came out at Ibrox.

'Elland Road at that time was a cauldron,' recalls Wilkinson, 'but there is just something about the construction of [Ibrox]. I don't know whether they knew it when they were building it, but the acoustics were brilliant. Even compared to Wembley, it was an amphitheatre, a proper away ground. You felt you were in Rome.'

The hordes were stunned into silence after 66 seconds when Leeds took the lead. A corner was cleared to the edge of the area where McAllister timed his volley to perfection. It flew unerringly into the top corner past keeper Andy Goram, who could only stare with disbelief at the quality of the strike.

In the stony silence, there was a lonely cry of 'Yesssss'. It was Gordon Strachan's father, Jim. Rangers great John Greig came down from hospitality and asked him if he was a Leeds fan.

'Nah, I'm Hibs but I just f***ing like to see you lot lose.'

Boosted by the goal, Leeds played some decent football, hinting that they might score again. The tide turned when a Lukic error gave Rangers a way back after 21 minutes.

When Ian Durrant swung a corner towards the centre of the box, the keeper lost its flight in the floodlights and punched the ball into his own net.

Jon Newsome headed the ball against the frame of the goal and then Strachan saw a goal disallowed for offside, but Leeds were floored eight minutes before the break.

Ally McCoist scored his 25th goal from 21 matches after Lukic parried a David McPherson header.

There were no more goals, and there was every hope that Leeds could turn the tables at Elland Road.

The fans poured into the stadium in good heart, confident that they would cheer Leeds to victory.

Beforehand, Wilkinson told his players, 'This is a chance to succeed, not a chance to fail. It's like Frank Sinatra, saving his best song till last, this has to be about Leeds United giving it their best from the first whistle.'

Hodge thought a more cautious approach would have been better advised. 'I was always sceptical about going at teams in a helter-skelter way. I agreed with what Brian Clough had said years before when he explained that he'd wait until the last minute of the second leg to win a European tie. We only needed a 1-0 win to go through on the away goals rule so patience should have been part of the game plan.'

Leeds' optimism lasted three minutes – former England striker Mark Hateley gave Rangers a boost with a goal that rivalled McAllister's Ibrox effort for quality.

'The first thing that comes to mind when I think of that night,' recalled Wilkinson, 'is Hateley scoring a goal, the likes of which he had never scored before and never scored since. He took it down 25 yards out, half-turned and volleyed into the top corner. There was a stunned silence.

'Once that first goal goes in there is a whole different complexion on the game. It made us do everything we didn't want to do. It was like trying to carry a ton weight up the down escalator.

'When a team goes 1-0 up in the leg after having started out 2-1 ahead in the tie, it makes the game go a certain way. I have seen teams concede three or four goals in circumstances like that, but all of our lads kept going.'

Leeds' gung-ho approach allowed Rangers to play a waiting game, always ready to break quickly. Goram had an inspired evening, repelling everything that Leeds could throw at him. Cantona, Speed and Strachan were all denied.

Rangers were at it again just before the hour, with Durrant leading a breakaway. He fed Hateley, who moved out wide on the left before looping a perfect cross to the back post for McCoist to head home.

Leeds weren't yet ready to surrender and nearly fired back immediately but Goram turned Wallace's effort against the post after a scramble in the Rangers box.

Cantona flashed a shot past Goram following a Chapman header with five minutes remaining, but the game was long gone and a passive crowd accepted their fate.

It was a bitter pill to swallow and crushed Leeds' fragile confidence, as acknowledged by Wilkinson. 'The result was damaging. We were unbeatable at home that season but couldn't kick a can in away games. A win over Rangers would have possibly given us the lift that we needed. It might have been one of those moments that sometimes happen in a season. Had we won that match we would have had bigger games to look forward to in the Champions League and that might have driven us on to perform better. Instead, we were back to being on the crest of a depression.'

An anonymous Cantona had a miserable evening. When Wilkinson substituted him, the Frenchman stormed down the tunnel in rage.

It was a pivotal moment – Wilkinson was frustrated at the way that Cantona drifted out of games, especially away from home. He had always been sniffy about the manager's expectations of his defensive contributions, much to Wilkinson's irritation. He could just about tolerate that while Cantona was effective at the other end, but when the brilliance stuttered, he became convinced that Cantona was an expensive luxury at best, a liability at worst.

The Frenchman had driven a coach and horses through the team spirit that propelled Leeds from the Second Division to the title. The whole was far greater than the sum of its parts, but it threatened to unravel when Cantona emerged as the star. He was an aloof loner, more interested in showcasing his repertoire than adhering to the game plan. Wilkinson was acutely aware of this and knew he couldn't hold the camp together while Cantona was around.

To get the best out of the Frenchman, Wilkinson would have to change his entire approach and that went against the grain.

Leeds reverted to type, firing balls up to Chapman, whose partnership with Cantona was fractious. Rumours of off-field squabbles and an affair with Chapman's wife, actress Leslie Ash, became hard to dismiss.

Things came to a head at the end of October. Wilkinson was preparing the squad for a game at Queens Park Rangers and scheduled a meeting with the players in their London hotel.

Wilkinson beckoned Cantona over in the lobby. He was ignored. 'Can't have seen me,' thought Wilkinson to himself as he gestured again. Again, the Frenchman seemed not to see. Becoming irritated, Wilkinson tried again, only to be blanked once more. He saw red. 'You've asked for it now, my friend.'

As was his wont, Cantona arrived late and strolled nonchalantly into the team gathering. Dress code meant nothing to him, and he was wearing a big coat, a supercilious look on his face. As the players fell silent, waiting with bated breath to see what Wilko would do, you could cut the atmosphere with a knife.

'Good afternoon,' sneered Wilkinson, looking purposefully at his watch.. 'Glad you could join us.'

He produced Cantona's passport and whizzed it across the room in his general direction. 'I gather you want this. I know you've got your tickets, so get yourself a taxi, f*** off to France and don't f***ing come back.'

Cantona took a few seconds to twig that he was being asked to leave. He took the passport and left without a word. Wilkinson warned the players to keep the incident quiet, adding that the Frenchman thought he was bigger than the club and would play no part at Loftus Road.

Cantona was unavailable due to a 'groin strain', according to Wilkinson, despite scoring for France in a World Cup qualifier against Finland. Cantona's attitude left him speechless with rage. Frustrated by the refusal to apply his capabilities in the interests of the team, Wilkinson omitted him entirely from the squad to face Scunthorpe in the League Cup on 27 October.

Cantona returned but was dropped again after a League Cup defeat at second-tier Watford. United's winless streak stood at seven, and Wilkinson told the press he was off to a health farm for the weekend to recover.

He talked of signing Swedish internationals Patrick Andersson and Joachim Björklund to solve a defensive crisis, but they were unimpressed. 'It was midnight, and he was in his dressing gown,' recalled Andersson of their hotel meeting. 'He thought he could discuss my future in ten minutes, but he was wrong.' Despite being offered £1,500 a week, the pair dismissed the notion.

Wilkinson wasn't concerned. Sterland was almost ready to make his comeback, while Dorigo's return to fitness meant the defence that finished the previous season was reunited, with Newsome at right-back.

During the international break, Wilkinson said, 'I just worked with the back four all week. We tried to get two or three things clear in our minds, establish a positive attitude. Success can be a poor friend, a very effective enemy. We have to knuckle down, close ranks and dig in.'

Leeds had leaked 16 goals in seven games and had just two clean sheets in 23. Arsenal arrived at Elland Road having won their previous six games, and everyone anticipated the worst.

Wilkinson gave David Rocastle his first Premier League start in the absence of Cantona and Wallace. The midfielder said he had 'nothing to prove to Arsenal ... It wasn't as if I was a flop there.'

Leeds, on the other hand, had plenty to prove after a dreadful run. They did so in spades, emerging with a 3-0 victory.

Their cause was helped by an injury to keeper David Seaman, euphemistically described as to his 'side'. Chapman's studs punctured Seaman's scrotum.

Early in the second half, as Arsenal prepared to face a corner, Tony Adams signalled frantically to the bench that Seaman couldn't continue. Lee Dixon and Steve Bould joined in with 'stretcher' gestures, but Leeds ignored their opponents. Strachan clipped the corner to the near post where Whyte flicked it on, high and looping into the six-yard box. Seaman winced in pain as Fairclough buried his header.

August 1962 – 18-year-old Howard Wilkinson warms up for Sheffield Wednesday

August 1989 – Howard Wilkinson taking pre-season preparations very seriously

5 May 1990 – Lee Chapman has just headed the winning goal at Bournemouth to secure the Second Division title

5 May 1990 – Mel Sterland, Vinnie Jones and Chris Fairclough celebrate promotion after beating Bournemouth. The trio were stalwarts of a magnificent campaign

18 September 1990 – David Batty in front of the classic blue façade at Elland Road. Despite being often at odds with the manager, Batty was a key member of Wilkinson's midfield for five years

27 Jan 1991 –Gordon Strachan rages at a poor decision during the FA Cup-tie at Arsenal. Strachan was the man who transformed Leeds following his move from Manchester United

7 Dec 1991 – Physio Alan Sutton prevents Howard Wilkinson from getting too close to a match official at Luton

8 February 1992 – Eric Cantona appeals for calm before his Leeds United debut at Oldham. Within ten months he was off in a controversial move to Manchester United

26 April 1992 – Chris Fairclough and Gary Speed congratulate Jon Newsome on his goal at Sheffield United on the way to Leeds' title-deciding victory

2 May 1992 – Howard Wilkinson, Bill Fotherby, Peter Gilman and Gordon Strachan show off the Barclays championship trophy

8 August 1992 – Howard Wilkinson leads his team out at Wembley for the Charity Shield game against Liverpool

9 October 1992 – Howard Wilkinson with goalscorer Carl Shutt after European Cup victory against VfB Stuttgart at Camp Nou, Barcelona

17 September 1994 – Howard Wilkinson lets his frustration show during a 2-1 defeat at Coventry

14 October 1995 – Tony Dorigo slides in on Arsenal's Ray Parlour. The Aussie was one of the world's best left-backs in his heyday

17 November 1995 – Bill Fotherby and Howard Wilkinson pose with Tomas Brolin after a move which was later described as Leeds United's worst ever transfer

24 Dec 1995 – Tony Yeboah beats a stranded Peter Schmeichel to put Leeds ahead on their way to victory over Manchester United. Yeboah was the jewel in the Leeds crown in the mid-90s

9 September 1996 – It's a sad walk past the Leeds United trophy cabinet for Howard Wilkinson on the day he lost his job

Alan Miller came on for Seaman and within five minutes it was 2-0 after Chapman scored from Wallace's cross.

The outcome was in no doubt and McAllister added a touch of class with a superb third, chipped over the keeper. Three goals, three points, a clean sheet, and a victory.

'We'll tell in the next month whether it's all been worthwhile, or whether today was just one of those days,' said Wilkinson. 'It was very, very important to get a win, but probably just as important for us was the performance.'

Cantona's reaction to being left out was to demand a transfer, insisting on a move to Manchester United, Liverpool or Arsenal.

Fotherby scoured Italy, Spain and France for a buyer, but found no takers. It appeared that the uneasy marriage would continue.

Then there came a chance conversation with Manchester United chairman Martin Edwards. It's a little hazy as to whether it was Fotherby ringing to enquire about the availability of full-back Denis Irwin or Edwards trying to see if Leeds would be prepared to listen to offers for Chapman.

Leeds desperately needed a specialist right-back after Sterland broke down again, but Manchester had a greater problem.

They were struggling in eighth, with 17 goals from 16 games. When their summer courtship of Alan Shearer ran aground, Alex Ferguson settled instead for Cambridge target man Dion Dublin, only for the big striker to break his leg. Ferguson's immediate response was to pursue Sheffield Wednesday's David Hirst but there was nothing doing.

Ferguson was sitting next to Edwards when Fotherby called but said nothing. After Fotherby was told that there was no chance of signing Irwin and responded by confirming that Chapman was going nowhere, Ferguson passed a note to Edwards: 'Ask about Cantona.'

Gérard Houllier had tipped Ferguson off about Cantona's dissatisfaction with life at Leeds as the pair watched the Rangers–Leeds game. When Ferguson asked how good Cantona was, Houllier extolled his virtues.

Fotherby was taken aback by Edwards' request but agreed to go away and 'see what I can do'.

Wilkinson was open to the offer. A payment of £500,000 was about to become due to Cantona and there was a fear that the Frenchman would repeat his trademark disappearing act. Wilkinson told Fotherby to do the deal.

Fotherby went back to Edwards, saying that he could shake hands on a fee of £1.6m.

'We'll give you a million.'

'Can't do a million, but we can do 1.2.'

'A million is as far as we can go, Bill.'

There was a long pause at the other end of the line. 'Okay, but do you mind if we say you've paid £1.2m?'

'That's your business, Bill, say what you like, but we'll only pay a million.'

And with that, a landmark transfer was done – Eric Cantona became a Manchester United player on 26 November, with Ferguson proclaiming it 'an absolute steal'.

'I don't know why I love you, but I do,' became a bitterly remembered quote in the history of Leeds United.

'Sometimes people just move to a certain club at a certain time and become something they would never have been anywhere else,' said Fotherby. 'The fact it was Manchester United gave it an edge, I suppose, but they were the ones who made the offer for a player our manager did not want.

'Howard was an absolute perfectionist. He wanted his players to be disciplined and adhere to a certain team pattern. Eric just didn't fit it. Alex Ferguson gave him a free role and probably wasn't quite as strict with Eric as Howard would have been. Eric liked to play to the crowd. That wasn't Howard's way at all.

'All the conversations with Howard and Mick Hennigan were, "If you can get Cantona out of Leeds, get him out." On our training ground they would go through set plays and moves. Howard was very strict. He would say, "You, Cantona, you stand in front of the centre-half." Cantona would reply, "I don't do this" (and then spit). He wouldn't stand there and head the ball. He walked off. This made them want him out. He was causing a little bit of friction.'

With the benefit of hindsight, the decision seems bizarre. Certainly, Leeds fans thought so – losing their talisman, especially to their fiercest rivals, was too much to swallow.

'There was no alternative,' insisted Wilkinson. 'The reality was that Eric was in France because I'd left him out. So, he'd gone back to France, history was repeating itself. All his previous clubs had done the same. The club we bought him from had incurred considerable financial loss in a similar situation. He said he wasn't coming back to play for us.

'It wasn't personal at all. In terms of making money, the situation was that if we could have not got some money for him at that time, history said that we'd lose everything. We'd lose the million we'd paid for him, because he'd sit on his backside in France until such time as the situation was resolved by us saying, "Well, look, we can't go on paying his wages. We'll do what everyone else has done: let someone else have him and see if they can deal with any problems they may have."'

The transfer stunned the Manchester United squad.

Lee Sharpe was taken aback by the news. 'I replied: "Yeah, right – absolutely no chance!" I turned on the radio and there it was: total shock. Then there were all the media stories about his past and we were like: "This bloke's a total nutter, what are we doing?"'

Even Ferguson had reservations, admitting that he felt 'not quite panic, but uncertainty as to whether we had done the right thing'.

According to McAllister, his players sided with Wilkinson. 'The Leeds players have been a bit upset by some of the remarks Eric is alleged to have made since he left Elland Road. I'm personally surprised that he has declared he was never given the ball to his feet when he was with us. That, really, is an insult.'

Fotherby was adamant. 'Our fans were bothered. They were really bothered. But I would do exactly the same again.'

One man was even more bothered, as revealed by Nigel Pleasants. 'The commercial guy who looked after the shop nearly topped himself as he had just bought 7,000 Cantona Leeds shirts about a week before the deal. The shop was stocked out with unsaleable Cantona merchandise and they all went to kids in Africa in the end.'

Cantona, for his part, was blissfully content. 'It became more and more clear that he wanted to get rid of me. Wilkinson tried to explain his decision by peddling the rumour that I did not accept his authority and that he must be the only boss. To justify his version of events, he had to let me go to one of his greatest rivals for a sum which was far lower than my value. This was clear evidence that he was ready at all costs, even financial, to ensure that I left.'

The departure of Cantona eased dressing-room tensions, but Leeds were bereft of confidence and struggling to put results together. There was no revival, no recovery, just a grim battle to avoid a relegation that seemed to be inexorably creeping up on them.

Wilkinson was irritable, at a loss to understand how his champions had collapsed so badly.

As ever, Wilkinson allowed his frustration to spill over at the expense of Steve Hodge.

The midfielder got the sharp edge of Wilkinson's tongue when his temper flared during a friendly at Rotherham. He was one of the substitutes. Wilkinson's half-time tirade halted when he spotted Hodge behind him. He thundered, 'I'm talking to you as well! You're a part of it! Yawning in the background!' He turned back to continue his rant then paused, turned back to Hodge and said, 'You probably didn't deserve that, but you got it anyway.'

Hodge, when not playing, used to watch home games from one of the boxes behind the goal. After one such match, he waited there to get the scores from the other teams in the relegation battle. When he then walked into the team meeting, he faced more biting remarks.

'Here he is,' chimed Wilkinson, 'late as ever. This is what today's result means to him, f*** all!'

The team scraped enough points to keep out of immediate danger. A 5-2 victory against Blackburn on 10 April, courtesy of a Strachan hat-trick, was vital. It was also their final win of the season.

United's 17th-place finish was the lowest by defending champions since Manchester City were relegated in 1938. When one considers that City were just 16 points behind new champions Arsenal, you could make a case for Leeds making the poorest ever fist of things.

They were in danger until their penultimate game, when an own goal from Phil King earned a draw at Sheffield Wednesday and formally ended the threat.

It's unclear why Leeds did so badly, whether it was the disruption caused by Cantona, a failure to win away or the defensive uncertainty caused by the outlawing of the back-pass to the keeper. It could have been the instability caused by the unavailability of Mel Sterland – Wilkinson never resolved the issue, variously trying David Batty, Jon Newsome, Scott Sellars, Ray Wallace, David Kerslake, Chris Fairclough, David Wetherall, David Rocastle and Gary Speed in the role. Sterland was limited to five starts, and the chopping and changing created a lack of continuity throughout the side.

Even Wilkinson could not put his finger on the cause, saying, 'A combination of all that, really, a combination of all that.'

It wasn't all doom and gloom. Wilkinson was heartened by the progress being made by his youngsters. 'I think from around about October of this season, I became increasingly aware that some of the kids here were doing well and watching some of their games and watching them train, you start to nurture that little warm feeling perhaps that maybe you have got one or two half-decent players coming along.

'But you never know. All you can judge is what you are seeing at the time and then try and work out whether they are going to get bigger, whether they are going to get stronger or whether they are going to get more mature and fortunately most of them have done that, so during the past 12 months we have started off with a useful bunch and they have developed into a more then useful bunch.'

When asked about the way Leeds fell off the cliff, Wilkinson's eyes betray his sorrow. The championship should have been the start of it all, but in some ways it was the end.

For a man with reverence for footballing dynasties, it was too depressing for words.

'If you think about from the 50s in England, there have been four or five. Revie was one, Clough was another, Bill Shankly was another, Alex was another. And afterwards, if you look at the history, it's taken, when someone's moved in, it's taken a long time, and lots of managers for it to get back to anywhere near where it was, apart from Liverpool. Culture teaches us all. Whatever subject you want to talk about, in order, as it were, to become educated with regard to that subject or topic, where it involves people, culture is very, very important. And for me, those examples I've just given, the people going in were going into a club, which had a very, very strong culture.

'What happens, as far as I'm concerned, is when those coaches ended, if you like, and those legends ended, and the people they leave behind have become engrossed in, saturated by the culture that that person created. No matter what you do, you can't recreate that. And you have to recognise that that's going to be a problem. Was I aware of that when I went to Leeds? No, although I did know and understand how much, how important it is for the person who's in charge of anything, anywhere, anybody, that they have to represent what it is they want.'

In retrospect, was 1992 a case of too much, too soon?

'Yes … it was always going to be very hard to, as it were, maintain that. And then the other thing that was happening was that there were people coming into the game with loads of money. All of a sudden, we're not in keeping with the size of the club we were these days. What we'd done, created an expectation which came five years ahead of that group of youngsters that, you know, emerged later and went on to play for their various countries.'

Would he have traded long-term sustainability for the peak of winning the title?

'If you could have guaranteed me doing what it is I wanted to do, then yes, but you can't. I couldn't sit in the dressing room and say, "Listen, fellas, in order that we're going to be as good as we can be in five years' time, we're going to lose next week."'

Wilkinson, ever the pragmatist, struck while the iron was hot, took what he could and bided his time until the tide began to turn.

Kidulthood

*We were doing what we said we were going
to try and do, which were producing. There
were some very, very good young players in
our youth team, very good.*

FROM THE start, youth development was at the core of
Howard Wilkinson's ten-year plan.

'It was the big thing I wanted to make happen. We
combined with the local schools and that meant the kids could
benefit from living at Thorp Arch. Unfortunately for me, I
was not at the club when those youngsters started to come
through. When I left, I knew the club was 18 months away
from the Kellys, Woodgates, Hartes, Kewells and so on being
considered first-team regulars. It was a major disappointment
to leave, knowing what was ahead.

'In my final couple of years, the financial situation had
not been too healthy and we had to fill the team with senior
or older players. But I knew that would be rectified in time. It
was a case of being patient and treading water until the kids
came through. When that happened, I knew they would give
the club tremendous momentum.

'If we're going to make the best use of the children at our
disposal, the talented ones, the best way to do it is get them
all in the same school near to us. They can train with us in

the morning before nine o'clock and train with us after school after half past three. We can have an arrangement with the headmaster that some lessons they don't need, and so on and so forth.

'But what you've got to recognise is that the schoolwork … is just as important as the football work back at the club. What we're building is a culture and it's a culture similar to Leeds of old, similar to Liverpool of old, similar to Man City and so on. Now, it's a culture which actually creates, it shapes the people within it.'

Wilkinson's passion for youth development is undiminished, and there is no greater advocate in the game.

Only the great Don Revie ever achieved more success at Elland Road than Wilkinson, but he believes it was his influence over the youth set-up that had the greatest ramifications.

'When I took over there as manager in 1988, they signed 18 schoolboys. How many of those do you think were offered a professional contract? Just one. Out of 18. I was amazed. What are we doing, promising kids failure?

'There was not enough teaching going on, you know, in a round sort of way. What do I mean by that? Well, apprentices would come in, sometimes they'd have to clean boots, sometimes they helped the ground staff and so on and so forth and they were called apprentices. I thought, well, there's more to becoming an elite athlete than that, than just being able to perform. You can't train to be an Olympic 400 metre runner to win a gold medal and, as it were, just be someone who can run. There's lots of other things that have to be dealt with in achieving that sort of elite performance. We need coaches now, if you like, to recognise that they've got more than just the football aspect to deal with in terms of this individual, this youngster, recognising that he needs to take and should be taking ownership for his performance and understanding what goes with that. Through that not only will his performances improve but you'll start to recognise that things like diet, lifestyle, also actually comes into their head.

'I was determined there had to be a better way.

'We discussed a lot about the importance of ethos, mindset, education and development. We worked hard to create the right culture in which they would thrive.

'On the coaching side, I brought in Dick Bate first, and then Paul Hart. When they asked me what the job was, I kept it simple. "You teach the boys to play. I teach them to win."

'Towards the end of my time as Leeds manager, we signed seven boys as apprentices. Six of them played first-team football. It was a great generation.

'The idea was that it would produce enough players to sustain the club's continued success. Someone sent me the other day a list of those players who came from there and made it in football. Jonathan Woodgate, Ian Harte, Stephen McPhail, Harry Kewell, Alan Smith, Paul Robinson; they came through and made a very good team. It finished second in the league and got to a Champions League semi-final. I think that was one of the reasons the FA latched on to me in 1997.'

When Wilkinson arrived at Leeds United, the players were training on Fullerton Park behind the West Stand. Wilkinson was appalled and told Leslie Silver bluntly that the club needed a world-class, purpose-built facility to progress.

'I always felt you want the ground to be a special place. If you go into the ground every day, it's where you work. It shouldn't be where you work. You don't rehearse a show for three months on the Palladium stage. The Palladium stage is for the dress rehearsal and "we're on!" It's a magical place and you want the ground to be like that. That was just part of the move to Thorp Arch. That was a bigger idea given the game was changing, we needed to get in there now and put our marker down in terms of youth development and producing our own players, and if they don't play for us, let's sell them and let them play for somebody else. But let's get a training ground that says "excellence", let's get facilities that say "excellence", so that when people walk into them to work, the standards you require of the individuals are met by the standards in the environment.

'There was no attraction to Fullerton. We used to take them training on cricket pitches that let us use their outfield, we used to go all over the place searching for surfaces, training up at Horsforth in pre-season. All over the place just looking for somewhere different, somewhere where they wouldn't walk up them steps like they did at Fullerton and look at it and mutter, "Oh, what a sh*t heap!" Also, it's difficult when you're in the dressing room Friday morning, the floor's covered in muddy shirts and boots and everything else, and then you're back in there Saturday morning. I just felt it was far better to come into a dressing room that looks as if it's been waiting for you for a week.

'We eventually found the right location and built a new state-of-the-art training ground and academy.'

Thorp Arch, situated near Wetherby, 20 miles outside the city centre, was the chosen base for a new complex. When finished, the facility boasted new changing rooms, an indoor pitch, a swimming pool and a number of outdoor pitches. In 1994, the club moved training operations to the site.

Coach Peter Gunby, who moved to live on site with wife Maureen, was a crucial figure throughout. He took on the role of housemaster, taking care of the youngsters, whom he continued to look after until his retirement in 2000.

Gunby had become part of the furniture at Leeds since joining in 1980. He and Maureen oversaw the conversion of Bill Fotherby's house into accommodation for young players. He kept a tidy ship, insisting all residents respected the property and played their part in maintaining the standard.

It was during this time that he and Maureen moved into Fotherby's former Roundhay home. The property had 12 bedrooms and was used as lodgings by youth players, who were cared for by Gunby and Maureen.

Gunby's efforts in setting rigorous personal standards for young pros helped turn them into men and saw him fondly remembered by many stars of the game.

Wilkinson: 'Peter Gunby and his wife, two really decent, good people, family people, gave those lads that sense of being part of a family, but a family with discipline. Peter took it upon himself to inspect their bedrooms every morning. He'd tell them, it's not good enough. But they weren't washing cars or painting white lines or helping cut the grass or sweeping the stands. They were learning to be footballers and if they failed at football, they were learning that it wasn't the end of the world.'

Thorp Arch is one of Wilkinson's greatest legacies and was a cornerstone of the club's development for the next three decades, serving as a beacon of youth development in the English game.

He is rightly proud of the facility and was appalled when the club almost discarded it under the regimes that followed Leslie Silver.

In late 2004, with a financial implosion forcing the club to sell Thorp Arch to raise money, it was reported that there was a possibility that houses might be built on a portion of the land. *The Guardian* got hold of a document which suggested that if planning permission was granted, a developer could build houses or offices on the valuable land.

Wilkinson cautioned that losing the facility to residential development would have wasted a £30m asset.

Although United received £4.2m from the sale, the buy-back clause related only to a portion of the site, with the possibility of eviction from the first-team training pitches.

'It's got all the ingredients of the plot for a tragic novel: Leeds going from rags to riches and back to rags again,' said Wilkinson.

'A good youth development system and facilities gives the club some heart and soul. It's a home and with that goes a tradition of developing a culture and identity for the club. It's something which is part of the process to having professional pride and a sense of responsibility, and that's hard to do in rented accommodation.

'If you have aspirations to be a big club, it demands excellent training facilities. Excellence is about maintaining quality in all areas. I'm no expert but if you had to start that facility from scratch again, the land, the planning permission and to develop the facilities would cost possibly more than £30m.'

Wilkinson's brainchild became the envy of the Premier League. It nurtured a new generation of talent, the backbone of the team that catapulted Leeds to glory around the turn of the millennium.

Long-time United follower Neale Sheldon recalls how Wilkinson engineered the move.

'One of [Wilkinson's] main gripes was the fact that supporters could watch first-team training on Fullerton Park. When Wilko was at Sheffield Wednesday, he had concrete fences put up around a couple of the pitches at Middlewood training ground to stop people watching.

'Thorp Arch was ideal for Wilko as it kept supporters away from the players and supporters away from youth matches on a Saturday.

'Wilko used to go potty when he took players to various destinations to train in secret, only to find the odd supporter had found the location.

'During Wilko's time, I managed to get to most of the "behind closed doors" friendlies, which irritated him greatly. I even did match reports and line-ups.

'Leeds sent fringe players and a few reserves out into deepest West Yorkshire, miles from civilisation. Parsley and Whitlow had just joined and needed to get up to speed.

'I followed the team coach to the venue. Pete Gunby and Dick Bate were supposed to be in charge but Bate decided to go in his car and got lost.

'So, there's me and Peter Gunby on the touchline. Whitlow picks up a knock and Gunby says, "Keep an eye on them and get the sub warmed up whilst I get Whitlow to the dressing room."

'Just as I've got Ryan Nichols warmed up and got the ref's attention to get Nichols on, Dick Bate turns up. Dick was a Wilko man, through and through, Lilleshall, the FA coaches, badges galore, but in reality, once you got to know him, he wasn't a bad bloke. Now Dick didn't bat an eyelid as I was sending on Nichols as sub, he just asked what the score was, then it suddenly dawned on him. "Where's Gunby and Whitlow?"

'Now after the match Dick has phoned Wilko to give him a report, before going off on a scouting mission. Dick has told Wilko that he'd more likely get a better report off that supporter from Stoke that was at the match.

'The first team were in action that night and Wilko had spotted me in the West Stand car park and came out to see me. His words were, "I suppose you will be giving a match report about a private match to everyone now, like you do for all those other matches you have been to." Then with a snap of the fingers, his bland, sarcastic tone changed, and I gave him a blow-by-blow account of the match.

'Wilko was a very hard man to pin down character-wise, quite an intense person. I'd have a heated argument with him one week, then the next week he'd be nice as pie.

'Another bust-up with Wilko involved the fencing-off of Fullerton Park for junior Northern Intermediate matches. I took exception to Wilko announcing that he had had numerous complaints and had decided to put up chain link fencing to stop supporters from watching youth matches from the roped-off touchline. We were like monkeys in a cage having to watch the match through the fence.

'That was basically Wilko's way, his way or no way. I took this matter up with Peter Gunby, club secretary Nigel Pleasants, board members, but to no avail. Wilko got his way.'

While Wilkinson relied heavily on Bate, his chief lieutenant was Paul Hart, a United centre-half in the post-Revie era.

After five years at Elland Road, Brian Clough had signed him for Forest a year after Leeds were relegated.

Hart remembers Clough's man-management skills positively. 'Nobody was exempt from his bollockings, which brought the dressing room closer in case it was your turn the week after. His bollockings were fearsome, but they weren't in abundance. And when he gave you a pat on the back, you felt six foot taller.'

Hart was signed by Wilkinson for Sheffield Wednesday in 1985 and was a mainstay for two seasons. He became Chesterfield manager in 1988 and stayed for three years, reaching the play-offs before a fall-out with the chairman led to his sacking in January 1991. He started a sandwich business to make a living before Clough rescued him from obscurity, appointing him youth coach at Forest. He worked with Clough for a year before joining Wilkinson in the summer of 1992 to head up Leeds' youth development programme.

While he learned much from both men, it was Wilkinson's understated style rather than Clough's eccentricities that struck him most positively.

Hart was regarded as one of football's brightest young coaches and he played a major part in Leeds' brief but dazzling blaze of glory.

'People showed an interest in me because I fitted the bill, and I still do, for developing a football club,' says Hart. 'I'm a builder, not a buyer. I always say I don't need lots of money, just a fair crack of the whip. I can develop a football club from top to bottom, and I'm one of the few who can, I think.

'I came five years into it, so it was already well in place. Howard said to me at the time, "We are 37th in the league right now but I want our youth development to be in the top three in the country." I asked him if we could compete – legally – with the Manchester Uniteds and clubs such as that. He said, "Yes."

'The big boost for us was winning the FA Youth Cup against Manchester United, against a team that included a lot of the boys who played against Juventus the other night. From that we were able to get into parents' homes and speak to them about what we were doing and what we would be able to offer their kids. The club had also just won the league, so they knew that we were doing something right. I worked with Eddie [Gray] for almost two years bringing them through.

'Like the Manchester United youth policy, it was nothing slapdash, nothing fluky. Whatever else is said about Wilkinson, the legacy he left Leeds was immense.'

1993 was the embodiment of all that. Leeds' teenagers made it to the Youth Cup Final where they faced a highly talented Manchester United side, the much-vaunted 'Class of 92'. In their side were Gary and Phil Neville, David Beckham, Paul Scholes, Robbie Savage and Keith Gillespie, all future internationals.

Several youngsters had already made it into Wilkinson's first-team selections, but he was not yet satisfied with the number coming through. He told Hart that his goal was to create a conveyor belt of talent.

'Paul was a great coach,' says Mark Tinkler, a star of that youth side. 'People talk about the influence Eric Harrison had on the Manchester United lads. Well, it was the same for us with Paul. He was really disciplined and demanded discipline from his players. You knew you had to go out on the training pitch every day and work as hard as you could. It wasn't enough just to have talent. You needed to work on the other side of your game.'

The group, which yielded other future first-teamers in Andy Couzens, Mark Ford and Noel Whelan, was reinforced by the signings of Kevin Sharp and Jamie Forrester. The pair had stunned the FA a year earlier when they rejected offers from several leading English clubs before joining French club Auxerre.

'We were probably the first English youth players to go abroad,' says Forrester. 'Auxerre's youth academy was excellent, way ahead of its time. It was an amazing opportunity.'

'The two of us were on top of our game,' says Sharp. 'Leeds had just won the championship and they asked me to play in a reserve game with players like Rod Wallace, Lee Chapman, David Rocastle and Scott Sellars. I played centre-midfield and got man of the match. I was due to go on trial at Arsenal the following week but Leeds said, "No, you're signing." I went to Stuttgart with them and then signed when I got back.'

'Leeds weren't really promoting youth players at the time,' recalls Forrester, 'but they really stuck their neck out for us. And I knew a lot about Paul Hart from his days at Forest. He was an excellent coach – tough but fair – and it seemed like the right place to be.'

Whelan was one of several Leeds youngsters who had been on trial with Manchester United in his younger days.

'I remember them showing me around The Cliff, and we walked into the indoor pitch and they said, "This is our big hope here." It was Beckham. He was hitting balls at the wall – small circles, big circles, practising, practising.

'But for me, Paul Scholes was the real stand-out. It was his passing and distribution but more than anything, it was the way he would always find space, even when he had three or four bodies around him. He had all the time in the world.'

The England Under-18 squad that year was dominated by players from the two clubs. 'We were all good friends, good professionals,' says Sharp, 'but there was a bit of needle there too.'

'In my ignorance, because I'd only just started as a youth coach, I didn't even realise [Manchester United] had won it the year before,' says Hart. 'I didn't know how good they were until I went to watch them in the semi-finals and I thought, "Gordon Bennett! They're not bad, this lot."'

The two-legged final brought a grand reckoning. In the dressing room at the end, coach Eric Harrison questioned Manchester's desire, told them that Leeds had 'wanted it more'.

And so they had.

While the Leeds first team was fighting relegation, their Old Trafford rivals won the inaugural Premier League title by a ten-point margin, becoming champions for the first time in 26 years. A week later, 30,562 packed Old Trafford for the first leg of the Youth Cup Final.

Leeds won 2-0 with goals from Forrester and Whelan. 'I think it was a shock to their lads,' says Whelan. 'There was always a big hype about Man United's academy. They probably thought they would walk it, but I don't think they had met a team like us before. We ticked every single box that night and they couldn't live with us. We could run, we could play, we could fight and they weren't ready for it at all.'

Phil Neville was taking his GCSEs. He did not play in the first leg but an injury to John O'Kane saw him called up for the second leg at Elland Road.

'At that time, the rivalry between Manchester United and Leeds was unbelievable,' he recalls. 'I remember my dad took me to a Rumbelows Cup semi-final at Elland Road a couple of years earlier and I couldn't take my eyes off the crowd. I was only 14 and I was petrified. You could feel that rivalry and that hatred.

'It felt just the same for that Youth Cup Final. I've played Champions League games away to Fenerbahce and Rangers and places like that. The atmosphere at Elland Road that night was right up there in terms of feeling that noise and intensity and hatred. It's one of those moments in my career where I look back and think, "Wow."'

The start was delayed due to an unexpectedly large crowd. There were 31,037 at Elland Road. Hart recalls, 'The East Stand was still being built at the time but they opened it anyway and we got a huge crowd. That's more than 61,000 across two legs for a youth game. It was amazing, genuinely amazing.

'Before the game, I said to the players, "How much do you want this?" and they all wanted it so badly. So I said, "Okay, I need you to do this, this and this." And they did it – to the letter.'

The game was shown live by Sky, and despite their first-leg disadvantage, the pre-match coverage was all about Manchester, with comparisons to the Busby Babes.

'I remember sitting in the changing rooms, tapping my boots on the floor,' recalls Whelan, 'and all I could hear was the singing, the noise, the stands above us … even now, I get tingles just thinking about it. That build-up, hearing the studs, walking out through the tunnel, and then it was just like, "Wow!"'

Leeds dominated midfield, with Ford and Bowman scrapping for everything. 'There were some tackles flying that night, I can tell you that,' says Tinkler.

'We had a fantastic team but over the two legs, Leeds bullied us in terms of physicality and game knowledge,' says Neville. 'Noel Whelan and Jamie Forrester up front were fantastic for them.'

Forrester widened the aggregate lead after 11 minutes with a spectacular overhead kick from Whelan's flick-on. 'I don't think I'd ever tried even one of those before,' says Forrester. 'I don't know how many times I tried in the years after that but I never scored another one like that. It's a special kind of goal for any player to score. To do it in front of 31,000 against Man United, live on Sky, that was even more special.'

When Scholes pulled one back, he risked life and limb with his celebration. Supporter Niall M: 'I remember Scholes tucking the penalty away and coming right up to the Kop and putting his finger to his lips to supposedly quieten the fans. The atmosphere was raw.'

Almost immediately, Whelan flicked on another high ball for Matthew Smithard to make it 4-1 on aggregate.

'I think it's fair to say they had a more talented group than we did,' says Sharp. 'But we had some good technical players in our group, too. Overall, I think we showed more desire than they did and they had two or three weaker positions where we exploited them.'

Hart agrees. 'We were physical. We could play but we were physically strong. I don't think the Manchester United boys had seen anything like it. At one point, two or three of them were down on their knees. We were just too strong for them.'

Phil Neville accepts that Leeds outfought Manchester. 'Eric Harrison ripped into the lads. He was saying, "It's not just about having the skill. It's about overcoming adversity."

He felt we'd been outmuscled and bullied by Leeds over the two legs.

'It was a big learning experience for all of us. We had been talked about. We were in the papers a lot. Losing that final to Leeds was probably a big jolt.'

Tinkler, Sharp, Bowman, Whelan and Forrester were members of the England Under-18 European Championship squad that won the tournament on home soil, alongside Gary Neville, Chris Casper, Butt and Scholes.

'David Beckham just missed out, which tells you what a strong squad it was,' recalls Forrester. 'And although we'd been rivals in the Youth Cup, we all came together for England. There was a good spirit in that squad.'

Whelan tested that team spirit to the limit. 'I took great pleasure in goading them on England duty!' he laughs. 'Gary Neville wasn't happy, so I used to give him some stick on the bus. They didn't always take it very well. They thought they were the bees' knees. Well, you've just been beaten not once but twice by a very good Leeds United team.

'We knew the rivalry was there. We just knew it. You couldn't take away the fact. When you watched the first team – and we were ball boys – that tension with both sets of fans, that tension on the field with the two sets of players.'

Supporters still speak avidly about that team and their victory.

Andy W commented: 'Really shows the potential that having a great crop of young players can have. I was at both games and the atmosphere was incredible.'

In March 1995, Wilkinson invited Leeds legend Eddie Gray to support Hart.

'He shocked me,' recalls Gray. 'I was doing a bit of media work and he phoned me up and said he'd like me to come down to the ground. I said, "I hope it's not anything I've been saying about your team because I think I've treated them quite fairly."

'He said it was nothing to do with that, so I came down and him and Bill Fotherby were in the office and he said to me, "I want you to come back to the club and work with me and Paul Hart. I want players at this football club that get me off my seat and excite me."'

Gray was perfect – he had built a side around youth after Leeds' relegation in 1982 and the fans revered him as a god.

While several members of the 1993 side enjoyed decent careers, the side that lifted the Youth Cup again in 1997 produced bigger names. It was the culmination of Wilkinson's ten-year plan, emphasised by their lifting of the Northern Intermediate championship.

Hart worked the players hard. 'There was loads of running, boys were absolutely busted.' He set high standards and demanded discipline.

One of the stars of that team, Wesley Boyle, recalled, 'We had a great team, we were just winning every game from the start of the season. It was such a good crop of players. If we got injuries, there were people coming in. We played a great passing game out from the back, just total football. It was really enjoyable to play in. Everyone was good on the ball. We all knew what we could do.

'We had probably one of the best youth teams in the country. Every player was outstanding technically. It didn't take an expert to see Harry Kewell was going to be a great player, and Jonathan Woodgate was the other outstanding player in that team, but there were other good players from 1 to 11 and even the subs. We were beating teams every week – we only lost one game that season.

'We got plenty of fans to our games anyway in the league. They came to the away games, all over the country. For the Youth Cup there was a big turnout for all the games. The whole club wanted us to go and win it.

'Some of the first-team players would call into the hotel when we were having our pre-match meal. Derek Lilley called in once to wish us good luck. Senior players came to the games to watch us, there was plenty of support from within the club.'

The largest crowd the teenagers had played in front of, 6,649, were at Elland Road to watch them beat Crystal Palace 2-1 in the first leg of the final.

The Leeds players outwitted a Palace outfit that was out to bully them. They simply shimmied away from all the muck and nettles.

After four minutes, Kewell tricked his way through a slew of opponents before laying on a superb ball for Boyle to score the opening goal.

Lee Matthews headed in from a Stephen McPhail cross after 21 minutes to make it 2-0.

Leeds were in command until Paul Robinson fumbled the Londoners' first shot of the evening. Richard Harris finished from close range.

McPhail dominated midfield but was booked for a second time for retaliating against some rough treatment and Leeds were down to ten. Palace had been the greater sinners, with 24 fouls to Leeds' 11, but such is the way of things.

Hart kept his players relaxed before the second leg, reminding them to battle hard for 20 minutes and then let their ability show.

'We couldn't wait to get started,' said Boyle. 'We were very confident; we knew we were a better team going into the second leg.

'The fans were staying at the hotel, waiting for us in the lobby before we left for the game. It was great to see them all with their flags. The coaches of all the other age groups were there, wishing us all the best. We had great support.

'It wasn't the best of games, just a battle. There wasn't much football played. Palace got close to us, always someone on you.'

Matthews grabbed the decisive goal with eight minutes remaining, his 32nd score of a remarkable season.

When asked to name his favourite player, Hart chose Alan Smith, who wasn't even in the side.

'He was already at the club when I went there. Eddie Beaglehole, the youth development officer, said to me, "You should see this lad, Alan Smith," and he was right. Alan progressed through the ranks, then went to Lilleshall, which he didn't fancy too much.

'We were delighted – we wanted him near us at the club. The thing about Alan was that he has a good attitude. I have heard him compared to Allan Clarke. He has got one thing that Allan Clarke had and that is a nasty streak – I think that's absolutely essential for any striker.'

Wilkinson has every right to be proud of his work at Thorp Arch. He would build on that legacy during his time with the FA.

'When you look at these dynasties, they eventually finish up producing their own. Don did it at Leeds, Alex did it at Man U, Liverpool were doing it well before, in terms of once Shankly got in there. Nowadays, it's good to see the Chelseas and the Arsenals producing and other clubs like them. It was like when I was at the FA, we talked about an England team of the future and that was why we came up with this notion of academies, that one of the by-products of academies ... would be better players for England. And I think in the last four years, we've really started to see that take shape. It's good now, to see the team sheets and look at them and say, goodness me. And, you know, it is happening, that different way of dealing with the younger players from 7, 8, 9, 10 years old, in a structured fashion ... they're following our principles rather than wins.

'In the end, bearing in mind you're dealing with human beings, you will start to see this. It's like behaviour in a good school, it's a school that's got a reputation for producing people who achieve, do as well as they can do. But at the same time they also produce people who, as it were, are not just academically contributing to the welfare of their society but they also contribute in the way that they've been brought up in a manner which is that we've got responsibilities. It's not good enough to just be clever, you know, and that principle applies everywhere. Football now, it's really got a grip.'

A feature of youth development that always rankled with Wilkinson was the term 'apprentice'.

'When I became FA technical director, we changed the name symbolically from apprentice to scholar. And in the new training ground that set the model for academies I built an accommodation block. We had a partnership with the local school. The lads joining us lived in the accommodation block; the partnership with the local school meant that we spent more time with them whilst they were schoolboys. They weren't travelling, it was just up the road to school and the training ground was just outside when they opened the door. Then we got a housemaster in.

'We weren't made of money; we had a debt that was far greater than it should be. There were boys, players at Leeds, who were being talked to by other clubs and told what they could get. So, it was difficult, but I always knew that we'd come through it and end up with the finished product that we required.'

It wasn't all roses; while the 1993 triumph sparked hopes among the fans, the players struggled to make a successful transition into first-team football.

'The Man United lads got into the team and stayed there,' said Tinkler. 'We all made our debuts for Leeds but it always felt it didn't really matter how well we did. The senior players would always come back in. It was a bit of a blow.'

'It was incredibly frustrating,' admitted Sharp. 'We seemed to go down the pecking order at Leeds, whereas Alex Ferguson at Manchester United thought, "I'll get rid of Paul Parker because that will help Gary Neville. I'll get rid of Mike Phelan, Darren Ferguson and Paul Ince because that will help Nicky Butt and Paul Scholes. I'll get rid of Andrei Kanchelskis because that will help David Beckham." Robbie Fowler was scoring for fun at Liverpool, Kevin Gallen the same at QPR. Sol Campbell got a proper run at Tottenham and never looked back.

'With us, it felt like we were fighting against the manager. We did really well in the reserves and we were all making a few first-team appearances and it felt like we were going to be a part of the first-team squad moving forward. But then the manager brought in a lot of older players, like Nigel Worthington, Carlton Palmer and Brian Deane. Nothing against those players but it ended my progress, Mark Tinkler's progress, Noel Whelan's progress, Jamie Forrester's progress. Howard Wilkinson did really well for Leeds and is rightly respected for that, but I don't think he was a big fan of the youth players.

'I believe we warranted more faith than was shown. At that time, Jamie Forrester was up there with Robbie Fowler as one of the best finishers in the country. Mark Tinkler could play centre-half or midfield. His vision and passing were top-level. To me, he warranted being a regular, particularly in the Leeds squad at that time. He could have had a long career at Leeds. We all played games here and there but it never felt like the manager really believed in us, which is what you need to feel as a young player. We never got a sustained run.'

Such recollections are at odds with Wilkinson's and conventional wisdom. Whelan felt it was unfair to blame the manager. 'I look back and think everyone was given an opportunity. If you get to put the first-team shirt on, there's your opportunity. You've got to take it. We got games but you're playing at the very highest level, the Premier League. After here, how many of them went and played at Championship level? Not many. Sometimes, it just doesn't work out.'

Hart: 'A number of those lads did play in the Premier League for the club, but even though they were tremendous players, it was possibly a step too far for some of them at that particular time. That's said with no disrespect and it's the nature of the beast. Many of them found football careers elsewhere and that's really what it's all about.

'Howard was brilliant. He was always helping and supporting us. He was so interested in it all. It was all part of his ten-year plan, to make sure that by the end of the 1990s, we were regularly feeding the first team with players from the academy. We did achieve that.'

What they also achieved was bringing a true shiver of excitement to Elland Road, reminiscent of Don Revie's transformation in the early 1960s.

Supporter Chris L: 'I was there at Elland Road that night, stood on the Kop with my school mates, it was incredible. We all wanted those kids to go on and be our heroes for the next ten years. Forrester's overhead kick still remains one of my favourites and one of the best goals I have ever seen live.'

Whether his face showed it or not, revolutionising the youth set-up excited Wilkinson, who credits his success in that area as the reason the Football Association asked him to become their first technical director, though he wryly added, 'It might also have something to do with the fact I was a frequent letter-writer to them during my time at Leeds, always complaining about something.'

Remake/Remodel

*I'd like to make Leeds United a winning
team again and if that means changes, then
changes there'll be.*

HOWARD WILKINSON was acutely aware that he had
to do something to reinvigorate his squad after the most
dispiriting of title defences. He would need to bring in new
blood 'and inevitably, as is football, that may mean some
people going out'.

Mel Sterland was one of them, in the saddest of
circumstances. Still only 32, Sterland's chronic injury problems
decided things for him.

He had four operations to try to sort out his ankle issues.
Wilkinson offered him a lifeline – a new contract if he could
prove his fitness. It was a test that Sterland could not pass,
ultimately prompting his retirement.

Stripped of his football career, Sterland faced an abyss
of uncertainty and despair. The sight of his training kit,
unceremoniously bundled into a black bin liner, was a stark
reminder of his lost identity. An overwhelming sense of dread
washed over him.

In his autobiography, Sterland lays bare the darkest chapter
of his life. He was consumed by such profound depression that
he teetered on the edge of suicide.

At the crucial moment, a familiar voice reached out to him. It was his mother, her voice echoing in his mind, as vivid as the memories he held of her. She chided him, reminding him of the family that needed him – his wife, his two children. Her words saved his life. He began to see a future that held value beyond the football field.

Wilkinson took a long, hard look at the rest of his players and came to the conclusion that a number had seen their best days – Chris Whyte (32), Mervyn Day (38), Lee Chapman (33) and Carl Shutt (31) were moved on. Dylan Kerr, a relative youngster at 26, also left, unable to convince Wilkinson that he would ever be more than a bit-part player.

Chapman was unhappy with the way his time at Elland Road ended, saying, 'One of Howard's coaching staff asked me, "The manager wants to know if you would put up with not starting half of the games this season."

'I said I wouldn't be happy at all and was transfer-listed. I think it was wrong to let me go.

'I get on with Howard now, but he just made some wrong decisions. Then again, don't we all?'

With age appearing to be such an issue, Wilkinson's signing of 35-year-old Arsenal legend David O'Leary as Whyte's replacement came as a surprise.

George Graham had decided that the talented Irish World Cup player had no more to offer, but Wilkinson considered him the ideal man to school his young centre-backs, Jon Newsome and David Wetherall. There were mixed views among the fans – some complained he was 'too old' while others insisted that 'you play with your head' at the back.

The pursuit of young Dundee United striker Duncan Ferguson was more logical. At just 21, he had years ahead of him, and 28 goals in 77 games north of the border told its own story. He already had two full caps. Leslie Silver underwrote the bid of £3.25m tabled by Bill Fotherby to get the man

Wilkinson saw as Chapman's like-for-like successor. The fee would have smashed the £2m record set by the purchase of David Rocastle.

Fotherby found terms easy enough to agree with Dundee United but talks with the player's agent broke down. Rangers, sitting on £5.3m from the sale of season tickets, came swooping in to snatch Ferguson for a British record fee of £4m.

Wilkinson confirmed that the Ferguson deal was dead after five weeks of talks and that he had been 'actively pursuing other options. We finally decided over the weekend, as a result of speaking to Ferguson and to his lawyer and his agent, that the best thing would be to withdraw from negotiations and pursue other options.'

With time running out, Wilkinson switched his aim to Sheffield United's Leeds-born striker, Brian Deane, who had been linked with a potential move to Elland Road in 1991. The fee was £2.9m for a player with three England caps and the distinction of scoring the first ever goal in the Premier League.

'I never asked to leave Sheffield United,' recalled Deane. 'I felt that I was part of the furniture, but the club probably needed the money and the deal was too good for them to turn down.

'It is every lad's dream to play for his hometown club. I was no different and couldn't wait to get started. I had been linked with moves here and there but Aston Villa and Leeds were really keen.

'It was probably the right time for me to leave. I knew there was interest from other clubs. I turned down a move to Crystal Palace to replace Ian Wright, who'd gone to Arsenal. I'm a Leeds boy and going there seemed like going home.'

Deane was regarded as irreplaceable by Blades manager Dave Bassett – he had been Sheffield's top scorer in four of the previous five seasons. 'Priceless,' Bassett said of Deane before telling his board that the club would be relegated as a result, a prediction that came true ten months later.

Deane saw the move as a dream come true, the Promised Land. Nonetheless, he admitted that he felt under significant pressure. 'Leeds had won the title a couple of years before and I was signed to try to help them do it again. I was also a Leeds lad and still live there, so I had pressure from people I grew up with who loved Leeds. I never had that much expectation at Sheffield United, as I was young and making my name in football.'

Deane had a difficult time at Leeds and admits to never showing his best. 'I went in there thinking I'd made it a little bit. I was slightly cocky and stopped doing the basics I'd got right in Sheffield. I didn't look after my body as well and my game dipped.'

Leeds already had a replacement for Mervyn Day, signing Brighton & Hove Albion goalkeeper Mark Beeney in April. The fee of £350,000 saved Brighton from being wound up by HMRC.

'Manager Barry Lloyd told me that he had given Leeds permission to talk to me and that he wanted me to negotiate a deal otherwise the club were history,' recalled Beeney. 'I didn't really have much choice because if I'd have turned down the chance I'd have been unemployed anyway with the financial situation at Albion.'

The most important change that summer cost Leeds not a red cent and owed everything to a hunch by Wilkinson.

Gary Kelly, a 19-year-old Irish forward, was signed in July 1991 from Home Farm, the Dublin club that produced many Irish stars over the years, including Johnny Giles. Wilkinson's summer gamble transformed Kelly's career.

With Sterland crippled by injury, David Kerslake was brought in from Bristol City to replace him in March but he had been a disappointment.

Wilkinson looked at Kelly, struggling to make his way in the reserves, and had a sudden brainwave.

While Kelly was signed as a forward, Wilkinson saw something else and told him, 'Gary, all through pre-season, you're going to play right-back.'

'Nah, nah.'

'Listen, Gary, trust me, you're going to play right-back. You're good in the air, you're quick, you're mobile, you're agile and, I'll be frank, I think you'll be a better full-back than you are a wide player.'

Wilkinson's experiment was a success – Kelly's experience as a forward made him an intelligent reader of the game and gave him a keen appreciation of what attackers feared most, while his exceptional pace allowed him to recover dangerous situations and turn defence into attack.

Wilkinson spotted Kelly's potential – if he couldn't make things happen in attack, he could see what others were about to do and stop them.

'The following summer, he was at the World Cup,' recalls Wilkinson. 'He got picked in the World Cup team when they pick the best players in the World Cup. He was just your ideal player – high performance, didn't take up a lot of your time, because he was low maintenance. He came, trained, listened, asked questions, went home, turned up the next day, and reliable, massively reliable.'

Kelly took to the role so well that he was a fixture at right-back for the next decade.

Wilkinson had no hesitation in picking him for the season's opening game, against Manchester City at Maine Road, a ground where United's two previous visits had brought 4-0 defeats. O'Leary and Deane also debuted, while Noel Whelan was drafted in for his second game to partner Deane.

The new-look team took the pitch in a bold new away kit with shirts of wide blue and gold stripes. Another innovation was the Premier League's introduction of squad numbers. Kelly sported 22 and Whelan 25. O'Leary wore the No 6 shirt and Deane donned 9.

While Deane marked his debut with a goal, Leeds had a frustrating afternoon. They dominated but were unable to turn their dominance into goals, thanks mainly to a man-of-the-match performance by City keeper Tony Coton. While Deane toiled on a warm afternoon, denied the service he had thrived on at Bramall Lane, Strachan, Speed, Dorigo, Whelan, Fairclough and substitute Wallace all went close.

'When playing for Sheffield United,' said Deane, 'the lads would play the ball up to me at every opportunity whereas at Leeds, the midfield four liked to keep possession, pass the ball around and get it out wide. It took me a while to adapt.'

In defence, O'Leary gave evidence of his cool head and class in a promising partnership with Chris Fairclough.

John Lukic was rarely troubled, yet Leeds nearly paid for their profligacy in front of goal. City scored three minutes from time with their second chance of the game. The away end was silenced when Lukic could only parry Mike Sheron's strike and Garry Flitcroft netted the loose ball.

It would have been a crime to return across the Pennines empty-handed, and Leeds poured forward in search of an equaliser.

Deane appeared to have snatched it after pouncing on a muddle in the City defence. He was wheeling away to celebrate when referee Dermot Gallagher awarded a free kick for a foul on Coton that no one else spotted.

Yet Leeds were not to be denied – following an injury-time corner, Deane scored from a yard when Coton could only block Speed's point-blank header.

A midweek victory against West Ham suggested that all was right with the world, but then Leeds were blown away 4-0 by Norwich at Elland Road. Worse, O'Leary was forced to limp off after damaging his Achilles tendon. It would be six months before he returned to first-team action.

Further defeats followed at Arsenal and Liverpool, and even beating Oldham could not ease concerns that this would be another tough season.

Lukic was dropped for the Latics match after conceding eight goals in three games. It was the first league game he had missed since returning to Elland Road in 1990 and Mark Beeney was given the chance to stake his claim.

'I didn't think [Lukic] was performing as well as he could,' said Wilkinson. 'I thought that was having an effect on other people and I decided that the best solution was to have a change.'

The clean sheet suggested that Beeney and the new centre-back pairing of Newsome and Wetherall would have a big part to play in the coming months.

Leeds had not won away from Elland Road in 17 months and 24 attempts, but a trip to struggling Southampton on 11 September offered a golden chance to end the hoodoo.

Wilkinson said as much beforehand. 'If we don't win at Southampton, we might try what Don Revie did, by getting someone in to exorcise the evil spirits.' He had tried everything – changing routines, hotels, travel arrangements, training, anything he could think of to rid Leeds of their malaise.

'It was just like winning the FA Cup,' beamed Strachan after a 2-0 victory. 'I don't think there were celebrations like this when we won the league title. In terms of satisfaction this was one of the best wins of my career. Now we have broken this barrier there is no reason why we cannot start to become a power again.'

Wilkinson started with the team that beat Oldham and Strachan was a pivotal figure as they bossed the opening half. He should have given them the lead, but his shot cleared the bar by inches, while Deane's effort struck the body of Tim Flowers with only the Southampton keeper to beat.

There was some anxiety that failing to convert such chances would result in another frustrating away day, but Leeds finally broke the deadlock on 51 minutes. Deane got the goal, rising at the far post to glance home a Batty cross.

Southampton improved and put United under pressure, but Leeds held firm and sealed the win with a minute remaining.

Strachan robbed Francis Benali on the dead-ball line and waltzed past Simon Charlton before finding Speed, who crashed home his sixth goal in five outings against Southampton.

With the away jinx broken, it was a riotous journey home.

The performance suggested that the togetherness and determination of the championship season endured despite the squad changes. The combined benefits of tighter defence and a reinvigorated attack hinted that the title hangover might finally be over, but further change was in the offing.

During the 2-1 victory over Sheffield United which followed, David Batty seemed to be favouring his right arm, holding it by his side. Celebrating McAllister's goal after five minutes, Batty put his left arm around McAllister's shoulder, protecting his right. When a team-mate caught his right hand as he celebrated Strachan's winning goal, Batty winced and snatched it away. He got through to full time without letting on what had happened.

Messing about pre-game, Batty had injured his wrist in attempting to save a McAllister shot. He knew what Wilkinson would say if he had cried off and admitted what had happened, so he said nothing. The next day, Batty admitted everything to Alan Sutton and an X-ray revealed two broken bones in his hand. Batty was out for the next four games.

Wilkinson felt compelled to toy with his tactics in the absence of Batty and O'Leary, opting for a 3-5-2 system with Chris Fairclough joined in the centre of defence by Newsome and Wetherall.

The switch suited the players, making them tighter at the back and stronger in midfield, the overlapping qualities of Kelly and Dorigo offering width and verve.

Even when Batty was fit, Wilkinson persisted with the formation, appreciating the benefits. A few weeks later, he was left with little choice – Batty said farewell to his hometown club when Blackburn spirited him away in a whirlwind £2.75m deal.

The midfielder had been devastated by the inadequacy of Leeds' title defence. 'The bottom line is we were crap. We couldn't win away from Elland Road and I suppose that in itself put a big question mark against the mental strength of the squad. Whatever the reasons, the seeds of doubt had been sown in my mind and in Wilko's. For all I know, he had already decided that I might be dispensable.'

Batty came on as sub in a game against Blackburn in October and later that evening took a call from Rovers manager Kenny Dalglish, who told him that Fotherby had confirmed that Leeds would sell for the right price.

'Once I knew Leeds were prepared to let me go, I was on my way; I wouldn't want to play for someone who did not want me.'

There had been summer speculation of interest from Liverpool and Sheffield Wednesday and now Leslie Silver told the press, 'We have a large overdraft at the bank … and whilst our bankers have not put pressure on us, I have always believed in balancing the books. The offer for David Batty was too good to refuse.'

For years, Silver had bankrolled the club – he advanced a loan of £850,000 during the championship season to help finance Wilkinson's transfer spree. Despite his largesse, there had been a change in approach. He either could not or would not continue to foot the bill. Weighed down by a £4m overdraft and further loans of £1.2m, the club had little option other than to sell players to fund the transfers required to ensure Leeds remained competitive.

The ongoing development of the stadium by Peter Gilman's firm was a drain on funds, as was the somewhat curious purchase of Fotherby's house for £265,000. Both arrangements reeked of nepotism. There were rumours that Fotherby had been trying in vain for ages to sell the house and had duped Silver while Gilman was accused of exploiting his position on the board to secure lucrative contracts.

Many saw the sale of Batty as an extraordinary move, a bland acceptance that Leeds United had become a selling club.

Wilkinson had wrung significant value from the players he brought in during his first three years in charge, but they were past their sell-by dates, and some of the manager's recent forays into the market had been haphazard.

He took a £100,000 hit on the sale of Scott Sellars and a similar markdown when he moved David Kerslake on.

Only the sale of his crown jewels could raise the sort of money needed to buy the players Wilkinson now sought. Batty was deemed dispensable, despite claims that Wilkinson tried to persuade him to stay.

News of the transfer provoked a revolt among the fans, for whom Batty was a cult favourite. According to an *Evening Post* survey, keeping Batty was supported by 1,952 with only 114 favouring a sale.

The result might have warmed Batty's heart, but the deal was already done, and the first brick had been removed from the wall of the title-winning midfield.

The changes continued.

With O'Leary still out and Sterland seemingly never coming back, Wilkinson signed Sheffield United defender John Pemberton for £250,000. He had been a difficult opponent when Leeds played the Blades at the end of the title season, defying them at one end and then forcing an own goal out of Lee Chapman. Pemberton was nothing if not committed to the cause and the spirit he brought to every game compensated for his lack of skill.

David Rocastle's nightmare stay at Elland Road ended in December, just as he appeared to be making a fist of things. He moved on to Manchester City in a straight player exchange deal for England wide man David White, both players valued at £2m.

Despite loud accusations from some corners of the stadium that 'you don't know what you're doing', Wilkinson weathered the storm over Batty. His change of formation sparked an upward trend in performances – the Oldham victory at the end of August began an unbeaten run in the Premier League that lasted 14 matches. Leeds were second in the table and goals were flowing, with nine men contributing.

Momentum was halted when Leeds lost at Norwich on 13 December. The victory came against the run of play, with Leeds denied by the woodwork and a man-of-the-match display by goalkeeper Bryan Gunn.

As Wilkinson said, 'You can analyse and scrutinise but at the end of the day what made the difference was luck – we didn't have it and Norwich did.'

Chris Sutton gave the Canaries the lead shortly before half-time, but Strachan and McAllister set up Wallace for a sharp equaliser midway through the second half.

Leeds failed to capitalise and were punished in the final ten minutes – Efan Ekoku tucked home the rebound after Beeney saved his first effort.

The Whites retained second spot, but they were 13 points behind runaway leaders Manchester United after 20 games – the Old Trafford side had dropped just 11 points and looked likely to romp home in their defence of the title.

Leeds recovered to beat Arsenal at Elland Road, with McAllister taking a leading role. He opened the scoring and it was his searching free kick that forced a second-half own goal out of Tony Adams following Kevin Campbell's equaliser.

The Scot's performance gave weight to stories that a number of European clubs were interested in his services. Sven-Göran Eriksson was said to want McAllister at Sampdoria and the midfielder admitted speaking to Sevilla, but nothing came of the speculation.

The next four games were drawn and Leeds slithered down to fifth as the New Year began.

Among those draws was a goalless affair at Old Trafford against Manchester United.

Steve Hodge remembers how Wilkinson instructed his team to go man-for-man in the game. Hodge's task? To deal with the formidable Roy Keane, something he managed admirably. While the game wasn't great to watch, Wilkinson's tactics were spot on.

In the course of a heated battle, Hodge slashed Eric Cantona to the ground, something you could get away with in those days. A moment captured by a photographer for posterity followed as Cantona, wagging his finger in admonition, stomped over to Hodge, burbling, 'Hodgey, non, non, non, non, non.' He shoved his noble finger up Hodge's plebeian nose.

Hodge's impressive return to the team propelled them to an unbeaten streak against heavyweights Arsenal, Newcastle and Manchester United. However, as the players warmed up for a televised Sunday game against Blackburn, Wilkinson tapped Hodge on the shoulder. 'If Speed is fit tomorrow, he plays.' Hodge was out in the cold again.

Wilkinson's words weren't unexpected – Hodge had never bonded with a man whose style and attitude he didn't care for and he had always been a peripheral figure. He played a few games in the first weeks of the New Year but was then frozen out.

Hodge's Leeds career was on its last legs. Wilkinson delivered the harsh news in a meeting at the end of the season. 'We won't be offering you a new contract and you're free to leave.'

The sting of rejection deepened as Hodge drove back to his home in Nottingham; he discovered from a radio report that he, along with seven other players, had been released. It was a further blow to learn that Stoke and Southampton had shown interest in him weeks before, but Wilkinson had told them he was unavailable.

After being loaned out to Derby the following August, Hodge left for good two months later, signing for Queens Park Rangers for £300,000.

One man who had found his niche was David White. He was going nicely, scoring three times in his first eight appearances, but Leeds' form was patchy. The third of White's goals came in an FA Cup replay at home to Oxford as Leeds bowed out after extra time.

The visitors were stranded in the bottom two of the second tier and should have been easy meat.

Wilkinson ranted, 'Our front two gave us nothing. When I changed things, the game changed and we started to do a lot better.'

Brian Deane and Frank Strandli were the guilty men, both subbed off midway through the second half.

Norwegian Strandli had joined Leeds from IK Start early in 1993 – despite scoring on his debut against Middlesbrough, he never blossomed in his time at Leeds.

Wilkinson also berated Beeney, who had gifted Oxford their opening goal, and dropped him.

Wilkinson had sharp words for his defence. 'We committed suicide with some of our defending. We fell into every trap, snare and ambush Oxford set for us. I went through the wringer and we had only ourselves to blame for the defeat.'

Lukic, a fit-again O'Leary and Wallace were recalled for the Premier League clash with Liverpool.

Leeds stormed back to form. After ten minutes Wetherall swept home at the back post from McAllister's curling free kick. And it was McAllister who sealed victory in the closing minutes when Leeds broke away, sliding the ball low past Grobbelaar.

The victory took Leeds up to fourth and they built on it, losing just one of the following ten fixtures, including thrilling victories against Aston Villa, QPR and Tottenham.

Wilkinson had other things to think about. Following Graham Taylor's resignation as England manager, former Leeds boss Jimmy Armfield was asked to prepare a shortlist of potential replacements. Wilkinson was put forward, along with Terry Venables and Gerry Francis. Venables had been interviewed and was clearly the favoured candidate, but the overtly conservative FA was concerned about the Londoner's business reputation.

According to Venables, 'They blew hot and cold from one day to the next and kept Howard Wilkinson and Gerry Francis on a reserve list for the job, just in case. Behind the scenes, they remained very positive, but kept telling me that they had "difficulties" and asking me to wait a little bit longer, and then a bit longer still.'

Venables was eventually confirmed in post, but only after ten weeks of haggling. He had to accept a condition that he would forfeit the job should any allegations of financial impropriety be proven. He also agreed to being excluded from all the FA's commercial activities.

Venables was annoyed by the FA's insistence that he drop his court action for unfair dismissal as Spurs' chief executive. He vetoed the FA's plan to engage Wilkinson as technical director, which would give him responsibility for overseeing the national coaching network.

The Leeds board offered Wilkinson a new contract in a move calculated to deter him from pursuing the FA's interest. It would keep him at Elland Road until 1997 and made him one of the best-paid soccer bosses in the country with an annual salary of almost £300,000. Wilkinson was happy to accept, saying, 'There was never really any doubt that I would sign … but there was no need to rush things.'

At the end of April, Manchester United ended Leeds' unbeaten run at Elland Road. Wimbledon, Sheffield Wednesday and Liverpool chased Leeds down hard for fifth place over the closing weeks but the three-match unbeaten spell with which the Whites finished was enough to settle the outcome, even though the position did not carry European qualification.

It was a significant improvement but Wilkinson confessed to feeling disappointed. 'When you look back over the season, we had to scrap for almost every result. We have not had a Shearer, a Wright or a Cole to assist us, unlike our main rivals just above us in the table.'

The positive upturn allowed Wilkinson to put the previous season's nightmare behind him, but he wasn't fooled. He knew he needed a stronger squad and spent the summer working on it.

Out went Strandli, Newsome and Ray Wallace – the £1m received from Norwich for Newsome helped fund a transfer kitty.

Wilkinson's priority was in attack but his initial signings were in deeper positions, the Sheffield Wednesday pair, Carlton Palmer (£2.6m) and Nigel Worthington (£325,000).

The fees paid were typical of the over-inflated valuations of British players. Chelsea broke their club record when they paid £2.3m for Watford striker Paul Furlong – a couple of years earlier he had been operating in non-league football.

Manchester United's Brian McClair and Danish international Brian Laudrup were rumoured to be on the shopping list while Wilkinson admitted, 'Buying abroad can be cheaper and sometimes it is warranted.'

Neither signing delighted the Elland Road faithful – Carlton Bloody Palmer was considered a poor replacement for Batty, an ungainly figure, all arms and legs and gangly awkwardness, with a head that appeared too small for his body.

One manager claimed: 'He covers every blade of grass out there, but that's only because his first touch is so crap!' A pundit suggested that 'Palmer can trap a ball further than I could kick it.'

Wilkinson, like Graham Taylor before him, clearly saw something that others didn't. He said: 'Carlton was in some respects a bit like Vinnie. He's not shy and that's still the case. He was a good athlete, a very good athlete, and at that time he could play centre-back and he could play midfield. And I thought we needed legs and someone who could get about the pitch, but at the same time had a bit about him in terms of influencing others. When Vinnie was around, there were better players than him in the group, but the group recognised what he brought to the party personally. My view of Carlton Palmer was that that's what could happen.'

Wilkinson had recruited Worthington from his native Ballymena to join him at Notts County in July 1981 and then took him to Wednesday in 1984.

He appeared much older than his 32 years and was derided as 'not good enough', a 'typical Wilkinson signing', only brought in because of misplaced loyalty to old favourites. The manager was unapologetic.

Wilkinson had brought in Australian international Geoff Sleight as chief scout in place of Ian MacFarlane. He had first come across Sleight during his time at Mossley. Sleight took over as caretaker manager when Bob Murphy left in November 1976 but Wilkinson replaced him permanently a month later.

In his time supporting Wilkinson, MacFarlane arranged trials for Jari Litmanen and Sami Hyypia, the Finnish pair who found fame at Liverpool. Wilko didn't see enough in either man to offer a deal.

Sleight was sent to check out talent in Australia and South Africa, the *Yorkshire Evening Post* confirming the news that he had 'been running the rule over an international striker and a midfielder. In addition, United have their eyes on another overseas international, who I understand is a central defender-cum-midfielder.'

On 21 June, the *Evening Post*'s Don Warters reported, 'Leeds United revealed today that a £250,000 deal to sign a top South African striker has been agreed with the player and his club.'

Philomen Masinga was the man in question, an international who plied his trade with Pretoria's Mamelodi Sundowns.

Sleight was also interested in Kaizer Chiefs defender Lucas Radebe, though that information didn't leak into the public domain for several weeks. When it did, it was widely assumed that Radebe was an afterthought to keep Masinga company, much as Rod Wallace's brother Ray had been in 1991.

In reality, Sleight had been told by South Africa captain Steve Komphala that Radebe was the best player in the country. Wilkinson recalled, 'Geoff phoned and said he was impressed with Phil but that he had seen another player he thought was an even better prospect. That was Lucas. He said South Africa were going to Australia and he'd like to go and take a second look at him, so I agreed. As it turned out, Lucas didn't travel so it was a wasted journey but we still decided to sign him on Geoff's say-so.'

Radebe was apprehensive about the new world he had entered and worried that Wilkinson and Mick Hennigan didn't rate him. He was mistaken – Hennigan told the media, 'I really like Radebe. He's got the lot. Pace, strength, skill, vision. Of the pair, he's the one to watch.'

The £250,000 fee was a bargain to rival that paid for Gordon Strachan five years earlier, although the main beneficiaries would be Wilkinson's successors.

Having recruited the pair, Leeds had to contend with the vagaries of work permit rules. Nigel Pleasants led on the task, saying later, 'I don't think it is as stringent now, but you had to do things like provide evidence of three players you had tried to sign in the same position from this country before they would issue a permit.'

Masinga's application was straightforward, and he scored freely in United's pre-season preparations. For Radebe, it was a protracted affair, taking until the first week of September to resolve. By then, Masinga had already made his mark, scoring in United's defeat at Chelsea.

But it was Noel Whelan who was making the real waves.

He missed the opening-day goalless draw at West Ham but came on as a sub for the home game with Arsenal. Within minutes, his speculative 30-yard effort had found the net thanks to a misjudgement by England keeper David Seaman. The late goal was decisive in a game that had been drifting to a draw.

'The gaffer told me to go out and enjoy it, to play my normal game and not worry about making mistakes,' said the

19-year-old. 'I knew time was running out and when Gary McAllister flicked the ball on, it bounced up for a nice half-volley. I thought, go for it.'

Whelan started the next game against Chelsea alongside Masinga with Deane injured. Whelan and Masinga both scored to give Leeds a two-goal lead, but the Blues took the points after a second-half collapse.

Whelan had done enough to secure a place. He scored the winner at Palace and then gave an outstanding performance in a memorable Elland Road clash with Manchester United.

The home crowd was stridently passionate, jeering Eric Cantona every time he came near the ball, and rousing their favourites to greater efforts. The visitors' decision to force Leeds to attack the Kop in the first half elicited a chorus of boos, setting the scene for a fierce confrontation.

Whelan started well and looked razor-sharp, snapping into David May inside the first minute as the Manchester defender dallied on the ball. May was not the last man that Whelan would harry on a memorable afternoon.

Leeds forced a series of corners after White went close with a drive from the edge of the area. When Wallace earned another after 13 minutes, White whipped in a kick which Manchester struggled to clear. As it bobbled around the area, Wetherall scuffed a shot into the net.

He admitted it was a complete mishit and that he had 'closed his eyes and hit it'. That just made it all the sweeter for the fans.

Whelan had been on the sidelines at the time, having a dislocated finger repositioned, but was soon back to press the visitors, aided by Deane, who came on after half an hour for the injured White.

Whelan danced into the area and skipped around challenges as he bore down on the byline in the closing minutes of the half. He slid the ball across the box, but

Masinga and Deane fluffed their attempts and the visitors survived.

Peter Schmeichel furiously berated his defence for their slackness. When the resulting corner came in, Masinga nodded it goalwards to give Deane an opportunity, which he contrived to flick over the bar from barely a yard out.

Leeds had their vaunted opponents on the ropes and were sorry to hear the half-time whistle. Whelan was at it again at the start of the second half, receiving the ball on the left and slicing through the defence to hit the byline. His cutback to Deane was emphatically netted for 2-0.

Wilkinson was as animated as anyone had ever seen him, celebrating in front of the ecstatic fans.

Whelan, exhilarated by the results of his bravery, continued to be a thorn in Manchester flesh, displaying the kind of tricks and ball control that Cantona had once brought to Leeds' play. In one episode, he tormented three opponents in quick succession before being hacked to the turf.

Masinga manufactured a marvellous opportunity for Deane inside the six-yard area but the latter stumbled on the ball as he lost his bearings and Schmeichel gathered. Speed went close with a header and Leeds had their opponents exactly where they wanted them.

Such dominance couldn't last – with 12 minutes remaining, referee David Elleray ruled that Deane fouled Paul Ince in the box. Everyone in the crowd, including Sky commentator Andy Gray, knew that the foul was committed a yard outside the area, but the official would have none of it. The despised Cantona stepped up to halve the deficit.

That set up a frantic final ten as the visitors turned up the pressure. Lukic had blamed himself for two of the three goals conceded at Chelsea but showed that he still had much to offer in goal as Leeds withstood the storm to secure the points.

Leeds' first victory against Manchester United since 1982 was merited by a performance that demonstrated their enduring quality. The front three combined well, with Wallace a constant buzzing outlet in a midfield role. McAllister showcased his ability to run a game and Wetherall and Palmer formed a solid partnership in the centre of defence.

Whelan was at it again, his brace against Manchester City decisive as Leeds maintained their decent start. There were too many defeats for Wilkinson's liking (six from their first 17 Premier League fixtures, along with a Coca-Cola Cup exit against Third Division Mansfield), but Leeds were bouncing along in the top six, until a comprehensive 3-0 defeat at Everton in December dropped them to eighth.

Masinga had been missing since suffering injury at Sheffield Wednesday in September. He returned to the starting line-up a week before Christmas when Leeds were at Arsenal.

Leeds won 3-1 with Masinga scoring twice, denied a hat-trick by a fine save from reserve keeper Vince Bartram.

Again, Leeds threatened to kick on, but then went four games without a goal as their season teetered on the edge of collapse.

Whelan paid the price, dropped by Wilkinson after his form and goal touch deserted him. It was a disappointing turn of events after his heroics against the Manchester clubs. Whelan started just two games after the end of December as he slipped down the pecking order.

Master Blaster

I've never seen or worked with a finisher like him. He thinks he'll score every time he goes out there.

TONY YEBOAH towered like a colossus over everything Leeds United did in the mid-90s. He was the idol the supporters had dreamed of since Eric Cantona's betrayal in 1992.

Yeboah carried his god-like status lightly, as if he never truly appreciated how precious were his gifts. His shooting was a combination of beauty and awesome power, which owed everything to perfect timing. He was quick and light-footed, yet at the same time so squat and imposing that he was almost impossible to knock off the ball.

Bill Fotherby spent months searching for someone who might supply the goals that Leeds United sorely needed – his main interest lay in Serie A, but it was in Germany's Bundesliga that he struck gold in the shape of Yeboah. The main man at Eintracht Frankfurt, Yeboah finished as the country's top scorer in 1993 and 1994, netting 89 times in 156 games.

'I'd never actually seen him play but I watched him a lot on Eurosport,' recalled Howard Wilkinson. 'I remember thinking, "Christ, what a player!"'

Yeboah struggled at first in Germany before coming to prominence with Saarbrucken in a relegation play-off against Eintracht Frankfurt in 1989. Eintracht won the first leg 2-0 but Yeboah terrorised them in the return and scored a brace.

He joined Eintracht at the end of the season but had a difficult time winning the fans over. He was the club's first black player and experienced racism that was red in tooth and claw.

In 1994, he worked with Ghanaian Tony Baffoe and Senegal's Souleymane Sane on an open letter denouncing racism in German football. The letter was published in *Bild*, the country's leading sports newspaper, and advocated for a change in attitudes. It prompted DFB, the German football federation, and the Bundesliga to launch the 'Mein Freund ist Ausländer' ('My friend is a foreigner') campaign with each club's shirts bearing the slogan.

Anthony Yeboah House, a five-storey building adjacent to Frankfurt's train station, carries a massive mural of Yeboah's face along with the slogan, *Wir schämen uns für alle, die gegen uns schreien* ('we feel ashamed of all who scream against us'). It has become the symbol of tolerance and anti-racism, commemorating the cultural transformation Yeboah inspired in the city.

On 5 January 1995, Fotherby got his man – he agreed a loan deal until the end of the season with a £3.4m option to buy. Yeboah's fall-out with Eintracht coach Jupp Heynckes paved the way. Yeboah, along with team-mates Jay-Jay Okocha and Maurizio Gaudino, was punished for a perceived lack of effort with additional training. The three were suspended indefinitely after refusing to play against Hamburg.

Yeboah claimed to have rejected an approach from Bayern Munich before saying yes to Fotherby. The signing was long overdue with United scoring just 29 goals in their 22 games, and none in their previous three.

'I didn't know Leeds but when the offer came, I said, why not?' recalls Yeboah. 'I had a problem with the coach at Frankfurt, so I decided I want to play football, I want my peace.

'Initially, the trust from Leeds was not there so they loaned me for the first six months and had the option for another two years.'

Wilkinson was determined not to rush Yeboah, committing to getting him match-fit before playing him. It was three weeks before he was added to the bench and seven before he got his first start.

Alan Sutton recalled, 'When he first came, his fitness was awful. So, me and Mick Hennigan and the manager would be running around the track at Elland Road to get some fitness into him. I'd take him down this side and Mick would take him down that side, and then the manager down another to get some fitness into him.

'If you ever saw him in pre-season, you'd say he was useless. He once did his medial ligament, he told me, in a pre-season game and after that he played but he never went out of his way to do anything that was going to put him under pressure. But once that gun went, you saw a different person.'

Sutton asked him why he was not trying, arguing that pre-season was when players were trying to get fit.

'No, no, no, no, no, no, no,' came the reply. 'I got injured, my knee, no, no, I do not play pre-season, that's when I got injured.'

Sutton recounts a tale reminiscent of 1962 when John Charles exasperated Don Revie sideman Les Cocker.

On his first day in training, Cocker was stunned as Charles came out and started running gently on the spot, going through his customary warm-up. The Welshman stood there with his arms outstretched, shaking his wrists, while the other players stood open-mouthed.

'What the hell d'you think you're doing, lad?' asked an incredulous Cocker.

Unfazed, Charles replied, 'Juventus won the Italian league and cup on this stuff, boyo!'

Sutton on Yeboah: 'I'd take him running. We used to have a little thing, the Spofford railway track down between Wetherby and Spofford. All the runs I did were all measured out, time, everything. I remember measuring, it was, like, two and three-quarter miles right from where the old shed was up to Spofford and then two and three-quarter miles back. Everybody would run together out, and then everybody for himself coming back.

'Well, Tony, I mean, I must have been 40 years older than him, well, he's just dancing back, like, he's just dancing.'

'Hey, you're supposed to be getting past me.'

'Oh yeah, yeah, yeah, I'm all right.'

Noel Whelan was half a mile ahead, but there was Yeboah, bobbing along in a world of his own without a care in the world.

Wilkinson finally named Yeboah in his matchday squad on 24 January for the game against Queens Park Rangers. He was included on the bench, with Phil Masinga given the chance to stake his own claim as main striker. A week earlier, Masinga had come off the bench at the start of extra time in the FA Cup replay against Walsall. As the clock ticked down, Masinga netted three times in the space of nine minutes to settle what had become a bit of a struggle against the Third Division side.

Masinga was at it again, scoring twice as Leeds took a 4-0 lead against QPR. Wilkinson brought Yeboah on for the South African with six minutes remaining to get a feel of things.

'I knew German football and I understood it,' said Yeboah later. 'The style, the way they did things – in England it was totally different. I wasn't happy at first, not because I didn't like Leeds but because English football, the kick and rush, didn't come naturally to me. I didn't feel like I belonged there.

'But I played for the first time as a substitute against QPR, just a few minutes before the end of the game. There was no time to do anything but the crowd ... I don't know how much they knew about me or if they liked me but the way they treated me, the reception I got, was fantastic. It gave me strength. I was motivated. I thought, "You know what? I'll make this happen."'

Yeboah got another 20 minutes in the Cup against Oldham, again replacing Masinga, whose goal 12 minutes earlier had given Leeds a 3-1 lead. They were given food for thought when Carlton Palmer's own goal made it 3-2, but they held on for the win.

Draws followed at Blackburn and Wimbledon and then came a fifth-round FA Cup-tie against Manchester United at Old Trafford. With the game broadcast live, a national audience was curious to see what the newcomer had to offer.

It looked easy for the Red Devils in the first half, when Steve Bruce and Brian McClair were left free to score from corners. Knowing he had to change things, Wilkinson threw Yeboah on at the break.

They were a distinctly odd couple, stood on the touchline, waiting to come on – the coal-black Yeboah, stood calmly next to the pale-skinned, fidgety, grey-haired Nigel Worthington.

The sheer scale of Yeboah drew a huge gasp; his stocky build made him look more like a middleweight boxer or a bench press champion than a footballer. As he trotted on to the field, his unconscionably large thighs gave him a bow-legged look.

Within seven minutes, Yeboah had opened his Leeds account. He had already threatened with a header that had Peter Schmeichel scrambling to save. The goal when it came was untidy – unmarked at the back post, Yeboah bundled

David White's ball across the six-yard box into the net from a couple of yards.

There was a collective intake of breath at that point, but Manchester shrugged off the shock to seal the game with a third goal from Mark Hughes.

Yeboah was at it again during the week when Leeds hosted Everton. This time he was on from the start, playing alongside Masinga with Deane dropped.

Everton dominated the game, but a combination of powderpuff finishing and Leeds' fortuitous defending saw the game reach the final ten minutes with no score.

It was then that Leeds reaped the reward of fielding a natural goalscorer. Three Everton defenders conspired to mess up the clearance of a low cross and Yeboah finished expertly from six yards to wrap up the points.

Leeds drew blanks in their next two games but snapped back to form with a three-goal hammering of Chelsea at Stamford Bridge.

Yeboah was the difference, scoring after 25 minutes. Minutes later, McAllister doubled the lead, knocking the stuffing out of the home side.

Yeboah's second goal in the opening ten minutes of the second period was the icing on the cake.

Four days later, another Yeboah brace was the highlight of the 3-1 defeat of Leicester, and he delivered again at the weekend, scoring the middle goal in a 3-0 win over Coventry.

Such spectacular returns convinced everyone that there was a genuine world-class talent in the Leeds ranks. Certainly, his new team-mates were in no doubt.

'One morning I got a delegation asking to see me, Gordon Strachan, Gary McAllister and Gary Speed,' recalled Wilkinson.

'Can we see you, gaffer? Listen, we think you're being a bit hard on Tony, in terms of when we lose the ball. We know if he gets a chance he scores. So, we just wanted to tell you, it's not a problem when we lose the ball, that he's maybe not as committed as you might like. Because we know when he gets a chance he'll score and that's good enough for us.'

Wilkinson was not used to managing such exceptional talent, but he had to confess himself pleased with the show of team spirit.

'For me that was some of my beliefs being repaid because I always said to them, that being in this environment is a two-way thing. You are out there, you are doing it, you're feeling it, you're in the trenches, so your views are as valid as mine. So, if you feel strongly about something, for God's sake come up and say it. And so they did.'

A less assured leader might have interpreted the visitation as a challenge to his authority, but Wilkinson saw it as a manifestation of the lessons he had spent the previous seven years drumming into the squad.

And he could not complain at Yeboah's proficiency in front of goal, exemplified by his first-half hat-trick in the 4-0 thumping of Ipswich.

After four minutes, Yeboah took McAllister's pass in his stride, rounded the keeper and rolled his shot into an empty net. There was an inevitability to the way his instinctive shooting brought two further goals in the final ten minutes of the half. The only shock came when his second-half header was denied by the woodwork.

Wilkinson purred with satisfaction at the end, lauding Yeboah's finishing, and how it gave his side 'that little extra injection of confidence which comes from seeing good work produce something'.

A goal by strike partner Deane earned a surprise victory at Liverpool. He was the first Leeds player to score at Anfield since John Hawley in November 1978, and it was United's first success at the venue since 1972.

The news that Galatasaray of Turkey had attempted to lure Wilkinson away from Elland Road tarnished some of the lustre. Their offer of a £500,000 salary was appealing, but the manager shrugged it off, preferring to revel in the feats of Yeboah.

'My biggest desire is to make sure that Tony Yeboah remains at the club. I would not need to sign anyone in the summer if Tony agrees to stay on here with us. It is important from our point of view that Tony stays with us. I don't think he had a scoring chance at Liverpool but he still looked a very accomplished player. As I have said for the last 18 months, the only thing we really needed was goals and his arrival has tended to improve that.'

The Anfield encounter launched a nine-day proving ground for United's late push for a UEFA Cup spot. A home game with table-topping Blackburn and a trip to Newcastle were not for the faint of heart. Leeds were undeterred, drawing with Blackburn and then defeating the Geordies. Victories followed against Aston Villa, Norwich and Crystal Palace and a last-day draw at Tottenham secured fifth place and European football.

One man who would not be around for that challenge was Gordon Strachan.

Many expected the former captain to be groomed as Wilkinson's replacement, but that was not something that sat well with the fiercely loyal Strachan.

He spent most of the season in the reserves, nurturing the young talent that was emerging. His final appearance for the first team came on New Year's Eve after deciding to bring forward his retirement, citing a chronic back problem as the reason.

'I have decided I no longer have sufficient influence on first-team football at Leeds. I think, if you are a player with a club at any level, you must be an influence whether it be through playing ability or different qualities. If you are no longer an influence, it's time to move on.'

It was almost a valedictory speech – within weeks Strachan had negotiated an exit in order to work with old mate Ron Atkinson, newly installed as manager at Coventry.

Big Ron's offer of a position as his assistant and a promotion when Atkinson moved upstairs impressed Strachan. He was happy to take Coventry's shilling, though he took a cut on the salary he was on at Leeds.

'Sort of player-manager elect,' said Atkinson when pressed on Strachan's title. 'There were other clubs who wanted to do a similar deal with Gordon. One even tried to nick him from under our noses yesterday, but what swayed him was the guarantee that he'll take over.'

The lack of a competing offer from Wilkinson or the Leeds hierarchy rubbed the Scot up the wrong way.

'Gordon came to me for a chat,' said Wilkinson. 'We talked it over. He said he wasn't comfortable with being seen as my successor. It was other people making him uncomfortable at the club. I told him it didn't bother me, but the offer he'd been made at Coventry was too good and so he took it.'

'I looked at Howard some days,' mused Strachan, 'and the pressure he was under, and I thought, "I don't fancy this." But I like working with the players, and this way I can give the admin side the body-swerve yet still have an influence on the team.'

It wasn't the end of Strachan as a player; he was still playing for Coventry two years later as he turned 40.

Leeds supporters besieged the club's switchboard, but the deal was done by way of a free transfer in recognition of outstanding service.

* * *

Given the presence of Masinga and Radebe in the Leeds squad, there was an aptness about the club's choice of South

Africa as the location for their preparations for the 1995/96 season. There was a hero's welcome for national treasure Masinga.

'It was the sort of welcome that I've seen the likes of Pele and Maradona get,' beamed Wilkinson.

Masinga captained United for the occasion when they lost to his former club, Mamelodi Sundowns, in the pre-season United Bank Challenge tournament. They then missed out in a penalty shoot-out for third place against Benfica, but the trip was more about togetherness and team-building and that ambition was satisfied. The party went on to Germany for a friendly against Bayer Leverkusen, and the time away set the team up for a decent start when they returned home.

And when the gun went, it was all about that man Yeboah …

Boom, boom, went the Ghanaian on the first day, a towering second-half header at West Ham bringing Leeds back on to level terms after an early concession. That was a mere hors d'oeuvre, with Yeboah thrashing home a winner, catching a volley perfectly with his left foot as a cross dipped. Hammers keeper Ludek Miklosko never saw the ball until it was dropping down off the roof of his net.

'Christ, what a player!' thought the manager once more as Yeboah celebrated his strike. But much more was to come.

Liverpool were next up and represented a stern challenge. They had finished the previous campaign a point ahead of Leeds but hoped to do much better this time. The opening day had seen them defeat Sheffield Wednesday, the only goal coming from £8.5m new signing Stan Collymore.

The pre-game hype was all about what Liverpool would do to Leeds. Early on, it looked that way and Leeds were lucky when referee David Elleray chose to wave play on after John Pemberton clattered into Collymore in the first five minutes. Liverpool's penalty appeals were strident and they felt even more aggrieved when Collymore limped out of the game midway through the first half.

But the night would not be remembered for any wrongs done to Liverpool, imagined or otherwise. The lasting recollection would be the goal scored in the second half by Yeboah.

It came within five minutes of the restart as Leeds rushed on to the offensive. Tony Dorigo's hastily launched high ball to the edge of the Liverpool box was speculative at best, but Dominic Matteo gave the diminutive Rod Wallace the freedom of Elland Road to rise unchallenged and nod the ball on.

Yeboah had dropped off as though anticipating his team-mate's touch and came soaring into a strike from fully 30 yards. It was on his so-called weaker right foot but there was no hesitation or doubt in Yeboah's mind; he simply tore into the ball, catching it perfectly.

In a moment that became instant legend, Yeboah hammered the ball with merciless power towards the Liverpool goal. It crashed against the bar, back down against the line and then violently into the roof of the net, as if daring anyone to deny it.

As one breathless commentator noted, goalkeeper David James 'never saw it', groping helplessly at thin air, the ball finding the net with a 'whoosh' as a packed North Stand rose to acclaim the strike of a lifetime.

Yeboah wheeled away with a broad grin on his face, wagging his finger joyously in an 'I told you so' gesture. When the Ghanaian hit the ball, it certainly stayed hit.

'That's unbelievable,' said Sky commentator Trevor Francis. 'That's the goal of the season. If nothing more happens in this game, I shan't be disappointed, because I can say, I was here.'

The Independent's Guy Hodgson reported, 'Yeboah, showing no compromise to a range of 25 yards, thumped a right-foot volley that hurtled through the sultry air and crashed past David James with awesome ferocity.'

Wilkinson referred to Yeboah's 'whizz-bang' goals when he signed him, and this effort exemplified the phrase. 'It was a great goal,' said Wilkinson. 'A fantastic strike, out of the top drawer.'

The win took Leeds top of the nascent table, and they stayed there at the weekend, a 2-0 victory against Aston Villa delivered courtesy of goals from Gary Speed and David White.

They dropped their first points in a draw at Southampton and then lost at Tottenham. Yeboah scored Leeds' goal, a headed equaliser to David Howells' opener, but Teddy Sheringham's winner was even better, a cool nod from the back post across Lukic and in.

It was not the best of preparations for Leeds' return to European football. The draw pitched them against a star-studded Monaco side that had reached the last four of the European Cup the previous season.

Critics predicted a heavy defeat. United fans feared the worst but what they got was another masterly display from Yeboah.

His first goal came after three minutes – Yeboah calmly hooked home when the Monaco keeper spilled his attempted claim of Tony Dorigo's high ball as he crashed into defender Lilian Thuram.

It was 2-0 shortly after the hour when Yeboah cut in on to his left foot and curled a beauty inside the angle of bar and post.

Ten minutes from the end, Yeboah outpaced his marker to reach Speed's headed through ball and chipped over the keeper from the edge of the area.

It was a stunning hat-trick, and Yeboah jigged happily in front of the travelling Leeds fans to celebrate a clinical victory.

The supporters loved it, chanting Yeboah's name like a mantra throughout the game, rising to a crescendo every time he found the net.

'Tony's unique – not just different from other strikers, but better,' said Wilkinson. 'What you saw him do in Monaco, he did for four years in the Bundesliga. Routine goals from three yards, wallops from 20 or 30. Right foot or left, headers. The lot.

'As it turns out, Tony looks a bargain at what we paid. But it doesn't matter what he's worth because he's here now and we won't sell him. Maybe it's a case of right place, right time.'

Wilko felt that with Yeboah around, Leeds had it in them to recover the heights of 1992, but he was less pleased with the way that league form dipped – defeat at home to Queens Park Rangers followed by a goalless draw with Notts County at the same venue. The booing that resonated around a sparsely populated Elland Road summed up a highly uncomfortable night; United found it impossible to break down a County defence that kept a clean sheet for the eighth time in 11 games.

Just as Wilkinson was starting to fear the worst, United returned to winning ways at Wimbledon, courtesy of another hat-trick from Yeboah.

On any other day, Carlton Palmer's opening goal, curled sweetly into the corner from 20 yards, would have been feted, but he had to give best to the Ghanaian.

Yeboah opened his account with a tap-in from a couple of yards, only for the Dons to pull one back from a corner.

Yeboah tried an audacious lob from the kick-off that barely cleared the bar, but that was just setting his sights. As the clock ticked down for the break, Yeboah chested down a rushed Wimbledon clearance some 40 yards from goal – surely he would lay it off to a team-mate, keep the move going? Not a bit of it. He cushioned it on his left thigh, swerved away from the defender that came to meet him and smashed the ball unerringly into the roof of the net from the edge of the D. It was an extraordinary strike, every bit as effortlessly powerful as the one against Liverpool, and again via the right foot that was supposedly reserved for standing on.

The strike was later selected as the Premier League Goal of the Season, and at the time Yeboah agreed that it was better than the one against Liverpool. 'I think the latest one was the best because I had to work for the kind of opportunity I needed.'

Because he was a Liverpool fan, he eventually changed his mind and named the goal against the Reds as his best.

Yeboah put the Wimbledon result beyond doubt in the 74th minute, completing his hat-trick with a neatly taken left-footed goal from the edge of the area. It brought his season's total to ten and his aggregate since joining United to a remarkable 23 in 26 games.

A delighted Wilkinson told the press, 'He's world-class. He has all the assets one looks for in the ideal striker. The second goal was just awesome.'

Wimbledon manager Joe Kinnear said simply, 'You can't legislate for people like Yeboah.'

It wasn't just his goals that stood out that day – Yeboah was at the top of his form, gliding over the pitch and harrying Wimbledon defenders at every turn. He was superb, the most perfect front man in football.

Brian Deane waxed lyrical about the Ghanaian. 'He had dynamite in both legs. As a player, he was a phenomenal talent. One of the best things about Tony was that he'd score a goal out of nothing. He often took the pressure off others, because we knew he could save us if we needed a bit of magic. He was so good at centre-forward that I got moved out wide to accommodate him. But I was happy to play alongside him. I've played with some terrific strikers, but he's up there with the very best.'

People were surprised when Wilkinson went for conservative defence against Monaco in the second leg, and he nearly paid the price. John Lukic was forced to give a man-of-the-match performance to preserve Leeds' aggregate lead.

Lukic, nearing his 400th first-team appearance for Leeds, said, 'That's what I am paid for. It is a team game. It is not about individuals. The team gained the right outcome over the two legs. If people want to say nice things about me that's fine, but I am paid to do a job.'

The game seemed straightforward enough until the 23rd minute, when Sonny Anderson's free kick got Monaco moving. It took a wicked deflection off United's wall and left Lukic flat-footed as it soared into the opposite corner.

Leeds had little to offer other than long-range efforts with Yeboah blotted out by Basile Boli.

Back in the Premier League, goals from Yeboah and Speed were enough to see off Sheffield Wednesday in front of a 34,000 crowd. The result took Leeds back into fourth, suggesting they could challenge for the title. They were only a couple of points behind pacesetters Newcastle and seemed set to push on, but a dismal October set them back on their heels.

They began the month with Coca-Cola Cup victory at Notts County, but suicidal defending left Wilkinson seething. Twice United took the lead, but each time they allowed County to equalise before Gary Speed got the winner from range with seconds remaining.

Wilkinson was in frustrated mood at the end, reacting angrily when the media asked why his men had struggled to put the game to bed. 'Well, you do if you defend like clowns. We had enough of the ball to win two matches, but each time we got our noses in front we committed crucial errors. But at the end of the day we got the result and we scored three great goals into the bargain. There have been occasions in the past in this competition, when we have played better than we did tonight and lost.'

Worse was to come with two heavy home losses. Arsenal came away with a 3-0 victory and then PSV Eindhoven tore Leeds apart, leaving Elland Road with a 5-3 win.

After six minutes, Speed's glancing header hinted that Leeds would do to PSV what they had done to Monaco, but four minutes later, Luc Nilis tortured Pemberton with a tricky run before Rene Eijkelkamp, playing instead of injured Brazilian superstar Ronaldo, fired home.

Speed went off injured after 26 minutes and PSV capitalised, going 3-1 up before half-time.

With nothing to lose, Leeds went for it. Yeboah launched a revival three minutes into the second half by creating a goal for Palmer.

When McAllister equalised after 72 minutes, a famous fightback seemed on the cards, but Nilis, the best player on the park, scored twice to end Leeds' interest in the competition.

Defensive ineptitude turned United's 100th competitive game in Europe into a night to forget, and Wilkinson knew it as he trudged his way back to the dressing room.

'It was a crazy tie for a European game,' the manager told the post-match press conference. 'It could have ended 7-6.'

League form collapsed – Leeds won just two of their next eight fixtures, the slump dropping them to ninth, while they lost 3-0 to PSV in the return leg. Goalscoring had become an issue, although the one Premier League strike that Yeboah managed was enough to beat Chelsea on 18 November, while a hat-trick from Gary McAllister saw off Coventry at the end of October.

Masinga had lost his way, having played just two games, while Deane had to wait until the beginning of November for his first goal of the season. Leeds had become overly reliant on Yeboah for goals, and when he stuttered, so did they.

Wilkinson knew instinctively that he had to quickly find a solution to what was becoming a serious problem.

Brolin

He is a class player, and I believe he will
prove to be an excellent buy for Leeds.

THE PHRASE 'fake news' could have been coined to describe the modus operandi of Bill Fotherby's career. Over the years, Leeds United's headline-generator-in-chief perfected the art of drumming up demand for season tickets by leaking stories about his pursuit of world-class players where a deal was 'almost done'. Curiously, the stories disappeared like smoke just as the renewal date passed.

The most extravagant of his strokes came in 1987 when Diego Maradona was the name bandied about.

Fotherby ran into Maradona's agent, Jon Smith, and asked about a potential deal. Despite being told that there was 'no chance' and being quoted a price of £8m, Fotherby would not take no for an answer.

'Everyone thought we were crazy. But I got Smith up to Leeds and we had lunch in the box, looking on to the pitch.'

'Look, Bill,' said Smith, 'we're bringing him over for a match between England and the World XI. Now, the possibilities of him having a game at Leeds … what could you do?'

'We can fix it up with the city council, make it a big do. But it mustn't leak out.'

Fotherby gave assurances about confidentiality, but the story spread like wildfire. 'Soon we were getting phone calls from Buenos Aires about Maradona,' smiled Fotherby. 'Directors of Arsenal and Tottenham are asking: "Are you going for Maradona? Where have you got the money from?"'

To Smith's mind, there was no chance of a deal coming off, but Fotherby ploughed on regardless.

'What if we paid him a lot of money? And we arranged a big house, spared no expense, that sort of thing, what about then?'

'I don't really know. Maybe.' Smith thought no more of it.

Don Warters broke the story in the *Yorkshire Evening Post*. 'Bill rang me one afternoon at 2pm and said Leeds were speaking to Maradona's agent about signing him,' he recalls. 'My first reaction was to say, "You what?" Bill, though, was adamant so I spoke to my bosses.

'Our last edition of the day had already gone but the decision was taken to run a special. We didn't want the story coming out anywhere else.

'Fotherby definitely believed he had a chance. He was a great salesman and a journalist's dream, in many ways. He knew the value of publicity and wanted Leeds United in the local paper.'

In time, though, even the super-optimistic Fotherby had to admit defeat. 'Things just petered out,' he admitted. 'It was a real shame as it would have been amazing for Leeds United. But even though the deal didn't work out it still earned us huge publicity that I believe helped play a part in the rebirth of the club under Howard Wilkinson a few years later.'

The incident only seemed to sharpen Fotherby's taste for such intrigues.

Tomas Skuhravy, Ruben Sosa, Paul Gascoigne, Peter Beardsley, Darko Pančev, Andrei Kanchelskis, Ruel Fox, Martin Dahlin, Faustino Asprilla – there was an endless litany of stories that suggested Fotherby was 'due to fly out to Italy' or some far-flung part of the world. Not one of those deals came to fruition, although the interest in Asprilla was genuine and only foundered when the Parma striker fell foul of local police authorities.

The transfers that did go through generally involved more commonplace talent, such as the journeymen from Sheffield, Paul Beesley, John Pemberton, Carlton Palmer and Nigel Worthington, usually described as 'typical Howard Wilkinson signings'.

The manager had the promise of United's youth development system to look forward to (or fall back on, depending on one's viewpoint) but most of his recruits were intended to buy time while the potential came to fruition.

In that respect, Tony Yeboah was highly unusual, a bona fide, ready-made superstar.

Wilkinson's aim in such moves was always to strengthen the squad. He wasn't looking for idols, just constantly seeking the perfect mix, something that would bring the sort of consistency and success he found at the start of his Elland Road career.

That aim appeared at odds with the story that broke in 1995 about Leeds chasing Queens Park Rangers winger Trevor Sinclair, priced by Rangers at £10m.

Fotherby told the media, 'We are keen to sell a number of our players and then we will be in a position to bring other players in.' Fotherby refused to name the players, but David White, Rod Wallace and Brian Deane were rumoured to be surplus to requirements. How such trading could be seen as strengthening the squad was anyone's guess.

1995 was mainly about reinforcing at the back. Chris Fairclough left for Bolton in the summer, allowing the club to recoup the £500,000 they paid for him in 1989.

When Ian Harte was promoted to the reserves at his expense, Kevin Sharp left for Wigan in search of first-team football. The £100,000 fee was seen as a pittance for a 21-year-old who had once been touted as the next big thing.

With David O'Leary finally accepting the inevitable and announcing his retirement through injury in September, Wilkinson forked out a million to bring in classy Oldham defender Richard Jobson. Beesley had been a £250,000 snip in August, teaming up with former Sheffield United team-mates Pemberton and Deane.

The biggest headlines were made by a move for Swedish World Cup player Tomas Brolin, a signing that appeased celebrity-hungry United fans.

Brolin's arrival prompted the departures of David White to Sheffield United and Noel Whelan to Coventry City.

There was huge anticipation at what Brolin would bring to the party. Few tears were shed over the departure of White, an inconsistent force during his time at Leeds, but there was genuine sadness at the loss of Whelan.

He was a home-grown talent who appeared to have a glittering future. Even the £2m fee was little consolation, though it was more than a year since his last Leeds goal.

Out of all the players from the 1993 Youth Cup squad, it hurt the Leeds fans most to lose Whelan; and it hurt Whelan the most to leave.

Leeds supporters adore one of their own and Whelan was one of the best, his avid love of United driving his stock even higher. While he almost joined Everton in his younger days, there was no contest after Leeds made their interest known. He scored six goals in one youth-team game – 'Howard Wilkinson said I should have scored eight' – and was only 18 when he made his senior debut.

Such initial promise faded and Whelan sensed that he was no longer part of the manager's plans.

'I got a call from Howard Wilkinson on a Sunday morning to say: "Can you come in?" Straight away I was sitting in my bed crying because I knew it was happening. I went into his office and he said they'd accepted an offer and I walked out.

'All of a sudden, you don't have your family or friends around. It's an exciting time but a lonely time for a young man as well. I was on about £1,500 a week at Leeds but moving to Coventry tripled or quadrupled that.'

When asked the reason for Whelan's departure, Wilkinson was cagey. 'I don't want to talk about Noel.'

Later in his career, problems were well documented – there was trouble on evenings out and issues with alcohol. Gordon Strachan took the extraordinary step of putting Whelan up in his house, accompanying him to training and imposing a strict curfew.

Whelan's demons were not widely known when he was at Leeds, and he was seen as a kid with huge potential; but signing a high-profile talent like Brolin was considered a coup and the fans waited with bated breath.

Brolin came to prominence with Sweden at Euro 92, scoring a breathtaking goal to put Graham Taylor's England out of the competition. His displays with a team that finished third in the 1994 World Cup further enhanced his reputation.

Brolin enjoyed a highly successful time at Parma, with Cup Winners' Cup and Super Cup medals before it all went wrong.

The signings of Faustino Asprilla and Gianfranco Zola saw Brolin shifted into midfield and then he lost his way completely. He broke his foot playing for Sweden in a Euro 96 qualifier in November 1994. He struggled to regain both fitness and a regular place. The signing of Hristo Stoichkov from Barcelona the next summer undermined his chances – coach Nevio Scala thought Brolin lacked the fitness to play in midfield.

The move to Elland Road appeared to suit both Brolin and Leeds. A lengthy conversation with Wilkinson led him to believe he would get plenty of playing time.

'The first thing he asked me was, "How much money do you want?"' recalled Brolin. 'I said the important thing was not the money but what my position in the team would be. He then got out some A4 sheets of paper and started to draw things.

'I was going to be the spider in the middle of the web, pulling the strings in midfield. I was the one who was going to play the decisive pass to Tony Yeboah. Everything was great.'

Wilkinson was evasive when asked later about the conversation. 'It's too long ago for me to remember the detail of what we talked about.'

Despite the media hype, Wilkinson and Brolin both had reservations. Brolin asked for, and was given, a contractual safety net, allowing him to leave in the summer if he'd not settled.

Vinnie Jones once said, 'Wilkinson's view was if a player had to think about signing for Leeds United, then he should be told goodnight.' In this instance, he ignored his gut and agreed to the escape clause.

Wilkinson confessed that 'it implied a doubt in commitment both on his part and on mine'. He went on to say that he had not been strong enough in the face of Brolin's demands to play, had given way too readily. 'Brolin wanted to be in and foolishly I went along with it. What happened with Tomas wasn't his fault, it was my fault, a mistake.'

At the time the deal was done on 7 November, the transfer appeared to make absolute sense. Brolin won several domestic and international honours in Italy with Parma, the lasting memories being the way he tortured Arsenal in the 1994 Cup Winners' Cup Final and then cut through the England defence to score a goal in a million. Leeds supporters drooled over the news. It was seen as a sure thing, a gamble that would pay off in exactly the way that Yeboah had. If only …

Brolin made his debut three weeks later as a late substitute at Newcastle. A 2-1 defeat saw Leeds slip to eighth.

Brolin's first goal came in a 6-2 defeat at Sheffield Wednesday on 16 December. Leeds were 3-0 down after 25 minutes when Brolin's big moment came, in bizarre fashion.

He rose above a defender to nod down a floated cross before following in. Wednesday keeper Kevin Pressman got to the ball at the same time as Brolin and the ball squirmed loose. Steve Nicol's clearance hit a grounded and unwitting Brolin in the face and rebounded into the net. His celebration suggested that the entire thing was planned.

'We played like a team who were capable of scoring six or seven goals, but unfortunately we defended like a team who would concede six too,' commented Wilkinson. 'I have to say that we were a bit unlucky at times. I don't think we deserved to get beaten 6-2.'

The debacle saw Leeds continue to slip down the table. They were without a Premier League victory in four weeks and stranded in mid-table as they prepared for the Christmas Eve game with Manchester United. There were fears that a fragile Leeds defence would be easy meat for the Red Devils.

The Old Trafford side were on a four-game winless run themselves and a side in transition – Alex Ferguson's growing faith in his youth-team graduates was underlined by the presence of Gary Neville, David Beckham and Nicky Butt, though his selection dripped with class in the shape of Peter Schmeichel, Denis Irwin, Roy Keane, Andy Cole and the despised Eric Cantona.

Wilkinson dropped Lukic and brought Deane back for Andy Couzens, but he stuck with Brolin and Yeboah continued to lead the line.

Whether it was Wilkinson's pre-match remarks or the bitterness of the club's rivalry with the men in red is unclear, but Leeds ripped into Manchester in front of a crowd fully committed to the cause.

Despite the lunchtime kick-off, the afternoon was bitterly cold, and the low, bright sun caused a few problems. Manchester struggled to settle, and Leeds enjoyed much of the early pressure, reaping material reward within five minutes. Gary Kelly's long throw earned a corner from a panicky defence, and Nicky Butt then conceded a clumsy penalty for handball.

Steve Bruce's vehement objections were futile as referee Dermot Gallagher stuck to his guns and Gary McAllister coolly despatched the spot kick into the top corner.

Leeds kept pressing; Deane chipped on to Schmeichel's bar with the keeper beaten. Despite the best efforts of Keane to get hold of the game, there was passion about the Whites' play. Some fierce Manchester tackles went in, but Leeds were too determined and canny to get themselves caught, often just stepping away from the challenge before it bit.

Despite their confident start, Leeds could not increase their advantage and they paid for their generosity after 30 minutes.

Butt robbed Dorigo and Speed as they tried to play their way out of deep defence on the left. He fed Cole, free around the penalty spot, and his swept shot beat Beeney and sent shudders of apprehension around the stadium.

The goal came as a wake-up call and Leeds reclaimed their lead within five minutes.

From Kelly's defensive clearance, Brolin won a header at halfway, and from there it was all about Yeboah. Parker missed his kick and Yeboah was on it in a flash, running at Irwin and turning him this way and that as he advanced on the area. Out came Schmeichel, big and extended, to try and get something on it, but there was nothing he could do. Yeboah masterfully clipped the ball over him and into the corner of the yawning net. It was a master craftsman at work, and how the Elland Road hordes bayed their adulation.

After the interval, Leeds' football was more controlled and conservative, and they absorbed all of the visitors' random assaults. Deane made it 3-1 with 73 minutes on the clock, climbing to power home a header after combination work by Palmer and Brolin. The Swede's deft chip begged to be buried and Deane did not need a second invitation.

Manchester United never suggested they could alter the outcome and Leeds comfortably held out for the victory.

It was a rare good day for Wilkinson that drab December, when Leeds found both form and mojo. The defence looked unusually sound, while Kelly and Dorigo spent most of the game driving forward down the wings. Palmer's play was atypically effective and McAllister's finest work came in the opponents' half. Deane and Yeboah combined well and, while Brolin often drifted out of things, he buzzed around and made things happen, playing his best game in Leeds colours.

A scowling Cantona's only contribution was to serve as the target for the loudest and most prolonged jeering from the crowd – his feints were ineffectual, his passing distinctly off-key.

After an exhilarating afternoon, Wilkinson was surprisingly downbeat, telling the media, 'It's easier to look good against a team who come here to try and win the match. If we've got one thing to learn, it's when a game is difficult to be won, you have to be patient and make sure above all else that you don't lose it. But finding that balance doesn't come overnight.'

A bright future seemed to beckon for Brolin – he had a positive second-half chat with Wilkinson as the game was halted to allow an injured player to receive treatment. Everything in the garden appeared rosy.

He retained his place and scored again three days later as Leeds won 2-0 at Bolton, hinting that they would soon be ascending the table. Such expectations were dashed when they lost at Everton and then figured in a New Year's Day goalless draw with reigning champions Blackburn Rovers. A fog-bound Elland Road hosted a dour encounter with few goalscoring chances worthy of the name.

The following weekend, in the FA Cup at Derby, Leeds seemed set for more misery after falling two goals behind within the space of a minute at the start of the second half.

Depleted by a knee injury to Igor Stimac and the dismissal of Gary Rowett, a ten-man Derby side dropped on to massed defence to protect their lead.

Suddenly, Leeds smashed their way back into the contest. Wilkinson introduced Wallace, but it was Dorigo, exploiting gaps down the Derby right, who made the difference as Leeds hauled themselves back to parity by the hour.

First, his drive was deflected to McAllister, who laid the ball off for Speed to score from 12 yards out.

When Yeboah spotted Dorigo overlapping again, the Aussie's low cross allowed Deane to equalise as Leeds' tails rose even higher. A draw seemed the likely outcome until the dying seconds when route-one football put Leeds ahead. McAllister calmly netted after Wallace headed on Beeney's huge punt.

Yeboah added insult to injury with a fourth seconds from time, lobbing his 15th goal of the season.

Wilkinson likened the game to Leeds' entire season. 'Very good at times and occasionally horrible. Enough to drive any manager potty.'

Wilkinson had left Brolin out of the matchday squad, considering him unsuited to the 'heated atmosphere' he expected at the Baseball Ground. Nonetheless, with Yeboah and Masinga departing for duty in the African Cup of Nations, the Swede looked forward to building on the promising start he had made to his Leeds career as the countdown began for the business end of the season.

Lower Than a Snake's Belly

You've got to make this more entertaining.
Go out and put in an own goal, then two
of you lie down, let Liverpool go three up
and everyone can go home happy, saying
they'd been entertained!

THE AFRICAN Cup of Nations frequently creates difficulties for English football, given its timing: smack in the middle of the season.

Certainly, in 1996 it set in motion a chain of events that created an implosion in what had been a promising season for Leeds United.

Howard Wilkinson paid the price for strengthening his squad with recruits from the continent. Leeds would be badly depleted in the three weeks between 13 January and 3 February – Phil Masinga and Lucas Radebe were away with South Africa and Tony Yeboah, the jewel in the Elland Road crown, led Ghana's attack.

Wilkinson negotiated a six-week loan agreement with former favourite Lee Chapman, now 36 and plying his trade with second-tier Ipswich Town, as insurance. It was hardly the most inspirational of signings. Even the folks at Portman Road thought so – Chapman had only played twice for them all season.

Wilkinson dismissed the criticism, obstinately insisting that 'if I call on him, he will not let me down'.

As ever, Leslie Silver and Bill Fotherby left the footballing decisions to Wilkinson, but it might have been judicious to intervene. His recent record in the transfer market was questionable. Yeboah had been a gem, but Wilkinson had been equivocal about Tomas Brolin – had he lost his touch?

The minds of Silver and Fotherby were elsewhere that January. The chairman's thoughts had turned to retirement while Fotherby was busy finalising a four-year sponsorship contract with the computer firm Packard Bell. 'It is the second-largest sponsorship in the Premier League,' he boasted, the deal worth £4m over four years.

Fotherby had accepted a five per cent reduction in his salary to appease the outrage caused by the disclosure that he was the highest-paid director in the Premier League. In terms of quid pro quo, he was entitled to a five per cent cut of the sponsorship deal.

Though the supporters grumbled and moaned, Wilkinson's choice of Chapman as his saviour went unchallenged.

The manager was unfazed – with Brolin, Brian Deane and Rod Wallace all available, the manager believed he could navigate the month safely enough.

Wilkinson's calculations were thrown out by a suspension meted out to Deane, which kept him out of the Coca-Cola Cup quarter-final with Reading and a Premier League clash with West Ham.

Masinga hadn't yet left for South Africa and started up front against Reading – it was he who levelled after the Royals took an unexpected early lead.

Reading strung five men across the back and negated Gary McAllister's influence by man-marking him. They sprang out of defence to score after Carlton Palmer surrendered possession in midfield.

Masinga equalised five minutes later, shooting home from six yards.

Leeds went ahead just before the break with a Gary Speed header, but they never truly had the game under control and were thankful to emerge unscathed.

Chapman's second debut for Leeds came against West Ham. He started brightly, setting up an early goal, but was sent off after 25 minutes for elbowing Marc Rieper in the face.

Chapman was mortified, saying, 'I was hyped up for this game and I'd just made a goal for Brolin. I've seen what happened on TV and it seems I did make contact with Marc's head with my elbow. The referee sent me off for intentionally elbowing him, but I'd never, never do something like that deliberately. It's very unfair.

'At worst, it was a clumsy challenge. It's so unfair because there was no intent to make contact. All I saw was the ball, it wasn't a red-card offence.'

Wilkinson was in denial, saying, 'I've known Chappy for many, many years. I know there is no way he would try to elbow someone. If that is what it looks like, it must have been purely an accident. He's very upset because it was a big day for him. When I've seen the TV re-run, I'll decide whether it's worth sending a tape to the referee.'

Brolin added a second goal to wrap up the three points, but Chapman's dismissal meant he would miss three games, though he could play against Liverpool the following week at Anfield.

Wallace and Brolin were deployed either side of Chapman in a system that was notionally 4-3-3 but more often drifted into 4-5-1 in a one-sided game.

As one paper reported, 'Brolin spent the game looking for a role to fill, Wallace a pass to collect and Chapman some way of convincing Wilkinson he has an ageing portrait in his attic.'

The formation might have made sense with a goalscorer supreme like Yeboah at the business end of things, but Chapman was by now a blunt instrument. He was yet to score in the current campaign and had managed just two goals in 1994/95, one of them while on loan at lowly Southend.

Neil Ruddock headed Liverpool into a lead on the half-hour and the Reds were dominant. They had to wait 30 minutes for a second, but then they were given the perfect opportunity. A penalty was awarded for Gary Kelly's professional foul on Rob Jones and the full-back was dismissed.

Robbie Fowler converted the spot kick, and Andy Couzens was brought on for a labouring Chapman as Wilkinson went on the defensive. He shouldn't have bothered – Liverpool added three further goals and ran out comfortable winners.

The manager's post-match comments that the dismissal significantly changed the course of the game were rose-tinted.

'Fifteen to 20 years ago he would have been one of those footballers who would probably have gone through their entire career without once getting sent off.'

Wilkinson should have been more concerned with his own prospects rather than Kelly's. Twice in the second half there were ironic cries of 'Wilko for England' from the Leeds end.

Days earlier, the manager had been interviewed by the FA for the new position of technical director. There was speculation that he was in the frame to replace Terry Venables, who had announced that he would quit as head coach after Euro 96. Kevin Keegan was favourite to succeed Venables, but bookies quoted Wilkinson at 8/1 for the job. He rejected the technical director role but that night at Anfield he could have been excused for reconsidering, so poor was his side.

There was a falling-out with Brolin, Wilkinson frustrated at the Swede's refusal to obey his edict regarding defensive duties.

Playing out wide exposed Brolin's twin flaws: a lack of fitness and a weight problem. So he came up with a plan to force the Leeds boss to move him back to the centre of midfield. 'I was going to be piss-poor against Liverpool.'

It worked – Brolin was the worst of a bad bunch and started only one more match before being consigned to the bench.

'Everyone thinks I was rubbish all the time at Leeds but there you can question the journalists,' insists the Swede. 'Against West Ham I scored both goals and was voted man of the match. The fans were singing my name. The papers wrote that I was a success. After the Liverpool game the Swedish papers wrote that I was rubbish. And they were right. But nobody – nobody – asked me why. How the hell can you go from being a success to being a disaster in one week? And, as I wasn't picked any more, everyone just assumed I was rubbish.'

When asked whether the board pressurised him to select Brolin, Wilkinson conceded, 'Well, to a degree, you know, I could sense that people were saying that, but the manager has to do what the manager thinks is right.'

Defeats followed at Nottingham Forest and Aston Villa. Brolin failed to even make the bench at Villa despite the threadbare nature of the squad, so furious was Wilkinson.

He had only 15 players available but had little hesitation in deciding that Brolin should be the one omitted. Seventeen-year-old Alan Maybury made his debut in a selection that included 20-year-olds Rob Bowman and Andy Couzens in defence while Mark Tinkler (21) came off a bench where Andy Gray (18) kicked his heels. Rumour had it that Brolin's only duty was to help carry the kit basket into Villa Park.

Unsurprisingly, Villa won 3-0.

'It was a question of seeing who was available and where I could play them,' commented an unrepentant Wilkinson. 'I thought the team would do better without Tomas. He was concerned at the amount of defending he would have to do and he said he might not be too good at it. I made the decision and he accepted it.'

United fans were beside themselves at what was going on – just when Leeds should be pushing on, they seemed to be falling apart. Questions were asked about transfer dealings and the quality of the squad. People liked the idea of bringing players on from the youth team, but they were not the short-term answer. It would be folly to pitch them in wholesale without proven players around them.

McAllister and Speed still had much to offer in midfield, but the journeyman nature of the rest of the squad was a cause for unrest.

With the return of Yeboah, Masinga and Radebe, there was some light at the end of the tunnel but even then there were issues. The two South Africans were due to catch a plane the morning after the African Cup of Nations Final, ready to play in the FA Cup against Bolton. The triumph of Bafana Bafana put an end to those hopes and Wilkinson was far from happy.

'Given the importance of the Bolton cup-tie,' he snapped, 'the least we were entitled to was for the players to be home on Sunday. We pay their wages. They have, in effect, been on loan to South Africa.'

With Pemberton, Dorigo and Jobson on the injured list and Ford and Beesley suspended, the squad was threadbare. Wilkinson's mood wasn't improved when he discovered Yeboah was carrying a thigh injury.

As it transpired, the freezing weather and six inches of snow on the Burnden Park pitch forced a second postponement of the Bolton game.

Yeboah marked his return with a goal in each leg of the Coca-Cola Cup semi-final against Birmingham as Leeds secured a place in the Wembley final.

It wasn't the easiest of passages – Birmingham rose to the occasion, particularly in the first leg at St Andrew's.

Former Leeds men John Sheridan and Chris Whyte were in the opposition ranks, but it was the little and large striking partnership of Steve Claridge and 6ft 7in Kevin Francis that offered the biggest challenge.

With a thunderbolt of a shot in the first half, Francis gave Birmingham a lead they held for half an hour.

Then Yeboah stepped in, equalising with a low angled drive and later forcing a second when his goalbound effort was headed past his keeper by the unfortunate Whyte.

Birmingham also played their part in the second leg at Elland Road – after Masinga wasted three early chances, the Midlanders found their feet in a goalless first half.

Six minutes after the resumption, City had an opening; the ball reached Ian Richardson ten yards out with just the keeper to beat, but Lukic blocked his shot.

That was the Blues' big chance – within two minutes, Masinga got the first goal. Yeboah's shot was deflected to McAllister, whose effort was blocked by the keeper and Masinga was perfectly placed to slot home the loose ball.

The die was cast almost immediately when Yeboah scored with a scissors kick.

When Kelly brought down Sheridan, Birmingham were gifted an opportunity to make a game of it. Blues fans weren't hopeful, having seen their men miss 17 of their previous 25 penalties. Claridge kept the sequence going, hitting the foot of a post.

Brolin saw his first action in a month when Wilkinson gave him the final six minutes as substitute for Masinga and Deane made it 3-0 two minutes later.

Wilkinson: 'It's a dream come true for me. Everyone wants to play at Wembley and if you're a manager everyone wants to take a team there. To take one there for the first time after such a long career in management, unbelievable. An absolutely unbelievable day for me.'

Leeds made harder work of things in the FA Cup, needing two attempts to shake off Port Vale. The Potteries side had put out holders Everton in the previous round and rose to the occasion – future England international Steve Guppy came as close as anyone to settling the tie when his shot from six yards narrowly cleared Lukic's goal.

'We live to fight another day,' sighed a relieved Wilkinson. 'We had enough of the ball but the players didn't show enough imagination, they didn't take the initiative and they didn't show sufficient courage to win the game. But it's still all there for us – provided we don't die of disappointment in the meantime.

'Perhaps our style is better suited to playing away from home in the cups. You have to give Port Vale credit, but we weren't anywhere near good enough.'

Gary Speed fractured his cheekbone in the game, an injury which kept him out of seven games at a crucial time. The initial prognosis had been that it would end his season.

Two McAllister goals earned victory in the replay, setting up a quarter-final against Liverpool at Elland Road.

Understandably, given the ease with which the Merseysiders had despatched Leeds in the league, Wilkinson set his team up in a formation designed to make them difficult to beat. He matched Liverpool's three-centre-back formation and deployed Ford as a shield in front of them.

As they had done in the domestic cups all season, Leeds forsook their squad numbers and named shirts for the game, opting for the traditional 1 to 11 which allowed Yeboah to take Wallace's normal No 8 shirt.

BBC pundit Jimmy Hill led media condemnation of Leeds' negative approach, saying, 'I was utterly appalled by the quality of shooting from players who are on £10,000 a week in some cases.'

Wilkinson responded with weary sarcasm when asked whether he thought his approach had spoiled the match. 'Yes, it did, and I told my players at half-time that it all had to change and they had to be more entertaining. I told them to stick one in their own net, then for a couple of them to lie down for ten minutes or so while Liverpool ran in two or three more.

'Then everyone would have gone away happy – except for all those people connected with this club.

'We went to Anfield in the league two months ago and got turned over 5-0 after being in with a shout until Gary Kelly was sent off. Today we drew 0-0 and still everyone says we are rubbish. You can't win, but that's the way it goes.'

There was no ambition, no excitement and no goals, leaving the fans to ask, 'What do we do at Anfield?'

The answer was simple: lose 3-0.

A close thing was conjured out of nothing by Yeboah in the first half as Leeds settled to their containing game, but there was only going to be one winner from the moment that Steve McManaman beat Lukic just before the hour.

It wasn't that Leeds played badly, just that they so lacked ambition – Wilkinson's approach might have made sense with Dorigo in the side, but injury forced him to use the prosaic Worthington. One could feel only pity for McAllister, a single shining beacon in Leeds' turgid mess of a midfield.

Wilkinson's adoption of a 5-3-2 formation had its impact on Leeds' goal return. Leeds scored 28 goals in the first 19 games of the Premier League campaign, but only a dozen in the next 19. On ten occasions Leeds failed to trouble the scorers.

Minds were elsewhere, preoccupied with Leeds' forthcoming Wembley clash with Aston Villa. Here was a chance to shake off the gloom brought on by a record of just two league wins since Christmas. They came close to ending that streak against Everton, but had to be content with a 2-2 draw.

Wilkinson, without McAllister (rested), Speed, Dorigo, Yeboah (all injured) and Wetherall (suspended), included five players who had not yet turned 21. His reshuffled side performed admirably with Andy Gray showing touches that uncle Eddie would have admired.

Deane was convinced his two goals would seal his Wembley place. 'I scored both goals and I got man of the match, then I found myself getting dropped. I was on the bench. So from my point of view, I was just hugely disappointed in the tactics and how we had set up and I couldn't believe it.'

Deane and Brolin were named subs for the final, with Wilkinson opting for Gray on the right wing and Yeboah up front on his own.

There were doubts about Yeboah's fitness. Before kick-off, the Ghanaian pulled Alan Sutton to one side, complaining that his knee was not up to playing.

Sutton was reluctant to raise the issue with Wilkinson. He whispered to Yeboah, 'Look, go out there, start the game, see how you go, and then after ten minutes, whatever, if it's not right, go down. I'll prime Geoff Ladley, let him know that you might have a little problem.'

The problem Leeds had that day was far from little – the afternoon was an absolute nightmare.

Yeboah played the full 90, but for all he contributed, he would have been better off sitting in the stands. 'Why is Brolin on the bench?' jeered the Leeds support, as perplexed by Wilkinson's selection as the rest of the country.

Even by the yardstick of their recent performances, there was a torpor about Leeds; they were just not at it.

Gray was the only man who showed up, playing with the freshness of youth. Leeds had nothing else, conceding ground and possession to a Villa team on top form, on the way to a top-four finish and the FA Cup semi-finals. United had not a prayer, hammered 3-0, the score an understatement.

The crowd unleashed their bile on Wilkinson, accusing him of losing his way. His passage to the players' tunnel at the end was a sad one, head bowed as he was forced to soak up the hatred.

'Of course it hurt,' said Wilkinson. 'It seemed very personal to me and I don't think that anybody was left in any doubt about what they wanted. I'm the one who has to take the responsibilities when we win and when we lose but the biggest disappointment of the day was a massive one, we just didn't take enough responsibility out on the field. They say that your first time at Wembley passes very quickly, but it didn't for me. I don't think I will ever be able to look back and say I enjoyed it.

'What should have been a marvellous experience, win or lose, turned into a nightmare. I was emotionally disembowelled, close to walking away from it all.'

Even the more constructive United supporters harboured doubts. One said, 'Time for a change at the top of our club I think – Wilko has worked many wonders but now we need a fresh approach. What we saw on Sunday is something I've seen too often over recent months and years.'

Wilkinson conceded that a lack of continuity in selection had harmed United's season, that his hands had been tied by injuries and suspensions. He had hoped the occasion would have helped the players to shake off their woes 'but Villa got the important early goals, and goals turn games'.

He appeared a broken man, low in resilience, confidence and ideas, at the end of his tether. Whether there were genuine thoughts of resignation, only Wilkinson would know but there were no positives to take from the day, just a bitter, stinging sense of regret.

'We didn't show our best against Aston Villa, we got punished,' recalled Deane. 'I remember coming off at the end of the game and our fans were on the left-hand side as we were coming off and they were criticising the manager then. They were saying some not very nice things, and I was just disappointed from my personal point of view because I felt that I could have really made a better impact had I been on from the start. But I don't pick the team.

'It was sad really because Wilkinson had done a lot for Leeds United. He did a wonderful job. I think at that point, that was when the fans started to question certain things that were going on and there wasn't really a way back from there. I'll always remember we tried to blood some of the young players and the fans weren't happy.

'That obviously impacted on the performances of the young players and some of them didn't recover from that. So that was kind of the beginning of the end for me.'

At the end, Gary MacAllister walked sadly towards the Leeds support to acknowledge them. Despite the jeers, he knew it was the right thing to do but it hurt like hell.

Carlton Palmer pointed his finger in the direction of some of his colleagues. 'The lack of effort from certain players in such a big game was nothing short of a disgrace. When you look at that, you've got to say the criticism dished out to the boss at the end was also a disgrace.

'At least I competed, I tried. If you can come off at the end of a match and say that, then fine. But I don't think many of our team could at Wembley. Young Andy Gray came in and was our best player. That says it all about the rest of the team.

'I was very disappointed with the treatment the boss received. I can understand the fans' frustration, but it wasn't his fault. He couldn't have done more to prepare us properly and was let down by too many players failing to perform on the day.'

Bill Fotherby backed Wilkinson to lead the Whites into the next century, then rounded on Brolin and Yeboah for their pre-match threats to leave if Leeds missed out on Europe.

'It was very disappointing to read about star names hinting that they might be ready to move on if we lost at Wembley. That was the wrong approach to take into a big final like this.'

'If Leeds are not in Europe then it will be a very, very difficult situation for me,' Yeboah had said. 'I will retire in two or three years' time, and I need to be playing at the very top until then. I would have to consider my position carefully, because it is very important for me to be playing in European competition.'

Brolin echoed that lack of conviction. 'If you cannot play in a big game like this one then I have to think about my future. I think I will have to try and find another team.

'I will speak about my future after the last game of the season, but it is fair to say that it would be easier for me to say yes to staying if Leeds qualify for Europe. Every player wants to play in Europe; it is an important influence.

'I don't know where my future lies now. The manager thinks his way and I think mine – so maybe we should go our separate ways.'

Leslie Silver conceded that, 'If Howard comes in and says he's had enough, we'll sit down and talk about it,' before insisting, 'We want him to carry on.'

At the end of a week in which hopes of double cup success had been blown apart, there was a feeling of inevitability in the air.

There was not even the chance of a late push for Europe. Leeds were 15 points shy of the fifth place that offered a path, and the yawning blackness around them swallowed Leeds whole. They won just one of their nine remaining games.

When Saturday Comes carried what amounted to an obituary for the empire that Wilkinson built, imploring,

'Walk away Howard, be brave enough to be part of the solution.'

The following Saturday, Wilkinson was greeted by concerted jeering as he made his way to the dugout for the game with Middlesbrough. There was support from some sections of the crowd and Wilkinson acknowledged them gratefully, but he cut a crestfallen figure.

His mood was hardly helped on the Monday morning when Brolin gave an April's Fool interview to Swedish TV, claiming he was about to return home on loan. The Leeds switchboard was jammed with press inquiries. 'The chairman and managing director are finding it difficult to see the funny side of this,' sighed an irritated Wilkinson.

When Leeds lost 4-1 at Chelsea, police and stewards had to throw out Leeds fans who stepped up their anti-Wilkinson campaign. As the players came out for the second half, a massive security cordon was thrown around the Leeds bench to ensure Wilkinson reached it safely.

Still there was more to endure – Wilkinson and his far from merry men became pawns in the battle between Manchester United and Newcastle for the Premier League title with Leeds due to face both title-chasers in the final month.

By late January, Newcastle, managed by Kevin Keegan, had a 12-point lead. They were playing scintillating football but had been gradually hauled in by their dead-eyed stalkers – by the time Leeds travelled to Old Trafford on 17 April, Manchester United had gone three points clear.

Mark Beeney returned to the side following the hammering at Chelsea, but his night ended after 17 minutes. He beat Andy Cole to a through ball, but referee Keith Cooper ruled that he handled the ball outside the box and dismissed him. With no substitute keeper allowed, Lucas Radebe took over in goal. He had also replaced the injured Lukic the previous month against Middlesbrough.

It took the jittery Red Devils until the 72nd minute to capitalise by way of Roy Keane's strike.

Newcastle also registered a nervy single-goal victory, at home to Southampton, but the real action came later that night.

Knowing the pressure that Keegan was under, Alex Ferguson indulged in some scurrilous mind games, claiming the Leeds players had let Wilkinson down.

Ferguson audaciously asserted that his remarks were not intended to get at Keegan. Prior to the Manchester United–Leeds game, he took a call from David Walker of the *Daily Mail*. He was asked if he would offer a few words of encouragement for Wilkinson, a close professional colleague.

Walker and Ferguson discussed Leeds' recent results and their miserable position in the table. They agreed that the players were showing less than a do-or-die commitment on Wilkinson's behalf. Ferguson decided that anything he had to say would be best said after the match was over to avoid appearing to patronise Wilkinson.

'My remarks were never meant to have anything to do with Kevin Keegan,' wrote Ferguson in his autobiography. 'They were aimed entirely at Howard Wilkinson's players.'

Whatever the truth was, Ferguson's comments were calculated to ensure that Leeds would do everything to prove him wrong when they faced Newcastle.

That game didn't start well; Keith Gillespie gave Newcastle the lead in the opening minutes, but Leeds rallied, for once giving Wilkinson their all. They couldn't get back on terms, but there was no lack of commitment.

Following the game, Sky's Andy Gray and Richard Keys interviewed Keegan. He lost it completely, launching into a rant, his eyes bulging with distaste for Ferguson.

After he admitted that his players had been below their best, Keegan let his emotions get the better of him. 'A lot of things have been said over the last few days, some of it almost slanderous, and we've never commented, we just got on working, trying to pass the ball like we do in training ... You've got to send Alex Ferguson a tape of this game, haven't you? Isn't that what he asked for?

'When you do that with footballers, like he said about Leeds ... I'll tell you something, he went down in my estimation when he said that. We have not resorted to that, but I'll tell you, you can tell him now if you're watching it, we're still fighting for this title, and he's got to go to Middlesbrough and get something, and ... and ... I'll tell you, honestly, I will love it if we beat them, love it!'

Fergie's remarks about his fellow professionals had Keegan spitting, wide-eyed with rage.

Keegan said in later years, 'It was pure emotion pouring out, heart-on-the-sleeve stuff, but that was the way I felt and I wasn't going to bottle it up just because the general rule in football seemed to be that Alex Ferguson was untouchable.

'Initially, I felt sorry for Howard Wilkinson and the Leeds players because, as far as I was concerned, Fergie was using them for his own means. I was less sympathetic, however, when I read in one of Alex's books a few years later that he had asked Howard if he could have a pop, and that, incredibly, the Leeds manager had no objection.

'That was out of order. If any manager had asked the same of me, I would have pointed out that if anyone was going to have a go at my players, it should be me. But he and Howard were close, whereas Howard was no friend of mine, and it turned out they had cooked it up in advance. My emotions were running high. In the heat of the moment, jabbing my finger for extra emphasis, it must have been television gold for the watching millions.'

Wilkinson admitted that Ferguson's comments had hit home. 'It's the old saying, if the cap fits. But if you're a footballer the best place to talk is out there. From a manager's point of view the best people to do the talking are the players.'

He said that Manchester United could have few complaints about Leeds' efforts, although he admitted, 'In the last 20 minutes we didn't threaten them as much as the Leeds team going full sail might have done. But in the circumstances maybe we weren't in a position to do that – we didn't have that in our armoury. After the goal they settled down and we became too anxious in our passing. We gave the ball away too easily. But the way they closed down was the best I've seen from them this season.'

One can only speculate as to why Wilkinson gave the nod to Fergie, if he did. Surely, in another season, when he was more like his true self, Wilko would have said no or snapped back with an acid note of sarcasm.

But this was a different Wilkinson, totally deflated at the end of a dispiriting season that began so well, promised so much, only to vanish into the ether like a puff of smoke.

The Sell-Out

The last board of the football club had one agenda, this board has another agenda.

'Don't hurt her, please don't hurt her. She's an old woman.'

'Keep it shut and don't struggle, Grandad, and no one'll get hurt.'

Leslie Silver stared at the figure hunched in front of him, his features hidden by a balaclava. He knew better than to fight back; it would make no difference to the callous thug in front of him. But he was so concerned about wife Sheila …

She sobbed, half in fear and half in pain, as her wrists were bound. Silver scowled angrily but bit his lip. There was little he could do even if he wanted to.

A peculiar idea came into Silver's mind. This was so much like what had happened to him at Leeds United.

When he first took on the role of chairman, he'd been tortured by young thugs, left in no doubt that they would 'do him' if they got the chance. That was all in the past, of course, but still he felt as trapped in the boardroom as he did right now, held prisoner in his own home as an armed gang ransacked the place, pilfering all they could find. He didn't need this, at his time of life, he thought to himself. 'Is it worth all the aggro?'

On the evening of Monday, 11 March 1996, Silver and his wife had been watching television in their downstairs lounge. At 9.30, they heard footsteps from the stairs and three masked men burst into the room, ordering the couple to lie face down on the carpet.

Silver was blindfolded and handcuffed to a door in the snooker room while Sheila was forced to reveal the location of the safe. Sheila was ordered to hand over the keys to the safe, which contained jewellery worth more than £200,000. Sated, the thugs made their escape, leaving the keys to the handcuffs.

Silver managed to reach the phone and dialled 999. The whole affair lasted around 20 minutes, but it felt like an eternity for the traumatised couple.

It was one of several house robberies targeting football people at the time. Police told Silver they knew who committed the crime but lacked the evidence to charge them.

The after-effects haunted Silver for a long time. There were many sleepless nights.

He'd found it equally hard to drop off the day before, tossing and turning as he relived the despair of United's deadly drab goalless draw against Liverpool.

He'd expected Leeds to be going at it hell for leather, still in two domestic cup competitions and with a place in Europe to play for. But Howard Wilkinson had let him down.

Chastened by the experience of a 5-0 hiding at the end of January, Wilkinson had gone for a cautious approach, designed to negate Liverpool's smooth game. It was desperately unambitious stuff and Leeds never looked like scoring, pilloried for their lack of ambition.

Wilkinson sarcastically waved aside the criticism. Silver hadn't been amused by his acidic comments. For once, his patience with his manager's eccentricity was exhausted. The burglary had put the icing on the cake of a disastrous weekend.

Silver is greeted by Bill Fotherby when he ventures into Elland Road for a brief chat a few days later.

'Are you okay, Leslie? Sounds like it was a nightmare?'

'It was, Bill, it was terrifying. There was no violence, but it was brutal. The worst part was being separated. Played havoc with my heart, it did.'

Silver had a cardiac issue the previous year and a check-up ended with the doctor advising him to take things easy.

'No chance of that with Leeds, of course, is there?'

'Might be time to think about selling up, Leslie.'

'Not this again,' thinks Silver to himself. He's had enough of Fotherby's nagging about putting the club on the market. But then, other things cross his mind ...

The following couple of weeks saw Leeds crash out of the Cup in the Anfield replay and then depress everybody with their abject surrender to Villa at Wembley. With one win in five games, they plummeted into the bottom half of the table.

Silver had had enough. He announced in early April that he was stepping down after 14 years as chairman, with Fotherby taking temporary charge.

Silver insisted his decision was purely for health reasons and that he would retain his shares in the club 'for the time being'.

In this context, 'the time being' meant until the summer – Silver had decided to take Fotherby's advice and sell.

The sale of Silver's 33 per cent stake offered the opportunity for a bidder to acquire a controlling interest.

Richard Thompson, owner of Queens Park Rangers, was touted as a potential buyer, though Silver indicated there were several interested parties. 'There are all sorts of suggestions about who might want to buy in,' he said. 'None have got beyond the talking stage, although one may soon. When I do come to sell my stake, then there is no way I will let it go to someone who doesn't have the best interests of Leeds at heart. The change of shareholding will not change the existing structure.'

Rothschilds, the club's financial advisers, assured the board that there would be interest in the market. Vice-chairman Peter Gilman, the other member of the gang of three who held the controlling management shares, was positive about the suggestion, particularly once Rothschilds provided an estimate of the likely selling price.

All three men were well aware of the depth of the supporters' disregard for them. That was nothing new with a football club – directors were universally reviled, labelled as egomaniacs, rich men who wanted a shiny toy but knew nothing about the game – but there was a particular edge to the situation at Leeds.

Fotherby attracted the most bile. He was widely regarded as a bullsh*tter, if not an utter liar. There were rumours that he had put little cash into the club when he joined the board (the accounts suggested just over £20,000) and sold his house in north Leeds to the club for £265,000. The house had been on the market for more than a year without any interest.

Appointed managing director in 1990, Fotherby drew an annual salary of £350,000, making him the highest-paid director in the Football League.

Gilman, too, was heavily criticised, accused, like Bob Roberts before him, of benefiting from development work at Elland Road.

Gilman was chairman of GMI Construction, which won a contract to build the East Stand. It sparked accusations that Fotherby got a backhander from the deal.

The club appointed local quantity surveyors Richard Cavadino & Associates to act as 'employer's agent' for the project, responsible for selecting contractors to bid for the design and construction of the stand and to evaluate the tenders.

George Wimpey put in a price of £3.5m but the contract was awarded to GMI, despite an estimate of £5.5m. Richard Cavadino claimed that Wimpey's bid 'did not comply with the club's specification'.

A similar event occurred in 1984, when Manston was awarded a contract for the construction of executive boxes at a cost of £186,000. Gilman was the chairman of Manston but resigned to avoid criticism.

When he was quoted as saying, 'Directors have risked millions so if they ultimately make millions, it seems a fair result,' United supporters feared the worst.

When the club was put up for sale, three interested parties emerged. A Norwegian group quickly fell by the wayside, clearing the field for a battle between London-based media rights company Caspian Group plc and Conrad plc from Manchester.

Conrad owned the Le Coq Sportif sports brand and the Bobby Charlton football schools. One of its other subsidiaries was chaired by former Leeds captain Trevor Cherry. Among Conrad's key leaders was Manchester United non-executive director Michael Edelson, a venture capitalist.

Edelson's Old Trafford connections unsettled Silver and Fotherby, who resisted all overtures.

The main attention was on Caspian, which owned the rights to such children's television characters as the Wombles and Paddington Bear. Their interest was driven by Richard

Thompson, who had sold his shares in QPR and joined the Caspian board, though City high-flier Chris Akers was the nominal figurehead.

Thompson, eyeing the money about to pour into the game, persuaded his colleagues to scour the market for a club.

Caspian saw Leeds United as a major opportunity, particularly attracted by the opportunities afforded by the Elland Road stadium. They planned to buy the ground back from Leeds City Council if their bid was successful.

Caspian tabled an offer for the club amounting to £16.5m, also promising to clear debts of £10m and provide £12m for transfers. Money would be found by way of a public share issue, expected to yield £28m.

The offer would allow Silver, Fotherby and Gilman to bank £5.5m apiece and Silver and Fotherby were ready to accept.

The fly in the ointment was Gilman, who favoured Conrad, arguing that its offer was even more lucrative. Gilman denounced Caspian, claiming that they had a number of loss-making businesses and that their offer 'stinks for the fans and under-values the club'.

Caspian fired back, pointing out that Gilman Construction had taken £11.5m out of the club in building contracts, some 22 per cent of the firm's turnover.

Thompson's association with former Arsenal manager George Graham fuelled speculation that Graham would be installed to replace Wilkinson if the deal went through. Thompson knew Graham from his time at QPR and the two men both had flats in the same Hampstead development.

A deep schism developed between Gilman and his two colleagues.

On 4 July, the Caspian board announced its offer, which was endorsed by Silver and Fotherby, giving Wilko the green light to start spending.

Eleven days later, Akers wrote to potential shareholders to inform them that Caspian's entire issued share capital would be made available on the London Stock Exchange, with shares to be launched on the market on 2 August. He confirmed that Silver and Fotherby had both 'irrevocably undertaken' to accept the offer and to reject any rival bid. Akers admitted that he was 'currently considering what action, if any, he may take, including legal remedies, against certain of his fellow directors and their associates'.

Gilman argued that Fotherby and Silver breached an agreement that any sale required unanimous approval. So angry was he at what he perceived as betrayal that he immediately applied for a High Court injunction to halt the deal, hoping that the judge would force the other two to sell their shares to him. The legal action put a temporary halt to any further transfer activity. Wilkinson was left sitting on his hands for a month despite having £12m burning a hole in his pocket.

As early as May, Wilkinson had been looking for options to replenish his squad. He was said to be interested in Barcelona's £2m-rated Croatian international midfielder, Robert Prosinecki. He was touted as the ideal replacement for Gary Speed, who had negotiated a move to boyhood favourites Everton.

Speed's departure was a grievous blow for Wilkinson, severing an association with Elland Road that had begun in 1986 when he joined the youth scheme.

The Welshman had more than 300 first-team games behind him and was one of Wilkinson's favourites.

'I had to talk to Gary when he was 20, 21 and let's say he maybe was living the life that his film star looks suggested he might lead and that was totally different to Gary the footballer and Gary the person. I said to him, "You have all the qualities to become a very good player, to become a leader. One, because your values are good. Two, because in terms of the football side you turn up, you do what's necessary and more, so you do everything right. You'll eventually be a captain." He blushed and said, "Nah." I said, "Well, because you turn up here early, you leave the ground late and when you're on the pitch, you're playing for us, not for you. You'll become a role model in that sense."

'That's important, that you have people like that. And by the time Gary left ... I think he played in every position in the team apart from goal, you know, start off wide midfield and moving more central and on occasions when we needed it, I'd move him further up the front. He's played left-back and so on.'

Before his hands were tied, Wilkinson made Charlton midfielder Lee Bowyer Britain's most expensive teenager in a £2.6m deal and persuaded Liverpool striker Ian Rush to join on a free transfer.

Upon his return from holiday, Gary McAllister insisted he would remain 'for as long as Leeds want me', but the uncertainty brought by the legal dispute so frustrated the United captain that he tabled a transfer request.

Coventry City, building an 'old Leeds' community around Gordon Strachan and Noel Whelan, offered a fee of £3m and a salary of £16,000 a week, double what McAllister was picking up at Leeds.

Wilkinson begged him to honour the remaining three years of his contract. McAllister promised to stay if Leeds extended his contract, increased his salary and committed to investing in the squad following the takeover.

Reasoning that £3m was a good price for a 31-year-old, the manager reluctantly sanctioned the sale. 'His contribution has been enormous since I signed him,' he said. 'I am very sorry to see him go but I am powerless to do anything about it.'

Wilkinson used the money to bring in Crystal Palace's Nigel Martyn, one of the finest keepers in the country.

Martyn was grateful for the opportunity to play in the top flight again after losing a play-off final with Crystal Palace.

'I think he felt that perhaps the team was a little bit stale at the time,' says Martyn. 'It needed freshening up. He wanted to bring new faces in. He wanted me to be one of those new faces to give the club a boost, because he felt there was some good youngsters coming through with a good blend of senior players. His vision was he could see us building in the early part and then hopefully pushing to be a top-four club.'

Martyn and Bowyer were signings of the highest quality, but losing McAllister and Speed tore the heart out of the side, though there had been comments from some that 'Speed needed to leave two years earlier; he had started to get the bird from fans.'

Speed acknowledged as much, saying, 'I don't think Howard Wilkinson lost the plot, which has been suggested. It was the players' fault. Once we'd won the league, I think we felt we were better than we were. We won it because we worked so hard for each other. We had Strach and McAllister, who could do a bit, skill-wise, but the rest of us were really just hard workers. After we'd won it, we all got it into our heads that we were so good that we didn't need to work that hard anymore, and as soon as we lost that we were ordinary.

'For my part, I wasn't training properly, and my attitude wasn't what it should have been. I stopped working at the game. I had an attitude problem and needed to leave to put it right.'

The departure of neither Speed nor McAllister was down to Wilkinson, but their decisions to move on were seen as an indication of the manager's waning powers.

The High Court approved the Caspian takeover on 25 July, much to Gilman's disgust. Wilkinson immediately broke

Leeds' transfer record, paying Manchester United £4.5m for left-winger Lee Sharpe.

Replacing Speed on the left flank was a must do. Sharpe had lost his way after a bright start to his career but was seen as young enough to recapture the qualities that brought him eight England caps under Graham Taylor.

Part of Sharpe's motivation for agreeing to the move was to secure regular first-team football and attract the attention of new England manager Glenn Hoddle.

Sharpe was hardly the type of player normally associated with Wilkinson, but the manager was unusually positive, saying, 'Glenn phoned me last week and expressed his disappointment at the dearth of left-sided players. I said to Lee, slightly tongue-in-cheek, that I would phone Glenn and tell him we might have solved his problem. Prior to his illness and injury, on that side Lee had no peer. When Gary Speed left, I was obviously looking for a left-sided player and, when you looked at the list, it was difficult to get beyond Lee Sharpe.'

'I just felt I'd had enough of Fergie,' said Sharpe when asked about why he moved. 'I couldn't figure out why I was playing bad one week and really good the next and I wasn't getting any help from him. So I left, thought I needed pastures new and if someone was gonna buy me for a few quid, maybe they'll be on my side a bit more.

'After about three weeks, [Howard] came up to me and said, "Listen, son, I know I've paid a lot of money for you – I knew you were good but I didn't know you were this good. Get yourself fit, that left-hand side of the pitch is yours, go out there, score some goals and enjoy your football. I'm really glad you're here."

'I remember standing there, shook my hands and thought, "Oh my god, it's like I'm in heaven."

'It wasn't all positive. I had fans telling me to f*** off back to Manchester. One guy came up to me in a bar and said,

"Once a scum, always a scum." Ten years later, that same person apologised to me.'

Wilkinson was upbeat about a new start, telling the press, 'I said after the League Cup Final defeat that we would have to start again, and that's what we've done this summer, started again. A lot of the off-the-field things I wanted to achieve have been achieved, but not all of them. If I could wave a magic wand this afternoon, I would probably sign two more players, but I can't.'

Ian Rush claimed in his autobiography that he had been promised the chance to succeed Wilkinson.

'What made the offer so appealing was that I would understudy Howard with a view to succeeding him as manager within two to three years. My aim was to work towards gaining the UEFA Pro Licence. I felt I would learn a lot under Howard, who was widely respected throughout the game. He was nothing like the Sergeant Wilko character he had often been portrayed as by the press. He loved football, cared about the game and his players, and was full of innovative ideas. His enthusiasm and energy was infectious.'

Wilkinson strongly refuted that version of events, adamant that Rush was 'just coming in as a player'.

Wilkinson was also disparaging about the new owners, saying, 'I paid the price when Caspian bought the club and the chairman afterwards always expressed his regret. Within about 18 months he'd told me that he wished it had never happened. It was a time when clubs thought that was the way to go. Okay, there was the Champions League semi-final but when you look at where they were and then we look at where they were afterwards and what was the trigger, well that was really the trigger. Whatever you think, with the benefit of hindsight I know, the three who were running that football club ran it properly and for the right reasons. They ran it because Leeds United was their club.

'Since they became a plc, they peaked at the semi-final of the Champions League, but since that brief dalliance with glory, it's been a gradual decline. I don't know who's the winner in all of this.'

Wilkinson suggests that despite the emergence of the youngsters, the substance of his plan was ditched. 'The whole idea was that the kids would be the heart of the team. They should be protected and we should make sure that they stayed at the club while we established ourselves financially. We were about 18 months from having all those young kids in the side. Harte and Kewell had made their debuts, Bowyer was in the team. We knew about Woodgate and Robinson, Smith was a prominent kid at the time.'

When Wilkinson told a reporter in 1999, 'There are so many people that deserve credit for the way the kids have emerged into such good players,' David O'Leary scoffed at the suggestion.

'They were only 13-year-olds when he had them,' said O'Leary less than graciously. 'A lot happens from then on. This is my team now. I have worked with them for the last two years with Eddie Gray.'

Wilkinson insists that his long-term vision was scuppered by the club's 'bet the farm' obsession with big signings and even bigger wages. The lopsided distribution of Sky's squillions created a yawning abyss between the game's haves and its have-nots. In later years Peter Ridsdale would gamble everything to keep Leeds in the former camp and his boundless ambition committed the club to more than a decade of chaos and instability.

'When I took over, I spent a lot of time talking about the monster on the horizon called satellite television,' Wilkinson said. 'Anyone with half a brain could see that once it was established there would be a need to keep a lid on the revenue.'

'Twere well it were done quickly

*It's like being on Death Row in an
American jail. You are waiting for the door
handle to turn, not knowing whether it's a
reprieve or just your final breakfast before
being executed.*

HIS EYES were empty and black, his face ashen white. At that particular hour, on that particular day, he would have preferred to be somewhere else, anywhere else, other than Elland Road for this, his final curtain call. It was an unbelievably sad day for Howard Wilkinson.

He'd had some time to get used to the idea, knowing full well what the new owners had planned, but it still hurt like hell when the axe fell.

He realised his days were numbered when he was tipped off by a managerial colleague. 'I got a phone call from a very good friend of mine who's also an extremely successful manager. He told me he had it on good authority that my job had already been offered to another high-profile manager who at that time was out of work. From then on, it was clear I was on borrowed time. It's the first time in my life I've not driven to work thinking how lucky I was.

'The players got to know it, too. The football grapevine is unbelievable. It was a great example of a lack of cohesion brought about by a lack of trust. When that feeling's gone from a team, flying is impossible.

'The chairman and another were still fighting for me to stay at the club. So, I had to go through pre-season and the start of the season knowing that this was highly unlikely.'

For many Leeds fans, Wilkinson had been on borrowed time since the awful spring. His chances of reversing United's decline had been holed below the waterline by long-term injuries to Tony Dorigo and Tony Yeboah.

The striker had been plagued by persistent knee trouble and not played a minute since the Coca-Cola Cup Final disaster in March. He required an operation to clear up the issue.

'It's not the best way to go into the season but, hopefully, the surgery will sort out the trouble,' said Wilkinson. 'It's not really possible to say how many games Tony will miss.'

Another issue was Tomas Brolin's petulant refusal to participate in pre-season, pointing to the lack of togetherness in the camp.

Nigel Pleasants recalled: 'Brolin was the most difficult character I have ever dealt with. He was an absolute nightmare. He went back to Sweden insisting he needed treatment but never came back. I had to keep issuing him with suspensions every two weeks.'

Wilkinson fined Brolin a week's wages – around £12,000 – for missing pre-season training and revealed that he was seeking guidance from the PFA on the legality of withholding his wages. He told the press that he would rather have any other player in his team than Brolin. By the time the Swede left the club for good, they had docked £72,000 from his wages.

Wilkinson was unable to obtain a fresh work visa for Phil Masinga. He blamed government red tape and considered appealing after being told by the Department of Employment that he couldn't keep the striker.

A request for a new permit was rejected because Masinga hadn't played in 75 per cent of United's games. Accepting defeat, the club offloaded Masinga to St Gallen in Switzerland.

It seemed as if everything that could possibly go wrong was doing so, that the world was conspiring against Wilkinson.

It would have been cleaner if Caspian had shown their hand and gone for a clean break in the summer, allowing Wilkinson to leave with dignity. They declined to do so, and he had to stagger on into the new season.

It was as if the money men were waiting for an excuse to sack Wilkinson, as if fearing an insurrection that only they considered likely.

Caspian were mistaken if they thought that the manager would sign his own death warrant – the first few weeks of the season brought some promising results.

The opening game, away to Derby, offered a glimpse of what Wilko's new Leeds would be like. The manager gave immediate debuts to Martyn, Bowyer, Sharpe and Rush. It was alarming to see a Leeds side completely shorn of the title-winning midfield. Rather than McAllister and Speed, Mark Ford and Andy Couzens partnered Bowyer and Sharpe.

Ford, perpetually referred to as a 'tigerish midfielder', was touted as a successor to Batty but possessed neither his class nor his capability – his shaven head was likely to persuade an undecided referee to go for a yellow or red card rather than a quiet word. Couzens was a local graduate from Wilkinson's youth scheme, but he was no McAllister.

Bowyer was something else entirely. The new man enjoyed a livewire debut, demonstrating the all-action, heart-on-sleeve commitment that would endear him to the Leeds faithful. He was an instant hit.

It was Derby's first season in the Premier League and that was evident in the first half, though Leeds only had an own goal to show for it, Jacob Laursen cluelessly diverting Bowyer's low centre past his own keeper.

A quarter of an hour into the second period, Brian Deane was stretchered off after receiving a boot in the groin. Eighteen-year-old Irish left-back Ian Harte came on to replace him; Sharpe, who had been playing wing-back, moved forward.

Fourteen minutes after entering the fray, Harte thundered on to a short pass from Bowyer to hammer the ball in right-footed from 25 yards. At 18 years, 352 days old, he became United's youngest opening-day scorer since Tommy Wright in 1984.

2-0 and the travelling fans were ecstatic – this was a course of events that few had expected.

The game should have been done and dusted. One had to go back to December 1994 to find the last time that Leeds had squandered a two-goal advantage in the Premier League. Derby had other ideas and were level within six minutes.

After Rams manager Jim Smith used his permitted three subs, his team quickly exploited a defence that suddenly began to leave huge gaps at its heart.

Given an acre of space, Dean Sturridge beat Martyn with a chip from the edge of the area. Then Richard Jobson's slack back-pass straight from the restart left Martyn in no man's land. Paul Simpson beat him to it and snatched the equaliser.

Leeds fans feared the worst but hope was renewed with five minutes remaining when Bowyer crowned his debut by netting Leeds' third goal.

There was to be no happy ending – three minutes later Sturridge notched his second after escaping the clutches of Lucas Radebe deep inside the area.

A downbeat Wilkinson told the media, 'We've got a point, a lot of good things in the game,' but he was clearly deflated at his defence's negligence.

United looked what they were: a team in transition.

Deane's injury was far more serious than it first appeared – an absence that would stretch on for weeks forced Wilkinson into a short-term solution. Desperate times call for desperate measures, but the month's loan of 34-year-old England centre-forward Mark Hateley brought only contempt from the terraces. Few could comprehend the logic of bringing in a man whose only contribution in his spell at Queens Park Rangers had been to elicit cries of scorn from his own supporters.

Hateley debuted in midweek at home to Sheffield Wednesday but could offer little on a night when yawning defensive deficiencies allowed the Owls to win 2-0. Everything could have been very different if the woodwork had not denied United on three occasions.

Caspian representatives began sharpening their knives but had to sheathe them when Leeds' first win bonus came from a televised match at home to Wimbledon.

In the first half, a section of United fans sided with Caspian, chanting the name of Kenny Dalglish. As if in sympathy, the players did Wilkinson few favours – they quickly abandoned any pretence of playing football and settled instead for lumping the ball long in the general direction of the Dad's Army of Hateley and Rush.

Sharpe, however, decided after 58 minutes that this was a night for intelligent football after all. He took a lay-off from Rush, shifted to his right to evade a defender and curled a beautiful shot into the goal. It was enough to secure the points.

When Harte headed in from a curling Sharpe free kick to secure victory at Blackburn, it seemed a corner had been turned.

Certainly, the players thought so.

'The dressing room after that game, you'd thought we'd won the league again,' recalled Wilkinson. 'Bill [Fotherby] came in the dressing room afterwards and from his reaction you would have thought we had won the Cup. One or two of the players were looking at him and thinking, "What's wrong with him?" But Bill had known that had we lost, the powers that be would have got rid of me. To be fair to Bill, he had been saying "Over my dead body" that a change would be made.

'I have to admit I had been threatening to leave myself for six to eight weeks before I eventually did go. The takeover had started to create unrest in the boardroom and performances on the pitch were up and down. I had also become increasingly aware towards the end of the previous season and during the summer that the people who looked like taking over had got someone lined up to come in as manager.'

Wilkinson – never sacked, never relegated – acknowledged that forthcoming home matches against Manchester United and Newcastle, sandwiching a trip to Coventry, were 'daunting fixtures. The team has got to win – it's as simple as that. When the season started, the fans weren't saying, "Well, what a summer of frustration, upset, hold-ups, limbo, injunctions, not being able to sign players, not knowing who's in charge, it's been." Whether that's fair or not doesn't come into it. No one ever said it would be.

'George Graham has turned down Manchester City, and I probably know more accurately than the media why he's done that, but I'll bet that at some stage it's reported that the reason is that he's been offered the job at Leeds United.'

The People quickly obliged with exactly that prediction.

A year earlier, Leeds had led the Premier League with nine points from three games. Since then, 38 matches – the equivalent of a full season – had delivered just 36 points. Relegation form.

'My players thought they were as good as people said they were,' admitted Wilkinson when asked what had gone wrong. 'They forgot why they got those victories. We also had the African Nations Cup, which meant we lost three players for a month, and Yeboah got injured the day after the Coca-Cola Final and we never saw him again. It was a roller-coaster season.'

When asked what kept him going, Wilkinson responded: 'I like the job, and surrender would have been a greater blow to myself than carrying on. My feeling is that after three days, I'd wake up thinking, "I'm bored to tears – why did I give in to them?"'

Pride, he said, did not come into it, merely a desire to finish what he had started.

'The directors held the view that good managers are hard to find. And my CV isn't exactly disastrous. We had a commitment, a long-term plan that we laid down very early on, and we were only part of the way through it. You could get someone new in and change things for a few months, but you've still got the same problems.'

Wilkinson reminded the media of his achievements since 1988, of the exciting talent streaming off the conveyor belt – Andy Gray, Mark Ford and Ian Harte had already gained international recognition. Mark Jackson, Jason Blunt and Harry Kewell were tipped to follow, while Wilkinson's coaching staff were hopeful that talented Irish teenager Stephen McPhail would fill the void left by McAllister.

Wilkinson was painfully aware that the vultures were circling, but he couldn't fathom 'the level of hostility, bile and bitterness' in many of the letters he received. Though he could 'understand' supporters' frustrations, he saw the booing at home games as damaging.

For all the talk of losing his job, Wilkinson appeared unfazed. 'I don't worry about it because I can't do anything about it. I'd rather be working than not, but I've been in management since I was 28 and some would say that by the law of averages, I'm going to get the sack at some point.

'Of course, I've still got ambitions. I want the championship again and I'd like to win a cup. I haven't altered my view about what I'm doing at Leeds United since the day I arrived. The only way I'll change is if someone says, "You're no longer in charge."

'A manager's not self-employed. If he's not in the directors' hands, he's in the players' hands. And if he's not in the players' hands, he's in the fans' hands.'

One reporter asked Wilkinson if he would ever write the story of the years following the title, to explain the restrictions he was under, the forces working upon him.

'You can spend your life trying to self-justify,' he said. 'But the question you always ask yourself is, "If I do this, if I say this, will it be in the best interests of the club going forward?" If the answer to that is "No", then you don't say it, and you don't do it.'

Wilkinson was in good form, if a little philosophical, buoyed by the thought that if his side won their game the following Saturday lunchtime, they would go second.

The fact that Leeds' opponents were reigning champions Manchester United made victory implausible, but Wilkinson knew that every dog could have its day and victory against Fergie would be one in the eye for his critics.

Such optimism was rapidly extinguished.

Karel Poborsky, who had played for the Czech Republic in Euro 96, was one of the individuals Wilkinson had his eye on during the summer. Wilko could only sit on his hands as Ferguson signed Poborsky and a slew of other new players, including the Norwegian, Ronny Johnsen, from Besiktas.

It was these two who forced the opening goal in the first minute after a comedy of errors – Johnsen had a free header at Poborsky's corner, but Ford cleared it off the line. Johnsen tried again. Harte did his best but could only send the ball into the net off the back of Martyn's head.

David Beckham, part of England's future, began to make Carlton Palmer, a relic from England's past, look like the dinosaur he was, while Ryan Giggs, Jordi Cruyff and Nicky Butt took hold of midfield.

That allowed Eric Cantona, Wilkinson's *bête noire*, to show off his talents. However, despite launching one brilliant move with the back-heel that came so naturally to him, the Frenchman was found wanting when it came to the penalty that was awarded to the visitors. The home crowd bayed with derision as he stroked the ball wide of the post.

It was a momentary reprieve – within three minutes of the resumption, Poborsky set up the second goal for Butt.

After 76 minutes, the Czech got on to the scoresheet himself, racing through a yawning defence before firing past Martyn.

From nowhere, Hateley shot against the crossbar to remind Manchester that there were two sides in the match.

It was an affront to Cantona, who poked home unmarked before throwing out his chest and raising his arms aloft in front of the crowd that once idolised him – a moment of naked insolence from a man who had no love for his opponents.

At that moment, Wilkinson's head slumped. He knew with crushing certainty that his reign was over.

The Manchester fans had been serenading him with jeers of 'Wilko for City', but now it was his own 'supporters' who turned on him, with chants of 'F*** off, Wilko' and 'Wilko out'.

He bore a haunted look as he told the media, 'They played with too much apprehension, fear, nervousness, and the thing you don't look when you play like that is a good player. It can look to the untutored eye that they can't play, they're not fit, not trying … but it's not like that.'

What Wilko could not say was what it was like.

On the Sunday, he broke the news to his players.

'I arrived at the training ground and Howard wasn't there,' remembers Ian Rush. 'This was unusual in itself as he was an early riser and was always the first to arrive. Eventually Howard arrived, gathered us together and said he'd come to offer his thanks to us all and say goodbye, as he had been sacked.'

'You're f***ing joking, boss?' blurted Carlton Palmer. Wilkinson assured Palmer that he wasn't.

'Everyone was shocked and genuinely saddened,' recalled Rush. 'The general feeling amongst the players was the Leeds board had bowed to a small section of disgruntled fans who knew, as Brian Deane put it, "bugger all".

'There was the usual woolly statement from the directors in such a circumstance, thanking Howard for all his efforts. The word was the board had just run out of patience.

'I felt that Howard had been a dead man walking for some time. In my opinion, the board were waiting for one bad result which would offer an excuse to get rid of Howard. The board must have done some preparation because in little over 24 hours, George Graham turned up and was introduced as our new manager.'

The curtain fell brutally on Wilkinson on the Monday morning. A press conference was hurriedly arranged so that he could sit alongside Fotherby as they broke the news.

'I'm very disappointed, very sad and obviously very shocked,' said a devastated man. 'The whole place is much healthier, more vibrant, a potentially bigger place than anyone ever dreamt it could be eight years ago. There aren't many clubs in a situation like ours who put up the vacant sign.'

Fotherby: 'This is the nasty side of being a chairman. It's not easy and this ain't come easy to me, but I had to think long and hard about it and make a decision. And I made my decision on Saturday. I believe it's the right decision for the club, for Howard Wilkinson, for everybody concerned. I felt we weren't going in the direction we should be going in. We have to have success and we haven't been having it.

'It was the hardest decision of my life. It was like tearing a part of my body away, but I had lost confidence, and I was not going to let us get into the situation where we were in that gluepot down below and couldn't get out.'

The decision hadn't been down to Fotherby or Silver, who retained a token seat on the club board until July 1999. It was down to the men who led Caspian, a public limited company making a very public execution.

'I enjoyed it enormously,' said Wilkinson of his final match, 'until it kicked off. The game itself and the aftermath were the low points of my career, and the temptation's always there to walk away from something when it gets unpleasant.

'A small section of our supporters have focused on me, focused their disapproval, their disappointment, their dismay. I think that started to affect the players.

'Caspian are involved in the City and have their ideas for the future of the club but, at a football club, what matters is the team, and if the performance is not as advantageous as they want it to be, they have to do something about it.

'I've been involved in football since I was 18 continuously. I've been involved in management since I was 27 continuously. I haven't had a break from it in all that time. I would like, if possible, to stand back, take stock, you know, maybe have a think about what's happening in football.'

Wilkinson was due compensation. His contract, signed in February, guaranteed him his full salary and bonuses until 1999 in the event of his dismissal. That would cost United £1.8m, and there were hints of a legal dispute. 'It's a big club and I hope we can sort it out in a gentlemanly way,' said Wilkinson.

With a weary sigh, sagging shoulders and eyes fixed sadly on the floor below him, Leeds United's best manager since Don Revie was gone.

A Post-Leeds World

As one door closes, another one shuts.

HOWARD WILKINSON'S years at Boston, Mossley, Notts County, Sheffield Wednesday and Leeds United were hugely successful. Even his final eight months at Elland Road could not taint his record. His job was lost because his face did not fit Caspian's shiny new business vision.

Out of work for the first time in four decades, Wilkinson was understandably reflective. He batted away an offer of the manager's job at Manchester City, a poisoned chalice that held no interest for him.

By the New Year, he was ready for his next challenge. A call from the Football Association was a welcome catalyst.

With director of coaching Charles Hughes set to retire within the following 12 months, the FA invited Wilkinson to become its first technical director.

Hughes, despite a reputation for organisation and hard work, had been roundly criticised for his remoteness from the professional game and archaic adherence to the teachings of Charles Reep.

Wilkinson went out of his way to counter accusations he would be a carbon copy of his predecessor. He told a press conference, 'Forget any preconceptions that you may have. Reserve judgement until you've read the script.

'A lot of assumptions have been made on my behalf about what I think and how I believe the game should be played. Someone told me once, never trust your assumptions because they generally lead you back inside your own head, which may not be a very "pleasant place to end your journey".'

As the assembled press men raised their eyebrows at a typically unfathomable Wilkinson quote, he quickly added, 'I think it was Eric who told me that,' a wry reference to Cantona.

FA chairman Keith Wiseman told Wilkinson that, 'Your job is to direct the production of a structure in England that will raise playing standards in our young players to world-class levels.' 'Is that all?' was Wilkinson's sarcastic response.

'I'd not long left Leeds United when I got the phone call asking me to meet with the chief executive of the FA. Really, at that time, I was looking to stay in management but as I listened, I realised this was an opportunity that interested me enormously. It was a blank sheet of paper. An opportunity to really create something … a plan for the English game.

'Eventually, I met with the FA and Rick Parry. It was clear they were aware of the transformation that was under way in France at that time. I agreed to join the FA on the basis that if English players and teams were going to thrive and succeed in the future, we needed a plan for the whole of the game.'

Wilkinson's responsibilities covered everything from the development of young players at grassroots level to supporting England manager Glenn Hoddle with the senior squad. It was the kind of role that Wilkinson had coveted for years, a lynchpin in the redesign of English football. His vision for such change was shaped by his relationship with Graham Taylor.

The pair were instrumental in the formation of the League Managers Association (LMA).

'When I was manager of Leeds United, Graham, Lawrie McMenemy, Olaf Dixon and John Camkin, who became the LMA's first chief executive, worked together on determining the feasibility of forming an association with relevant aims and objectives which all the managers would want to join. This work came to fruition when the LMA was officially formed in June 1992, with Graham as our first president.

'We agreed that it was wrong that the decisions that are taken in football are not decisions which benefit from the wisdom of people in the trenches. The Football League, the Premier League, whoever it is, make the decisions, and then their decisions impact on coaches and managers. Graham and I got together and said, "No, managers should have a voice." He and I decided that the LMA would be an independent body, would fight for the rights of managers to have an influence on the game.'

Wilkinson's involvement in the initiative prompted him to reject an approach from Arsenal in 1995.

The Gunners, searching for a manager with a proven track record, had money to spend and wanted Wilkinson to take over when George Graham was fired. The blank sheet of paper and free hand they offered was appealing, but Leslie Silver was dead set against giving the Gunners the opportunity to talk to his manager.

Wilkinson said later, 'The biggest career mistake I've ever made was not pushing hard enough to be allowed to leave to join another club when I was offered it. I was under contract at the time, it was the summer, the formal approach was made and rejected. Looking back, I should have pushed from my end.

'I didn't think it was setting a good example for me to do that when I was forming a group of people who wanted to have a greater say and a greater influence in what went on. It would be wrong to use the word moral, but it would allow people to say, "Listen to him spouting about managers' rights and so on and in the same breath he buggers off to Arsenal because it's a London club."

'Although Leeds could be big, Arsenal is and was big. I met Peter Hill-Wood for lunch and talked. I got a phone call from their secretary, Ken Friar, asking me to another meeting and I said, "I don't think it's right to do it now." We'd just started the LMA and I was chairman and I thought I couldn't say one thing and do another in terms of what the LMA wanted to stand for.'

Wilkinson admitted that ditching the day-to-day involvement of managing a football club in favour of an administrative role was initially difficult 'but once the crack of gunfire had gone from my ears and the smell of war from my nose, I found myself watching games from a different perspective. I was no longer thinking, "How can we beat them?" or "Could he do a good job for Leeds?" The more games I watched, the more attractive this job became. As a manager of a football club, the prime function is to win football matches. It can reduce the scope in which you operate. I was no longer developing my strengths.'

Wilkinson revealed that he would be operating at two levels. 'The first one is the game as it was and my brief was to produce a report which would attempt to … give our game at all levels a structure which we haven't had in the past. Over and above that, having tried to get the structure right, basically my job is then to try to ensure that we develop players better than we have done up to now and develop coaches who are better than the ones we've developed up to now.

'We got the report through the FA council in record time. Eighty voted for it, two against it, we hit the ground running and we've been running ever since. All the Premier League clubs have agreed that they're going to run academies plus maybe, I would anticipate, between five and ten Football League clubs, so we should start next season within the region, I would think, of 25 academies devoted specifically to the development of young footballers from seven or eight right through to 21.

'Since I took the job, I don't think there's been any serious proposal I've made which has not eventually been accepted. But you have to live in the real world and you have to have the patience to recognise what's possible and in what timescale. We're talking more marathon here than sprint. Undoubtedly these days, success at international level comes increasingly from taking a long-term view. If you look back over international football, very definite trends do emerge, and the successful teams fall in line with those trends – trends that you find very hard to buck – and for that to happen you've got to start thinking long-term.'

The Kafkaesque world of Lancaster Gate took some getting used to, but Wilkinson came to terms with it eventually. He contributed to the *Charter for Quality*, a blueprint covering player development, academies and 'the strategy for the development of international players and coaches'. The aim was to create a continuous stream of world-class international players and teams.

Sheffield Wednesday made a concerted attempt to lure Wilkinson back to Hillsborough after they sacked David Pleat in September 1997. FA director of public affairs David Davies hinted at legal reprisals, while Wilkinson committed his future to the FA, saying, 'I've got a contract with the FA. I am manager of the England Under-18 group and we have a game on Friday. The charter has gone through the FA and been accepted by the FA. I'm as committed to getting that charter organised as I was when I started. I was committed then, I'm committed now. What more can I say?'

Wilkinson was the driving force behind the development of St George's Park, a base for the national team. He persuaded the FA to buy 330 acres of east Staffordshire national forest for £2m in 2001, but the scheme was continually delayed by the protracted development of the new Wembley. The political shenanigans surrounding the new national stadium project, and disputes with its figurehead, Ken Bates, over the direction to be followed, scuppered many things.

When Glenn Hoddle was hounded out of the England job in February 1999 after controversial comments regarding disabled people, Wilkinson was asked to take the team for a friendly against France.

He told a press conference, 'When I got home last night, my wife questioned my sanity – but that's nothing new, she does that all the time. I could have said no to the job but I felt the downside was less than the upside. If we win, I will be able to put "England manager" on my CV, "beat the world champions". Then when the manager of Mongolia gets the sack, I can send that off.'

Wilkinson was widely criticised for recalling Arsenal right-back Lee Dixon a month before his 35th birthday.

England lost the game 2-0 and Kevin Keegan was appointed permanently the following week.

Keegan's tenure was not a happy one – he resigned abruptly following defeat in a World Cup qualifying game against Germany at Wembley in October 2000.

Wilkinson and the Under-21 squad he was then managing were sitting in the stands. They only learned of Keegan's resignation when they arrived at their London hotel. FA chief executive Adam Crozier and David Davies asked Wilkinson to meet them urgently at Burnham Beeches, headquarters for the senior side.

Crozier invited Wilkinson to take charge for the upcoming game with Finland. On the surface, Wilkinson appeared calm, but as he put the phone down, he thought to himself, 'Oh sh*t, here we go again.'

'The car radio was on as I was driven to Burnham Beeches,' recalls Wilkinson, 'and there was news of this

England player and that England player being injured. When I got there, things were worse than I anticipated. Kevin had a prior agreement with the players that they would go home after the German game and return to Burnham on Sunday evening. Most of them were already gone by the time I got there. I didn't know who was available. Contacting people on a Saturday night is not easy. I wanted to have a staff meeting and I had to read our reports on the Finnish side and then watch the videos of their games. What struck me most of all was the sense of disarray. Everybody was flat, not only because of the result but what happened afterwards.'

The appointment was slammed by *The Guardian*, which wrote of Wilkinson, 'Motivational skills: None, unless you are a believer in gobbledegook. Tactical awareness: Great, if you like the ball hoofed higher than a sponsor's blimp. Temperament: Drone, drone, drone (think William Hague). Verdict: Would be totally outclassed.'

Wilkinson was left with barely half of Keegan's original squad, with David Beckham a key absentee through injury.

The night before the game, Wilkinson was open with the players. 'Being honest, some of you may not be around to reap the rewards of a good result. But this is a crucial game, and the fact remains that we are all here because football is what we do and we're competitive people. The excuses are not valid. We have to perform.'

Played in a near gale-force wind on a hard pitch, the match was poor. England should have won, but Ray Parlour's strike with three minutes left was ruled out when the linesman failed to spot it had crossed the line after hitting the crossbar.

When Albania beat Greece, England were pitched to the bottom of the group.

'Overall, I thought the players did well and I told them that,' said Wilkinson. 'It was a crucial point. Germany played Finland twice in the group and couldn't beat them.'

Such facts didn't wash with the public and pundits, who considered victory a must. Wilkinson and his players were slated and the manager's reputation with the press didn't help his cause.

The Guardian was at it again immediately:

'Nothing could have better summed up the woolly thinking of Wilkinson, who sent out a team so lacking in midfield skills and balance that Kevin Keegan might have picked it. And it was obvious to everyone who witnessed England's dreadful performance that, if he throws his hat into the ring for the coach's job ... Adam Crozier should toss it straight out again.

'Wilkinson, who is one of the six men who will have Crozier's ear as he attempts to find Keegan's replacement, was noncommittal about his candidature afterwards, saying that all parties had agreed not to comment until they returned to England.

'A Wilkinson appointment, however, would be an affront to those who want to see the English game moved forward. Judging from his team selection and their performance last night, he would return it to the dark ages.'

A phlegmatic Wilkinson said, 'Even my closest friends wouldn't try to say I am good with the media. I felt I was going to be portrayed as uncommunicative, stubborn, dour and irascible, so what was the point? Why disappoint them? When I walked into the first press conference, I might as well have been a cardboard cutout of an England manager. They asked questions they would ask of a man who had been in the job for five seasons. It was stupid. Nobody seemed remotely interested in the fact that I was taking charge for one match.'

Wilkinson admitted it would now be 'difficult to qualify' for the finals but claimed that a draw was a reasonable outcome given the chaotic build-up. In retrospect, it was a point gained.

Without it, Beckham's free kick at Old Trafford later in the section against Greece would not have secured qualification.

In June 1999, Wilkinson had controversially decided to remove Peter Taylor, Hoddle's choice as manager of the Under-21 side, and take on the role himself. Wilkinson's spell was disastrous. He inherited an unbeaten team who were yet to concede a goal. Three of his six matches ended in defeat. The nadir came with a 4-0 humbling at home to Spain in February 2001.

Wilkinson was defiant. Despite seeing his side given a footballing lesson, he described it as 'a worthwhile exercise'.

After losing several regular players to Sven-Göran Eriksson's first senior squad, he said, 'It's better the game finished up like it did rather than us hauling back the deficit and everyone saying what a terrific fightback and being drowned in the euphoria of the result.

'If that was the case, they might have forgotten all the other bits. It was a bad performance, and the defenders found the tide coming in for half of the game. In that period, you were scratching your head and thinking of some players, "I've not recognised them."

'But I said to them at full time there were lots of pluses to take out of the game if we are prepared to learn from our mistakes. We were up against a very good side whose movement and passing was excellent, but they were also organised, determined and energetic in the way they went about getting the ball back. It's a case of comparing that with our passing and movement and we were almost clumsy at times in the first half. But the good thing is it was a friendly.

'The result was not foremost in my mind. At this level, winning is important but not the chief thing and we have a lot of talented players. We have a lot of people in the squad who hadn't played before and now they've got games under their belt. It's difficult to get cohesion, sometimes impossible. I can't pick players if they are not available.'

Wilkinson fell out with Crozier over the latter's decision to appoint Eriksson as England manager without consulting him and there were differences of opinion with the Swede from the start. Eriksson was an advocate of 4-4-2 and wanted the Under-21s to play the same way. Wilkinson stubbornly stuck with 4-3-3.

Eriksson got his way when David Platt was made Under-21 manager, much to the dismay of Wilkinson, who wanted to control this area. Platt appointed Steve Wigley as his assistant, only to discover that the coaching staff had been supplemented by Wilkinson nominee Les Reed.

During the World Cup campaign, Wilkinson argued again with Eriksson. He wanted FA-qualified coaches to be part of the scouting team who watched future opponents, but Eriksson insisted on using Dave Sexton.

Tottenham manager David Pleat commented, 'Howard Wilkinson has worked very honestly and genuinely to do ten years' work in two years with the academies. I hope, because of all the problems which could arise due to the introduction of Eriksson on a long-term contract, that Howard isn't sacrificed or he decides that it is time to leave his position.'

The lack of unity at Lancaster Gate was public knowledge. Sunderland took advantage when they came in with a shock move for Wilkinson.

After a disastrous start to the 2002/03 season, Sunderland manager Peter Reid was sacked after seven years in charge. Sunderland had lost five of their nine games and were deep in relegation trouble.

Even Wilkinson was taken aback when chairman Bob Murray invited him to take over. He had never intimated that he might be interested in such a job despite his frustration at the FA.

Wilkinson was aware that there would be no money in the transfer window, but he was positive. 'I relish the challenge ahead here at Sunderland. It is clear to me that this is a club with a proud tradition, huge and faithful support and in the Stadium of Light and academy, facilities that will be second to none. I see bright and exciting times ahead for Sunderland Football Club and its supporters.'

Those supporters were unimpressed with the appointment of Wilkinson and his assistant, Steve Cotterill. They wanted a big name to lift the spirits and a local radio phone-in show was swamped with complaints.

The bookies had heavily backed David O'Leary and Mick McCarthy, but there was a late surge of bets on Wilkinson. Ladbrokes reportedly slashed his odds from 33/1 to 10/1 in the afternoon prior to the appointment.

'If I've been one thing in my life,' said Wilkinson, two hours into the job, 'it's been honest. We don't see ourselves as messiahs. Steve and I are taking over a team that's fourth from bottom of the Premier League. So that's on our management CV now. It's on the players' CV now. The objective is very, very clear. We have got to get away from that relegation area as quickly as possible.

'I wouldn't have come here if I didn't think the club had terrific potential. But that's all it is: potential. I don't want to talk about where we might be 12 months from here. I don't even really want to talk about three months from here. At the moment, my horizon stretches to the West Ham game next week.'

Wilkinson's first act was to send the players out on a long run – the second thing was another run. 'They came back and their faces were purple,' said a witness. His priority was, as always, improving their fitness levels.

The early signs were good. The players' initial shock turned to respect. Wilkinson's first address went down well. There were smiles in training.

'I didn't realise how much I'd missed it until I got back out there,' Wilkinson told the press. 'I suppose that's the value of having what was a very worthwhile, interesting and, I hope, productive sabbatical as far as the FA and English football are concerned. But yes, I had missed it. I've been managing and coaching since I was 27.

'It's just nice to be out working with players, doing something that is second nature to you. I had culture shock at the FA. I always thought I was maybe a strategist, but I became a politician, a diplomat, a meetings man. It was hard work for me because it was a change in direction in my 50s that I had to think long and hard about.'

Young midfielder Paul Thirlwell has positive memories of Wilkinson's time at Sunderland.

'If you're at the bottom of the league it either goes one way or the other, and, unfortunately, he couldn't get us out of it. But it wasn't through a lack of effort, and Steve Cotterill was a good coach. For whatever reason it didn't work but I liked Howard. He had quite a dry sense of humour. He can come across as a bit dour, but day-to-day I found him quite humorous.'

Wilkinson's training methods included watching DVDs of geese flying in formation and using rugby balls in sessions.

'We were doing some quite strange things in training,' admitted Thirlwell. 'There was a lot of visualisation techniques, and he was probably a bit ahead of his time in terms of the ideas – but they were foreign to us. You kind of got the logic behind what he was saying, but when you're a young lad and you're looking around the room and you see everybody thinking, "What's happening here," it was a bit bizarre. I don't think we'd have been watching videos of geese under Peter Reid and Bobby Saxton, would we?'

Kevin Kilbane, a seasoned professional, acknowledged that Wilkinson wasn't wanted by the Sunderland fans, but he appreciated his structured approach to training. He also praised the increased emphasis on planning, team shape, set pieces and video analysis. While some players found the new methods tedious, Kilbane revealed that many welcomed the fresh approach.

Wilkinson's stay was a disaster. Cornered by reporters, he gracelessly snapped, 'What do you lot know anyway? How many caps have you won?'

'Forty-three actually, Howard, 15 as captain,' piped up *Daily Express* journalist Jimmy Armfield from the back of the room.

Wilkinson was sacked after 20 matches which yielded two victories.

'I am not surprised by anything that happens in football but still felt profound shock when it actually happened,' he said. 'I came to Sunderland with my eyes wide open and knew we would face difficulties but still thought that they could be dealt with in time.

'Sunderland was the worst [decision] I ever made because I made it for the wrong reasons. I didn't do my usual homework. I talked to them on Thursday night, said yes and was there on Tuesday morning. I made all the mistakes I hadn't made before.'

Undeterred by the experience, Wilkinson had two further spells in club management.

The first was a brief stint in China as manager of Shanghai Shenhua in the spring of 2004. His stay was cut short for 'personal reasons', understood to be illness within his family.

The following October, he agreed to hold the fort for Dave Bassett, now director of football at Leicester City, following the shock departures of manager Micky Adams and coach Alan Cork.

Two months later, Wilkinson returned to Notts County as a non-executive director. It was reported that Wilkinson would help out new manager Steve Thompson with coaching sessions.

Wilkinson abruptly resigned in September 2007, just hours after chairman Jeff Moore announced his departure.

As 2009 began, Wilkinson made a sentimental return to his spiritual home, Sheffield Wednesday, by then an ailing Championship club with massive debts.

When Wednesday were relegated in 2000, they were left with a bunch of expensive players without relegation clauses in their contracts. The position was compounded by the loss of broadcasting income when ITV Digital collapsed in 2002, its rights deal with the Football League bankrupting it.

Venture capitalists Charterhouse sold Sheffield Wednesday to three board members, triggering a dogfight that split the club.

Chairman Dave Allen stepped down in November 2007 and was replaced by Lee Strafford. He could not stop the rot but he healed the divisions.

Strafford and Nick Parker joined the board at a time when there were reports of 'significant progress … in the search for new investment'. Strafford benefited from having no ties with the former regime.

Strafford hired Wilkinson as technical adviser in January with two goals in mind: securing investment and developing a long-term football strategy.

'Howard brings with him a world-class CV,' said Strafford. 'This is a great move which adds value to everything we are doing. Howard will act as an adviser to the board as we figure out how to produce the infrastructure that will allow Brian Laws to best fulfil the potential of our football operations.'

There was talk of a 'complex deal to bring £50m to Hillsborough', with a four-party syndicate consisting of investment institutions and wealthy individuals.

Strafford set a March 2009 deadline for new investment, but that timescale was quickly abandoned when the club's principal creditors failed to agree on the parameters of an offer. Most creditors agreed to write off a portion of their debts – the Co-operative Bank, owed £21m of the total debt of £25m, consented to a reduction, but Dave Allen, owed £2m, stubbornly resisted.

When Strafford resigned on 17 May 2010, Wilkinson stepped into the breach as interim chairman.

On 11 August, the High Court granted the club 28 days to settle its debt to HMRC. The Co-op's Hugo Groves asked for the deferral of a winding-up petition after money from the sale of players was used to reduce the PAYE debt of £550,000.

The club had always been clear with the Co-op that they needed £3m of interim finance. They avoided administration after the bank agreed a facility to support the payment of £1.1m to HMRC.

'When we do get investment, they will have to show they can manage the club properly on a sound basis,' Wilkinson told BBC Radio Sheffield. 'Investment is crucial, but investment on its own will not solve the problem. We need to make sure above all that we do not get to a position where the future of the football club is as close to curtains as it has been this week. What you need, as well as investment, is sound management because we are not going to attract someone who is going to waste money.'

On 8 October, the club announced that it had secured investment from a consortium led by Leicester City owner Milan Mandaric, including an immediate advance of £2m to provide working capital.

The Co-op agreed to a settlement of £7m from Mandaric, who bought the club for £1 and poured in a further £18m. The outgoing directors agreed to walk away with less than half of what they were owed, although they would receive payment in full if the club was promoted to the Premier League.

Wilkinson told the media, 'I believe this to be one of the most important days in the recent history of our great club. Our trials and tribulations have been well documented, but I can now see a brighter future for Sheffield Wednesday.

'Our club has been on the brink of administration, and if this were to happen then so many people around our club would have suffered.

'I would like to put on record my sincere thanks to the departing and former directors of the club who are also the loan note holders. They have served the club loyally for many years without remuneration and have agreed to suffer a significant financial loss in order to allow this transaction to proceed. Their support throughout the many years of their service should not be doubted.

'On behalf of the board, I fully recommend this offer to shareholders, and to our supporters I again call on you to get behind our team.'

It was odd to see a man as steeped in football as Wilkinson suddenly transformed into a businessman.

Mandaric formally took over from Wilkinson on 7 December, after receiving the support of 99.7 per cent of voting shareholders.

Wilkinson said, 'It's time to start to think about the time when the club could begin looking to where Sheffield Wednesday should be, which is in the Premier League. Let's hope we go to where we want to go.'

By then, Wilkinson had moved on to his next challenge, becoming chairman of the LMA on 17 May 2010.

From his first day in the job, he was a powerful advocate for his profession, saying, 'I am very anxious to make [young coaches] aware of the downsides. In England, half of the managers who start in coaching are no longer in the game five years after they took that first job. Survival is, in itself, an enormous achievement. The stats show that the first-time manager who loses his job before 75 games, within five years of that happening, is no longer in the game in any capacity. And how many first-time managers do get past 70-odd games?

'Some people are naturally resilient, some are not, but the better ways of being resilient can be learnt. Ideally, when you say to yourself you want to be a manager, one of the questions you must ask yourself is: "Do I enjoy problems, and do I see them as an opportunity or something that I'd rather not have to deal with?" If you want to be a manager, resilience is absolutely essential.'

Wilkinson was certainly a resilient character, having survived every challenge that football could throw at him over his eight decades. There were regrets along the way, but Wilkinson had a great many more positive memories and relationships.

'The ultimate victory in competition is derived from the inner satisfaction of knowing that you have done your best and that you have gotten the most out of what you had to give.'

Judged by those criteria, Wilkinson was an incredible success – Notts County, Sheffield Wednesday and Leeds United all over-performed under his leadership and no one could have accused him of not making the most of the resources at his disposal.

Reflections

You can go to the pictures or read a book,
but football constantly comes back into your
mind. It's not a job, it's a life.

ARSÈNE WENGER'S impact on English football is undeniable.

Wenger joined Arsenal three weeks after Howard Wilkinson was shown the door by Leeds United; by the time 'Arsène who?' headlines were circulating in Fleet Street, Wilkinson had been peddling the value of sports science, personalised nutrition plans and statistics for nearly two decades. Wenger's studious image saw him nicknamed 'The Professor' at Highbury, but Wilkinson beat him to the punch on that one, too.

'In my early days at Leeds, somebody called me "the mad professor", because I brought in a urologist, tested players so that it could be worked out which was the best drink to rehydrate them.

'On my first day, I turned the kitchen upside down, and reorganised the food and the menus. What I did in training was also sometimes looked upon as a little strange or different. I was always fascinated by trying to find new ways to get that extra winning edge. I had to say to the ladies in the restaurant, "What they've been eating, they can no longer eat here."

'I had the kitchen staff in and explained to them that I didn't think they were bad cooks, I just thought they were cooking bad food and that from now on we're gonna go down the healthy diet road. Sports scientists were saying that the best time to re-energise in terms of food was immediately after performance, so there was a point where you were trying to get the players to eat a chocolate bar or something or other in the dressing room after a game and then that was shown to be not as effective as this and so on. And then you moved on and moved on.'

Seaweed tablets replaced the fish and chips. Wilkinson weighed the players every Monday, fining them £100 for every pound they were overweight. That regime once cost Mel Sterland £600 after a weekend of lager and curry.

Gordon Strachan: 'The fitness training was all about self-discipline. The leadership came from Vinnie, Kammy and Speedo.' He impishly added, 'Oh and Mel, of course!'

Wilkinson was the most meticulous, diligent and prepared of managers, obsessively buying into the adage that 'to fail to plan is to plan to fail'.

When Gary McAllister served as Wilkinson's captain, he said, 'His thoroughness is legendary and one of the most striking things about his managerial style. Nothing escapes him no matter how big or small a detail it might appear to be.'

McAllister described the dossiers that Wilkinson maintained on opposition teams. If it all smacks of Don Revie's famous approach, Wilkinson didn't hand them out and lecture his players like Revie did. Just like his predecessor, however, he used to arrange for the United reserves to play in the style of that week's opponents so that his first team could practise how to get the better of them in the days before the game.

The Leeds captain added: 'He's fairly intense before, during and after matches as well, but I can honestly say that

I've never seen him throw a complete wobbler the way he apparently used to when he was with Sheffield Wednesday. The lads have all heard the stories of how cups of tea went flying about the Hillsborough dressing room if things weren't going well, but he must have matured or something because our tea-set has remained intact! He has his moments at half-time if things aren't going well, but generally that comes in the shape of a reminder to players that they might not be doing their jobs the way he wants. The boss does it in front of everyone and names the lads he's not happy with, but it's a case of pointing things out rather than trying to belittle anyone.'

Wilkinson espoused the credo of marginal gains as popularised years later by cycling's Dave Brailsford. 'You have to accumulate success in areas which hitherto hadn't seemed to matter,' explained Wilkinson. 'Take every opportunity to add to your chances of success. It's just accumulation of small advantages, that's all that you're looking for. Eventually, the players buy into it, and it becomes second nature to them and then they start to moan if they don't get it.

'Arsène Wenger at Arsenal introduced psychological physical mapping. When players woke up in the morning they had to answer questions on a form on their mobile phones, always the same questions and that had to go into the club, and all that had to be done before a certain time so that by the time they got in the club, the sports support staff, that's sports medicine, sports science, etc., could look at all that and have an ongoing build-up in order to make sure that by the time they arrived at the club for training, all these things were noted and put back into the file.

'And out of that came the ability to say if you're at a club long enough, what we're seeing here is that this player is, the yardage he's covering, etc. Within margins, there's a point where we're recommending you need to rest him, for your good and for his good, he needs to have a week free or whatever. It's just become run of the mill now.'

Wilkinson was obsessed with understanding player motivation and behaviour so that he could wring the maximum out of each of them.

'What do you expect from him? What's his ten? If he's giving you his eight, his seven, his nine, week in, week out, you're okay, especially if he's a Gary Speed, who's not giving you other problems, or a Gordon Strachan. But if you've got the bloke that's giving you nine one week and then other times it's five or six or whatever, you've got a problem.

'If you sit down with a player and you settle for an agreed conclusion to the discussion which is how good you can be and what will it take to make you that good? What do you bring to the party because it's you who's got to do this? It's not me. I can try and be the catalyst but ultimately it's you. It's down to you and everybody's different on that score and football's different to working as a research chemist in some laboratory somewhere. Different qualities are required.

'Having football intelligence, in my opinion it's not an intelligence which is, as it were, "Ooh, it's up there in that box there, if you want football intelligence, get it out of number 43." But top performers do have this ability to make good decisions. They do have this ability to compute all these signals that are going on around them and come up with the best option.'

Wilkinson focused on creating the proper conditions, the correct tone, providing true leadership.

'One of the things I say is that in order to create the correct relationship with your players, in order to get the best out of your players, you have to go into work every day believing that you're going to be at that club for the rest of your life and yet at the same time accept that at the end of the day you may get the sack.

'If you lead people, what you say has to be said with a view to the long term. You can't live from day to day in football. Your position has got to be a position where the people you're dealing with, in terms of the group, us, not me, we, then that's very difficult. It undermines your position if players start to think, "Hmm, I wonder?"'

Wilkinson changed the culture at Leeds United, eradicating the dragging indiscipline that plagued the club in the 80s. He left other legacies. Despite claims made on behalf of Peter Ridsdale, Wilkinson was the architect of the European shield club crest which was introduced a couple of years after he left Elland Road and remained in place 25 years later. Taking his inspiration from a combination of the Italian national team's badge and the label off a bottle of wine, he worked with a graphic designer to sketch out the basic idea which was later adopted.

Given his head, Wilkinson could do remarkable things. He just needed the right sponsor.

He fully acknowledged his fortune in working for a chairman like Leslie Silver. The quality of their relationship, the positivity, respect and trust between them, left an indelible mark. Wilkinson was unequivocal about what would have been important to him if he had ever been an owner.

'Two things would matter for me. One, picking the right person, and two, being clear on what was important. Being successful in business, building a successful business, doesn't mean you're going to be a good football chairman. It's a help but it doesn't mean that you're going to be right. There's two things that matter if that person seriously thinks about it. He needs to recognise what matters and then he needs to recognise that selection of the person who's going to be the manager or coach has the qualities required to be successful, given he knows once we decide on what we're going to do, we are going to do it.

'That works in a factory, if you turn up at seven in the morning in the factory knowing that the place is run well and that in the current climate this guy is not going to panic, if he treats you fairly and well, if there's an illness in your family or whatever, it's a better place to work and I think that that helps you. If you were the owner of an ordinary business and you sacked five managing directors in the space of two years, people would look at you, wouldn't they? But in football that seems to be accepted, a chairman can sack five managers in two years and he's still there. It's his club, I suppose, but it just seems incredible. Like I said, I don't think they understand that very simple fact that if the person in charge is going to be as well-prepared to get the best out of that dressing room as is possible, that person has to, in order to get his ideas across, work as if I'm going to be here for the next ten years because I've got to have that attitude to convince them of what it is I'm doing, saying, etc. And for that to happen, the person above him has to recognise the importance of that but also has to prepare himself better.

'There's a cultural attitude in this country which is anti-coaching, or against having an analytical attitude to sport, and it does make life difficult because it colours everyone's attitude. It's come out recently when we've had foreign players who start to talk about the differences and make negative comparisons with the preparation they've been used to. It comes out with foreign coaches coming in – people like Arsène Wenger. The sort of preparation that he employs I don't think is that much different to the sort of preparation that others would employ, nor would it be fundamentally different to that which I would employ, but because Arsène's come in and done it, it's had a positive influence. People say, "Ah well, it's come from abroad, it must be good, it's worked there" – and I think that's good.

'Any situation where part of your responsibility is to get people to change or learn or adapt is a teaching situation, and I found that my teacher training and the degree course did have some benefits. I asked people for advice and the one piece of advice I really took to was the fact that the FA course in physical education and in teaching might be very helpful in terms of football coaching and management, and it was.'

Wilkinson makes fascinating and insightful company; he is refreshingly honest and open, generous with his time, constantly pondering on how he can help the sport he loves. When asked what advice he would give a young manager, he is candid.

'We have got some very good English managers, but you need opportunities and the British managers tend not to get the best jobs. When coaches talk to me, I say to them, "Listen, you're not gonna like what I'm gonna say, because you've got a wife and three kids or whatever, but if I were you, I'd go and start in Scandinavia." I can give you five or six good examples who've gone there over the years with no reputation, got a job and that's given them the opportunity to be at a club for longer than you get here and, whilst that's happening, they're learning and you never know, one day you might finish up as England manager.'

It's unheard of these days for any club to give a manager as long as Wilkinson or Alex Ferguson were given. Such honeymoons are now as rare as goals from David Batty, particularly at Leeds United, where Brian Clough and Jock Stein had six weeks apiece. Massimo Cellino hired and fired coaches like other people might change their socks, giving Darko Milanic just 32 days, one day more than Sam Allardyce's abortive rescue mission in 2023.

Wilkinson once said that there were only two sorts of manager: those who had been sacked and those who would be fired in the future.

Wilkinson is quickly into his stride when asked how long it is reasonable to give someone to have an impact.

'It depends where you're going, depends what's gone on before that, and so on. So, I can't say that. What I can say is, for you to get to really know them, and for them to get to really know you, you're talking 12 months minimum, because it's not like learning to drive. You know, there's no Highway Code, as it were. And, you know, people generally don't drive on the right side of the road, on the correct side of the road, and so on.

'I have a realistic view of football. I knew that what you do and what you build at any one time may never be finished. Nevertheless, if you're going to do your best for the players that you're working with, it's absolutely critical that when you get a job, you think you're going to be in that job the rest of your life. And you have to think every day when you go in, not about just today but about the next three months, six months, nine months, 12 months and so on. Otherwise, you won't be effective. Players will see through you.

'You have to develop this mindset where 'I'm going to work as if I'm going to be here forever.' But I have to accept that facts show that probably won't be the case. Nevertheless, in order to form the sort of bond I need to form with players and in order to get their respect, their trust, they need to know and understand that I'm in it for us, not for me. That's it, they need to know that when I speak, I'm saying honestly what I think, and that I do genuinely believe that if you're a manager of a football club, it's not me on a journey, it's us. And the players know it full well, that I'm the scout who's leading us on this journey through the backwoods and through the Sioux ambushes. One who might not be here and we've got to get another one.'

Wilkinson's modesty and down-to-earth nature shine through in all he says and does.

'I count myself very lucky, employed in football for 60 years, but never worked a day in my life.'

When asked about the management role in the modern era, Wilkinson reflects on how things have changed since his heyday.

'All you can say is that is very, very difficult at the moment for any manager to contemplate. Any manager taking the job, as far as I can see, would not know who he is going to be working for. And that matters enormously. That is the most important relationship within the football club.

'The important line of communication in the football club is between the decision-maker or makers and the manager.

'If there's uncertainty about first of all the people in that line or the way that line works, you are going to have a problem.

'In old-fashioned military terms, it's like having a general in the field or the trenches not knowing whose orders he is supposed to be following and sometimes, not being able to talk to anybody to see whether there is an order or not.

'Instability at the top of any organisation is not good news. It does not matter if it is business, or the church or government. If you get instability at the top, you have got a problem. The uncertainty just spreads down a chain and it affects people's mindset and their performances in any business.'

Wilkinson remembers his time at Elland Road fondly, proud that he made a silk purse out of a sow's ear, even though his chairman provided golden thread and silver needles.

While he achieved remarkable things at Notts County and Sheffield Wednesday, it's doubtful whether he could have repeated his success with Leeds United at any other club. The foundations were there, the owner was heaven-sent, and he was given a free hand.

'If you said to me, what do you think would be the ideal owner, I'd say you need somebody like Leslie Silver. What do I mean? Well, a benevolent, modest, but shrewd decision-maker who will weigh up what it is you're saying and then basically, not say to you, I don't think that's a good idea or a bad idea, he'll say to you, yeah, we can afford that or we can't. So do it, if we can. But that's not the sort of relationship you see too often.

'I got to start to believe that this man could be trusted, that he was genuine and that at his heart was the welfare of Leeds United and the fact that that affected him deeply. Leslie was a lovely man, a self-made man, a man of his word, a gentle person – his manner was very gentle – but he had a backbone and balls of steel. So, we bonded.'

However much Wilkinson owed to Leeds and Silver, one thing is certain. Few other men could have matched his achievements in those golden years at Elland Road, could have turned round an oil tanker in such dramatic fashion, could have built such camaraderie and team spirit, could have developed such a conveyor belt of young talent, could have invested as wisely as he did, could have delivered such wonderful memories.

Wilkinson deserves a thousand thanks for what he did for Leeds United.

'I have a really nice feeling when I think about my time there, recognising that I'm amongst people who actually recognise my part, the part I'm playing, don't just take me for granted.'

This humble man then added, 'I'm not sure anyone will remember yours truly – a lot of water has passed under the bridge in the last 25 years.'

There has, indeed, been an awful lot of water, but what a bridge was built by Howard Wilkinson, one of English football's greatest ever managers!

Bibliography

Adams, Micky, *Micky Adams: My Life in Football* (Biteback Publishing, 2017).

Batty, David and Thornton, Bill, *David Batty: The Autobiography* (Headline Book Publishing, 2001).

Chapman, Lee, *More Than a Match: A Player's Story* (Stanley Paul, 1992).

Coomber, Richard, *Lucas Radebe: From Soweto to Soccer Superstar* (Great Northern Books Ltd, 2010).

Crooks, Richard, *Wednesday v United: The Sheffield Derby* (Pitch Publishing Ltd, 2018).

Ferguson, Alex, *Managing My Life: My Autobiography* (Hodder, 2000).

Fisher, John, *Painting the Town Silver: The Life and Times of Leslie Silver OBE* (Beecroft Publications, 2015).

Gray, Eddie, *Marching on Together: My Life at Leeds United* (Hodder & Stoughton, 2001).

Hilaire, Vince and Maslona, Tom, *Vince – The Autobiography of Vince Hilaire* (Biteback Publishing, 2018).

Hodge, Steve, *The Man With Maradona's Shirt* (Orion, 2011).

Hughes, Charles, *The Winning Formula: Soccer Skills and Tactics* (Collins, 1990).

Jones, Vinnie, *Vinnie: The Autobiography: Confessions of a Bad Boy?* (Headline, 1999).

Kamara, Chris, *Mr Unbelievable* (HarperSport, 2010).